COMMONWEALTH GAMES
Peeping Through History

COMMONWEALTH GAMES
Peeping Through History

By

Laxman Singh

CYBER TECH PUBLICATIONS
4264/3, Ansari Road, Daryaganj, New Delhi-110002 (India)
Ph.: 011-23244078, 011-43559448 Fax: 011-23280028
E-Mail: cyberpublicationsdelhi@yahoo.com
Website: www.cybertechpublications.com

Commonwealth Games

Peeping Through History

Laxman Singh

First Edition 2011

Published by G.S. Rawat

For Cyber Tech Publications

4264/3, Ansari Road, Daryaganj, New Delhi-110002
Ph.: 011-23244078, 011-43559448 Fax: 011-23280028
E-Mail: cyberpublicationsdelhi@yahoo.com
E.mail: cybertechpublications@g.mail.com
website: www.cybertechpublications.com

Printed at: Asian Offset Printers, Delhi-53

Contents

Preface

Sports and games competitions are not merely game events, they bring together the participatns from different locales, thus enhancing mutual understanding, universal brotherhood and peace. They have been instrumental in shaping a new world order—in diplomatic as well as economic terms.

Commonwealth Games are the third largest multi-sport event in the world after Summer Olympic Games and the Asian Games.

It is remarkable to note that event was first held in 1930 under the title of the British Empire Games. The event was renamed as the British Empire and Commonwealth Games in 1954, the British Commonwealth Games in 1970, and gained its current title in 1978. Only six teams have attended every Commonwealth Games: Australia, Canada, England, New Zealand, Scotland and Wales. Australia has been the highest scoring team for ten games, England for seven and Canada for one.

The first edition of the event was the 1930 British Empire Games and eleven nations took part. The quadrennial schedule of the games was interrupted by World War II and the 1942 Games (set to be held in Montreal, Canada) were abandoned. The games were continued in 1950 and underwent a name change four years later with the first British Empire and Commonwealth Games in 1954. Over 1000 athletes participated in the 1958 Games as over thirty teams took part for the first time.

The event was briefly known as the British Commonwealth Games for the 1970 and 1974 editions and the 1978 Games, held in Edmonton, Canada, were the first to be held under the title of the "Commonwealth Games".

The present book compiles vital information on the beginning, growth and development of Commonwealth Games in historical perspective. The following chapters make core of the study—Introduction; Sports and Games: Key Aspects; Commonwealth Games: An Overview; Sports Competition; 1930 British Empire Games; 1934 British Empire Games; British Empire Games 1938; 1950 British Empire Games; British Empire and Commonwealth Games, 1954; British Empire and Commonwealth Games, 1958; 1962 British Empire and Commonwealth Games; 1966 British Empire and Commonwealth Games; 1970 British Commonwealth Games; 1978 Commonwealth Games; Commonwealth Games 1982; 1986 Commonwealth Games; 1990 Commonwealth Games; 1994 Commonwealth Games; 1998 Commonwealth Games; 2002 Commonwealth Games and 2006 Commonwealth Games etc.

No exaggeration, such works cannot be completed single-handedly unless consulting learnedworks penned by seasoned professionals and experts in the field. We have consulted a number of books, journals, newspapers and magazine articles besides plethora of literature available digitally at various web sources.

We express our gratitude to them all for subscribing their views and works. My colleagues, seniors, friends and family members have helped me a lot while working on this project. I am deeply beholden to them all. I am equally grateful to my publishers for publishing this work elegantly in the present shape.

—L.S.

PART - I

HISTORICAL PERSPECTIVE

1

Introduction

> "There never has been, there isn't now and there never will be, any race of people on the earth fit to serve as master over their fellow men."
>
> —*Franklin D. Roosevelt*

Since we intend here to discuss Commonwealth games, first it is necessary for us to understand what Commonwealth is?

In the following paragraphs we will acquaint you with the Commonwealth in historic perspective. Then we will elucidate the salient points of the main theme.

As the famous adage goes on, "the sun never sets in the British Empire", Commonwealth nations were one time the colonies of Great British Empire. Though some of the present members of the Commonwealth of Nations are exception to it.

The Commonwealth of Nations, normally referred to as the Commonwealth and previously as the British Commonwealth, is an intergovernmental organization of fifty-four independent member states. All but two of these countries were formerly part of the British Empire. The member states co-operate within a framework of common values and goals as outlined in the Singapore Declaration.

These include the promotion of democracy, human rights, good governance, the rule of law, individual liberty, egalitarianism, free trade, multilateralism and world peace. The Commonwealth is not a political union, but an intergovernmental organisation through which countries with diverse social, political and economic backgrounds are regarded as equal in status.

Its activities are carried out through the permanent Commonwealth Secretariat, headed by the Secretary-General, and biennial Meetings between Commonwealth Heads of Government. The symbol of their free association is the Head of the Commonwealth, which is a ceremonial position currently held by Queen Elizabeth II. Elizabeth II is also monarch, separately and independently, of sixteen Commonwealth members, which are known as the "Commonwealth realms".

The Commonwealth is a forum for a number of non-governmental organisations, collectively known as the Commonwealth Family, which are fostered through the intergovernmental Commonwealth Foundation. The Commonwealth Games, the Commonwealth's most visible activity, are a product of one of these organisations. These organisations strengthen the shared culture of the Commonwealth, which extends through common sports, literary heritage, and political and legal practices. Due to this, Commonwealth countries are not considered to be "foreign" to one another.

It is remarkable that while not all current members were once British colonies, the Commonwealth is generally considered to be the successor to the British Empire. In 1884, while visiting Australia, Lord Rosebery described the changing British Empire, as some of its colonies became more independent, as a "Commonwealth of Nations".

Conferences of British and colonial Prime Ministers had occurred periodically since 1887, leading to the creation of the Imperial Conferences in 1911. Thus, the formal organisation of the Commonwealth developed from the Imperial Conferences, where the independence of the self-governing colonies and especially of dominions was recognised. The Irish Oath of Allegiance, agreed in 1921, included the Irish Free State's "adherence to and membership of the group of nations forming the British Commonwealth of Nations". In the Balfour Declaration at the 1926 Imperial Conference, Britain and its dominions agreed they were "equal in status, in no way subordinate one to another in any aspect of their domestic or external affairs, though united by common allegiance to the Crown, and freely associated as members of the British Commonwealth of Nations". These aspects to the relationship were eventually formalised by the Statute of Westminster in 1931. Australia, New Zealand, and Newfoundland had to ratify the statute for it to take effect— which Newfoundland never did. Australia and New Zealand did in 1942 and 1947 respectively.

After World War II, the British Empire was gradually dismantled to just 14 remaining British overseas territories, still held by the United Kingdom today, partly owing to the rise of independence movements in the subject territories and partly owing to both the British Government's straitened circumstances resulting from the cost of the war and a progressive domestic movement to decolonise. In April 1949, following the London Declaration, the word "British" was dropped from the title of the Commonwealth to reflect its changing nature. Burma Myanmar, 1948, and Aden (1967) are the only states that were British colonies at the time of the war not to have joined the Commonwealth upon post-war independence. Among the former British protectorates and mandates, those that never became members of the Commonwealth are Egypt (independent in 1922), Iraq (1932), Transjordan (1946), Palestine (part of which became the state of Israel in 1948), Sudan (1956), British Somaliland (which became part of Somalia in 1960, although it has since declared itself independent as Somaliland), Kuwait (1961), Bahrain (1971), Oman (1971), Qatar (1971), and the United Arab Emirates (1971).

Further, it is pertinent to note that the issue of countries with constitutional structures not based on a shared Crown but that wanted to remain members of the Commonwealth, came to a head in 1948 with passage of the Republic of Ireland Act 1948, in which Ireland renounced the sovereignty of the Crown and thus left the Commonwealth. However, the Ireland Act 1949 passed by the Parliament of Westminster gave citizens of the Republic of Ireland a status similar to that of citizens of the Commonwealth in UK law. The issue was resolved in April 1949 at a Commonwealth prime ministers' meeting in London. Under this London Declaration, India agreed that, when it became a republic, in January 1950, it would accept the British Sovereign as a "symbol of the free association of its independent member nations and, as such, Head of the Commonwealth". The other Commonwealth countries in turn recognised India's continuing membership of the association. At Pakistan's insistence, India was not regarded as an exceptional case and it was assumed that other states would be accorded the same treatment as India.

In fact, the London Declaration is often seen as marking the beginning of the modern Commonwealth. Following India's precedent, other nations became republics, or constitutional monarchies with their own monarchs, while some countries retained the same monarch as the United

Kingdom, but their monarchies developed differently and soon became fully independent of the British monarchy. The monarch of each Commonwealth realm, whilst the same person, is regarded as a separate legal personality for each realm.

Commonwealth Now

As the Commonwealth grew, Britain and the pre-1945 dominions became informally known as the "Old Commonwealth", and planners in the interwar period, like Lord Davies, who had also taken "a prominent part in building up the League of Nations Union" in the United Kingdom, in 1932 founded the New Commonwealth Movement, of which Winston Churchill was the president. The New Commonwealth was a society aimed at creation of an international air force to be the arm of the League of Nations, to allow nations to disarm and safeguard the peace. Some of these ideas were reflected in the United Nations Charter, drafted in Dumbarton Oaks (21 August to 7 October 1944) and San Francisco (25 April to 26 June 1945).

After the war, particularly since the 1960s when some of the Commonwealth countries disagreed with poorer, African and Asian (or New Commonwealth) members about various issues at Commonwealth Heads of Government meetings. Accusations that the old, "White" Commonwealth had different interests from African Commonwealth nations in particular, and charges of racism and colonialism, arose during heated debates about Rhodesia in the 1960s and 1970s, the imposition of sanctions against apartheid-era South Africa in the 1980s and, more recently, about whether to press for democratic reforms in Nigeria and then Zimbabwe.

Goods

It is significant to note that Commonwealth's objectives were first outlined in the 1971 Singapore Declaration, which committed the Commonwealth to the institution of world peace; promotion of representative democracy and individual liberty; the pursuit of equality and opposition to racism; the fight against poverty, ignorance, and disease; and free trade. To these were added opposition to discrimination on the basis of gender by the Lusaka Declaration of 1979 (which mostly concerned racism), and environmental sustainability by the Langkawi Declaration of 1989.

These objectives were reinforced by the Harare Declaration in 1991. The Commonwealth's current highest-priority aims are on the promotion of democracy and development, as outlined in the 2003 Aso Rock Declaration, which built on those in Singapore and Harare and clarified their terms of reference, stating, "We are committed to democracy, good governance, human rights, gender equality, and a more equitable sharing of the benefits of globalisation." The Commonwealth website lists its areas of work as: Democracy, Economics, Education, Gender, Governance, Human Rights, Law, Small States, Sport, Sustainability, and Youth.

Through a separate voluntary fund, Commonwealth governments support the Commonwealth Youth Programme, a division of the Secretariat with offices in Gulu (Uganda), Lusaka (Zambia), Chandigarh (India), Georgetown (Guyana) and Honiara (Solomon Islands).

The Commonwealth has long been distinctive as an international forum where highly developed economies (such as the United Kingdom, Australia, Canada, Singapore, and New Zealand) and many of the world's poorer countries seek to reach agreement by consensus. This aim has sometimes been difficult to achieve, as when disagreements over Rhodesia in the late 1960s and 1970s and over apartheid in South Africa in the 1980s led to a cooling of relations between the United Kingdom and African members.

STRUCTURE

Head of the Commonwealth

Under the formula of the London Declaration, Queen Elizabeth II is the Head of the Commonwealth, a title that is currently individually shared with that of Commonwealth realms. However, when the monarch dies, the successor to the crown does not automatically become Head of the Commonwealth. The position is symbolic: representing the free association of independent members. Sixteen members of the Commonwealth, known as Commonwealth realms, recognise the Queen as their head of state. The majority of members, thirty-three, are republics, and a further five have monarchs of different royal houses.

Queen Elizabeth II, current Head of the Commonwealth

The main decision-making forum of the organisation is the biennial Commonwealth Heads of Government Meeting (CHOGM), where Commonwealth Heads of Government, including (amongst others) Prime Ministers and Presidents, assemble for several days to discuss matters of mutual interest. CHOGM is the successor to the Meetings of Commonwealth Prime Ministers and earlier Imperial Conferences and Colonial Conferences dating back to 1887. There are also regular meetings of finance ministers, law ministers, health ministers, etc. Members in Arrears, as Special Members before them, are not invited to send representatives to either ministerial meetings or CHOGMs.

The head of government hosting the Head of Government Meeting is called the Commonwealth Chairperson-in-Office, and retains the position until the following CHOGM.

Commonwealth Secretariat

The Commonwealth Secretariat, established in 1965, is the main intergovernmental agency of the Commonwealth, facilitating consultation and cooperation among member governments and countries. It is responsible to member governments collectively. The Commonwealth of Nations is represented in the United Nations General Assembly by the Secretariat, as an observer.

Based in London, the Secretariat organises Commonwealth summits, meetings of ministers, consultative meetings and technical discussions; it assists policy development and provides policy advice, and facilitates multilateral communication among the member governments. It also provides technical assistance to help governments in the social and economic development of their countries and in support of the Commonwealth's fundamental political values.

Marlborough House, in London, is the headquarters of the Commonwealth Secretariat

The Secretariat is headed by the Commonwealth Secretary-General who is elected by Commonwealth Heads of Government for no more than two four-year terms. The Secretary-General and two Deputy Secretaries-General direct the divisions of the Secretariat. The present Secretary-General is Kamalesh Sharma, from India, who took office on 1 April 2008, succeeding Don McKinnon of New Zealand (2000–2008). The first Secretary-General was Arnold Smith of Canada (1965–75), followed by Sir Shridath Ramphal of Guyana (1975–90).

Members

The criteria for membership of the Commonwealth of Nations have developed over time from a series of separate documents. The Statute of Westminster 1931, as a fundamental founding document of the organisation, laid out that membership required dominionhood. The 1949 London Declaration ended this, allowing republican and indigenous monarchic members on the condition that they recognised the British monarch as the "Head of the

Commonwealth". In the wake of the wave of decolonisation in the 1960s, these constitutional principles were augmented by political, economic, and social principles. The first of these was set out in 1961, when it was decided that respect for racial equality would be a requisite of membership, leading directly to the withdrawal of South Africa's re-application (which they were required to make under the formula of the London Declaration upon becoming a republic). The fourteen points of the 1971 Singapore Declaration dedicated all members to the principles of world peace, liberty, human rights, equality, and free trade.

These criteria were unenforceable for two decades, until, in 1991, the Harare Declaration was issued, dedicating the leaders to applying the Singapore principles to the completion of decolonisation, the end of the Cold War, and the fall of Apartheid in South Africa. The mechanisms by which these principles would be applied were created, and the manner clarified, by the 1995 Millbrook Commonwealth Action Programme, which created the Commonwealth Ministerial Action Group (CMAG), which has the power to rule on whether members meet the requirements for membership under the Harare Declaration. Also in 1995, an Inter-Governmental Group was created to finalise and codify the full requirements for membership. Upon reporting in 1997, as adopted under the Edinburgh Declaration, the Inter-Governmental Group ruled that any future members would have to have a direct constitutional link with an existing member.

In addition to this new rule, the former rules were consolidated into a single document. These requirements, which remain the same today, are that members must: accept and comply with the Harare principles, be fully sovereign states, recognise the monarch of the

Commonwealth realms as the Head of the Commonwealth, accept the English language as the means of Commonwealth communication, and respect the wishes of the general population with regard to Commonwealth membership. These requirements had undergone review, and a report on potential amendments was presented by the Committee on Commonwealth Membership at the 2007 Commonwealth Heads of Government Meeting. New members were not admitted at this meeting, though applications for admission were considered at the 2009 CHOGM.

The Commonwealth comprises fifty-four of the world's countries (including one currently suspended member), across all six inhabited continents. The members have a combined population of 2.1 billion people, almost a third of the world population, of which 1.17 billion live in India and 94% live in Asia and Africa combined. After India, the next-largest Commonwealth countries by population are Pakistan (176 million), Bangladesh (156 million), Nigeria (154 million), the United Kingdom (61 million) and South Africa (49 million). Nauru is the smallest member, with about 10,000 people.

The land area of the Commonwealth nations is about 31,500,000 km2, or about 21% of the total world land area. The three largest Commonwealth nations by area are Canada at 10,000,000 km2, Australia at 7,700,000 km2, and India at 3,300,000 km2. The Commonwealth members have a combined gross domestic product (measured in purchasing power parity) of $10.6 trillion, 66% of which is accounted for by the four largest economies: India ($3.3 trillion), the United Kingdom ($2.3 trillion), Canada ($1.3 trillion), and Australia ($800 billion).

The status of "Member in Arrears" is used to denote those that are in arrears in paying subscription dues to the Commonwealth. The status was originally known as "special membership", but was renamed on the Committee on Commonwealth Membership's recommendation. Currently, there is one Member in Arrears: Nauru. Nauru joined as a special member, but was a full member from 1 May 1999 to January 2006, when it reverted.

New members must "as a general rule" have a direct constitutional link to an existing member. In most cases, the existing member is a former colony of the United Kingdom, but some have links to other countries, either exclusively or more directly (e.g. Samoa to New Zealand, Papua New Guinea to Australia, and Namibia to South Africa). The first member to be admitted without having any constitutional link to the British Empire or a Commonwealth member was Mozambique, a former Portuguese colony. It was admitted in 1995 following its first democratic elections and South Africa's re-admission in 1994. Mozambique's controversial entry led to the Edinburgh Declaration and the current membership guidelines. In 2009, Rwanda became the second Commonwealth member admitted to not have any such constitutional links. It was formerly a Belgian trust territory that had been a German colony until World War I. Consideration for its admission was considered an "exceptional circumstance" by the Commonwealth Secretariat.

Applicants

Sudan, Algeria, Madagascar and Yemen have applied to join the Commonwealth. Of these four, Madagascar and Algeria were never British colonies or possessions. In 2006, Commonwealth Secretary-General Don McKinnon said Israel and Palestine could join the commonwealth.

Other eligible applicants could come from any of the remaining inhabited British overseas territories, Crown dependencies, Australian external territories and Associated States of New Zealand if any become fully independent. Many such jurisdictions are already directly represented within the Commonwealth, particularly through the Commonwealth Family.

France secretly considered membership in the 1950s, under the leadership of Prime Minister Guy Mollet. In the context of nationalisation of the Suez Canal, colonial unrest, and increasing tensions between British-backed Jordan and French-backed Israel, Mollet saw a union between Britain and France as a possible solution. A British Government document of the time reported, "The French would welcome a common citizenship arrangement on the Irish basis." The request was turned down by the British prime minister Anthony Eden, along with a request for Commonwealth membership, and a year later France signed the Treaty of Rome with West Germany and the other founding nations of the Common Market, later to become the EU (which the UK and Ireland joined in 1973, Malta and Cyprus in 2004) .

In recent years, the Commonwealth has suspended several members "from the Councils of the Commonwealth" for "serious or persistent violations" of the Harare Declaration, particularly in abrogating their responsibility to have democratic government. This is done by the Commonwealth Ministerial Action Group (CMAG), which meets regularly to address potential breaches of the Harare Declaration. Suspended members are not represented at meetings of Commonwealth leaders and ministers, although they remain members of the organisation. Currently, there is one suspended member: Fiji.

Nigeria was suspended between 11 November 1995 and 29 May 1999, following its execution of Ken Saro-Wiwa on the eve of the 1995 CHOGM. Pakistan was the second country to be suspended, on 18 October 1999 following a military coup by Pervez Musharraf. The Commonwealth's longest suspension came to an end on 22 May 2004, when Pakistan's suspension was lifted following the restoration of the country's constitution. Pakistan was suspended for a second time, far more briefly, for six months from 22 November 2007, when Musharraf called a state of emergency. Zimbabwe was suspended in 2002 over concerns with the electoral and land reform policies of Robert Mugabe's ZANU-PF government, before Zimbabwe withdrew from the organisation in 2003.

Fiji, which was not a member of the Commonwealth between 1987 and 1997 as a result of a pair of coups d'état, has also been suspended twice, with the first suspension being imposed from 6 June 2000 to 20 December 2001 after another coup. Fiji has been suspended once again, since 8 December 2006, following the most recent coup, this suspension only applying to membership on the Councils of the Commonwealth. After failing to meet a Commonwealth deadline for setting national elections by 2010, Fiji was "fully suspended" on 1 September 2009.

As membership is purely voluntary, member governments can choose at any time to leave the Commonwealth. Pakistan left on 30 January 1972 in protest at the Commonwealth's recognition of breakaway Bangladesh, but rejoined on 2 August 1989. Zimbabwe left in 2003 when the Commonwealth heads of government refused to lift the country's suspension on the grounds of alleged human rights violations and deliberate misgovernment. Although heads of government have the power to suspend member states from active participation, the Commonwealth has no provision for the expulsion of members. Until 2007, Commonwealth realms that became republics automatically ceased to be members, until (like India in 1950) they obtained the permission of other members to remain in the organisation. This policy has been changed, so if any current Commonwealth realms were to become republics, they would not have to go through this process.

The Irish Free State left the Commonwealth when it declared itself a republic, on 18 April 1949, after passing the Republic of Ireland Act 1948. South Africa was prevented from continuing as a member after it became a republic in 1961, due to hostility from many members, particularly those in Africa and Asia as well as Canada, to its policy of apartheid. The South African government withdrew its application to remain in the organisation as a republic when it became clear at the 1961 Meeting of Commonwealth Prime Ministers that any such application would be rejected. South Africa was re-admitted to the Commonwealth in 1994, following the end of apartheid earlier that same year. The declaration of a republic in Fiji in 1987, after military coups designed to deny Indo-Fijians political power there, was not accompanied by an application to remain. Commonwealth membership was held to have lapsed until 1997, after discriminatory provisions in the republican constitution were repealed and reapplication for membership made.

Commonwealth Family

Commonwealth countries share many links outside government, with over a hundred Commonwealth-wide non-governmental organisations, notably for sport, culture, education and charity. The Association of Commonwealth Universities is an important vehicle for academic links, particularly through scholarships, principally the Commonwealth Scholarship, for students to study in universities in other Commonwealth countries. There are also many non-official associations that bring together individuals who work within the spheres of law and government, such as the Commonwealth Lawyers Association and the Commonwealth Parliamentary Association.

1. Commonwealth Foundation

The Commonwealth Foundation is an intergovernmental organisation, resourced by and reporting to Commonwealth governments, and guided by Commonwealth values and priorities. Its mandate is to strengthen civil society in the achievement of Commonwealth priorities: democracy and good governance, respect for human rights and gender equality, poverty eradication and sustainable, people-centred and sustainable development, and to promote arts and culture.

The Foundation was established by the Heads of Government in 1965. Admittance is open to all members of the Commonwealth and (as of December 2008) stands at 46 governments out of the 54 member countries. Associate Membership, which is open to associated states or overseas territories of member governments, has been granted to Gibraltar. The year 2005 saw celebrations for the Foundation's 40th Anniversary. The Foundation is headquartered in Marlborough House, Pall Mall, London. Regular liaison and cooperation between the Secretariat and the Foundation is in place.

The Foundation continues to serve the broad purposes for which it was established as written in the Memorandum of Understanding:

2. Commonwealth Games

A multi-sport championship called the Commonwealth Games is held every four years; the last having been held in Melbourne, Australia, in 2006, and the latest due to be held in New Delhi, India, in 2010. As well as the usual athletic disciplines, as at the Summer Olympic Games, the Games include sports particularly popular in the Commonwealth, such as bowls, netball, and rugby sevens. Starting in 1930, the Games were founded on the Olympic model of amateurism, but were deliberately designed to be, as they are still renowned for being "the Friendly Games", with the goal of promoting relations between Commonwealth countries and celebrating their shared sporting and cultural heritage.

A Panaromic view of "Commonwealth" sports, Rugby Sevens at the 2006 Games.

The Games are the Commonwealth's most visible activity, and interest in the operation of the Commonwealth increases greatly when the Games are held. There is controversy over whether the Games, and sport generally, should be involved in the Commonwealth's wider political concerns. The 1977 Gleneagles Agreement was signed to commit Commonwealth countries to combat Apartheid through discouraging sporting contact with South Africa (which was not then a member), whilst the 1986 Games were boycotted by most African, Asian, and Caribbean countries for failure of other countries to enforce the Gleneagles Agreement.

3. Commonwealth of Learning

The Commonwealth of Learning (COL) is an intergovernmental organisation created by the Heads of Government to encourage the development and sharing of open learning/distance education knowledge, resources and technologies. COL is helping developing nations improve access to quality education and training.

4. Commonwealth Business Council

The Commonwealth Business Council (CBC) was formed at 1997 CHOGM. The aim was to utilise the global network of the Commonwealth more effectively for the promotion of global trade and investment for shared prosperity. The CBC acts as a bridge for co-operation between business and government, concentrating efforts on these specific areas enhancing trade, facilitating ICT for Development, mobilising investment, promoting corporate citizenship, and Public Private Partnerships. The CBC has a dedicated team, CBC Technologies, based in London and is focused on the international technology and global services industry throughout the Commonwealth.

5. Commonwealth War Graves Commission

The Commonwealth War Graves Commission (CWGC) is responsible for maintaining the war graves of 1.7 million service personnel that died in the First World War and Second World War fighting for Commonwealth member states. Founded in 1917, the Commission has expanded to construct 2,500 war cemeteries, and maintains individual graves at another 20,000 sites around the world. The vast majority of the latter are civilian cemeteries in the United Kingdom. In 1998, the CWGC made the records of its buried online to facilitate easier searching. Commonwealth war cemeteries often feature similar horticulture and architecture, with larger cemeteries being home to a Cross of Sacrifice and Stone of Remembrance. The CWGC was notable when first founded for marking the graves identically, regardless of the rank, country of origin, race, or religion of the buried. It is funded by voluntary agreement by six Commonwealth members, in proportion to the nationality of the casualties in the graves maintained, with three-quarters of the funding coming from the UK.

Commonwealth Culture

It is remarkable that mostly due to their history of British rule, many Commonwealth nations possess certain identifiable traditions and customs that are elements of a shared Commonwealth culture. Examples include common sports such as cricket and rugby, driving on the left, the Westminster system of parliamentary democracy, common law, widespread use of the English language, designation of English as an official language, military and naval ranks, and the use of British rather than American spelling conventions (see English in the Commonwealth of Nations). None of these is universal amongst, nor exclusive to, the

Commonwealth, but are more commonly found within its members than elsewhere.

1. Literature

The shared history of British presence has also produced a substantial body of writing in many languages, known as Commonwealth literature. There is an Association for Commonwealth Literature and Language Studies, with nine chapters worldwide and an international conference is held every three years.

In 1987, the Commonwealth Foundation established the annual Commonwealth Writers' Prize "to encourage and reward the upsurge of new Commonwealth fiction and ensure that works of merit reach a wider audience outside their country of origin". Prizes are awarded for the best book and best first book in the Commonwealth, as well as regional prizes for the best book and best first book from each of four regions. Although not officially affiliated with the Commonwealth, the prestigious Man Booker Prize is awarded annually to an author from a Commonwealth country or the two former members, the Republic of Ireland and Zimbabwe. This honour is one of the highest in literature.

2. Sport

Due to the legacy of British colonial rule, many Commonwealth nations play similar sports that are considered quintessentially "Commonwealth" in character, including cricket, both codes of rugby, and netball. This has led to the development of friendly national rivalries between the main sporting nations that have often defined their relations with each another. Indeed, said rivalries preserved close ties by providing a constant in international relationships, even as the Empire transformed into the

Commonwealth. Externally, playing these sports is seen to be a sign of sharing a certain Commonwealth culture; the adoption of cricket at schools in Rwanda is seen as symbolic of the country's move towards Commonwealth membership.

Besides the Commonwealth Games, a number of other sporting competitions are organised on a Commonwealth basis, through championship tournaments such as the Commonwealth Judo Championships, Commonwealth Rowing Championships, Commonwealth Sailing Championships, and Commonwealth Shooting Championships. The Commonwealth Boxing Council has long maintained Commonwealth titles for the best boxers in the Commonwealth.

3. Political System

Due to their shared constitutional histories, most countries in the Commonwealth have similar legal and political systems. The Commonwealth requires its members to be functioning democracies that respect human rights and the rule of law. Half of Commonwealth countries have the Westminster system of parliamentary democracy. The Commonwealth Parliamentary Association facilitates cooperation between legislatures across the Commonwealth, and the Commonwealth Local Government Forum promotes good governance amongst local government officials.

Most Commonwealth members use common law, modelled on English law. The Judicial Committee of the Privy Council is the supreme court of fourteen Commonwealth members.

Symbols

The Commonwealth has adopted a number of symbols

that represent the association of its members. Elizabeth II holds the position of Head of the Commonwealth as a symbol of the Commonwealth's free association, dating back to the London Declaration, issued in 28 April 1949. The English language is recognised as a symbol of the members' heritage; as well as being considered a symbol of the Commonwealth, recognition of it as "the means of Commonwealth communication" is a prerequisite for Commonwealth membership.

The flag of the Commonwealth consists of the symbol of the Commonwealth Secretariat, represented by a gold globe surrounded by emanating "rays", on a dark blue field; it was designed for the second CHOGM, in 1973, and officially adopted on the 26 March 1976. 1976 also saw the organisation agree to a common date on which to commemorate Commonwealth Day, the second Monday in March, having developed separately on different dates from pre-existing Empire Day celebrations.

Commonwealth Citizenship

In recognition of their shared heritage and culture, Commonwealth countries are not considered to be "foreign" to each other. When engaging bilaterally with one another, Commonwealth governments exchange High Commissioners instead of ambassadors. Between two Commonwealth realms, they represent the Head of Government rather than the Head of State.

In addition, some members treat resident citizens of other Commonwealth countries preferentially to citizens of non-Commonwealth countries. The United Kingdom and several others, mostly in the Caribbean, grant the right to vote to Commonwealth citizens who reside in those countries. In non-Commonwealth countries in which their own country is not represented, Commonwealth citizens may seek consular assistance at the United Kingdom embassy.

Now we wish to acquaint you with the sports and sports ulture in historical perspective before coming to the main theme of commonwealth games.

REFERENCES

Commonwealth Ministerial Action Group". Commonwealth Secretariat. http://www.thecommonwealth.org/Internal/38125/cmag/. Retrieved 2007-07-29.

Dale, William (July 1982). "Is the Commonwealth an International Organisation?". International and Comparative Law Quarterly 31 (3): 451–73.

"Harare Commonwealth Declaration". Commonwealth Secretariat. 20 October 1991. http://www.thecommonwealth.org/Templates/Internal.asp?NodeID=34457. Retrieved 2007-07-29.

Harold, Perkin (September 1989). "Teaching the nations how to play: sport and society in the British Empire and Commonwealth". International Journal of the History of Sport 6 (2): pp. 145–155. doi:10.1080/09523368908713685.

McKinnon, Don (February 2008). "A Commonwealth of Values: a Commonwealth of incomparable value". The Round Table 97 (394): pp. 19–28. doi:10.1080/00358530801890561.

"Singapore Declaration of Commonwealth Principles 1971". Commonwealth Secretariat. 22 January 1971. http://www.thecommonwealth.org/Internal/20723/32987/singapore_declaration_of_commonwealth_principles/. Retrieved 2007-07-25.

2

Sports and Games: Key Aspects

> "A Dwarf standing on the shoulders of a giant sees farther than the Giant, but if he stood upon his own basis, he would scarcely see at all. It behoaves him to remember that the Giant is Giant."
>
> —*Lewis*

In the preceding chapter we have tried to acquaint you with the 'Commonwealth of Nations,' wherein we have highlighted origin, growth, objectives and various activities of the commonwealth; and their relevance in the present world order is also emphasized.

Since the main theme of the present work is 'Games' (Commonwealth Games), it is necessary for you to acquaint with sports and games,—their origin, present modes and other salient features like sports diplomacy, nationalism etc. Here follows the narration.

In common parlance, a sport is commonly defined as an organized, competitive, and skillful physical activity requiring commitment and fair play. It is governed by a set of rules or customs. In a sport the key factors are the physical capabilities and skills of the competitor when determining the outcome (winning or losing). The physical activity involves the movement of people, animals and/or a variety of objects such as balls and machines.

In contrast, games such as card games and board games, though these could be called mind sports, require only mental skills. Non-competitive activities such as jogging and rock-climbing, are usually classified as recreations. Physical events such as scoring goals or crossing a line first often define the result of a sport. However the degree of skill in some sports such as diving, dressage and figure skating is judged according to well-defined criteria. This is in contrast with other judged activities such as beauty pageants and body-building shows, where skill does not have to be shown and the criteria are not as well defined.

Accurate records are kept and updated for most sports at the highest levels, while failures and accomplishments are widely announced in sport news. Sports are most often played just for fun or for the simple fact that people need exercise to stay in good physical condition. However professional sport is a major source of entertainment.

Coming to historical perspective, there are artifacts and structures that suggest that the Chinese engaged in sporting activities as early as 4000 BC. Gymnastics appears to have been a popular sport in China's ancient past. Monuments to the Pharaohs indicate that a number of sports, including swimming and fishing, were well-developed and regulated several thousands of years ago in ancient Egypt. Other Egyptian sports included javelin throwing, high jump, and wrestling. Ancient Persian sports such as the traditional Iranian martial art of Zourkhaneh had a close connection to the warfare skills.

Among other sports that originate in Persia are polo and jousting. A wide range of sports were already established by the time of Ancient Greece and the military culture and the development of sports in Greece influenced one another considerably. Sports became such a prominent part of their culture that the Greeks created the Olympic Games, which in ancient times were held every four years in a small village in the Peloponnesus called Olympia. Sports have been increasingly organized and regulated from the time of the Ancient Olympics up to the present century. Industrialization has brought increased leisure time to the citizens of developed and developing countries, leading to more time for citizens to attend and follow spectator sports, greater participation in athletic activities, and increased accessibility.

These trends continued with the advent of mass media and global communication. Professionalism became prevalent, further adding to the increase in sport's popularity, as sports fans began following the exploits of professional athletes through radio, television, and the internet—all while enjoying the exercise and competition associated with amateur participation in sports.

Remarkably, in the new millennium, new sports have been going further from the physical aspect to the mental or psychological aspect of competing. Electronic sports organizations are becoming more and more popular. Activities where the outcome is determined by judgement over execution are considered performances, or competition.

Now we come to sportsmenship.

Sportsmanship

Sportsmanship expresses an aspiration or ethos that the activity will be enjoyed for its own sake. The well-known sentiment by sports journalist Grantland Rice, that it's "not that you won or lost but how you played the game," and the Modern Olympic creed expressed by its founder Pierre de Coubertin: "The most important thing .

... is not winning but taking part" are typical expressions of this sentiment.

Sportsmanship is an attitude that strives for fair play, courtesy toward teammates and opponents, ethical behaviour and integrity, and grace in victory or defeat.

Violence in sports involves crossing the line between fair competition and intentional aggressive violence. Athletes, coaches, fans, and parents sometimes unleash violent behaviour on people or property, in misguided shows of loyalty, dominance, anger, or celebration. Rioting or hooliganism are common and ongoing problems at national and international sporting contests.

The entertainment aspect of sports, together with the spread of mass media and increased leisure time, has led to professionalism in sports. This has resulted in some conflict, where the paycheck can be seen as more important than recreational aspects, or where the sports are changed simply to make them more profitable and popular, thereby losing certain valued traditions.

Politics in Sports

At times, sports and politics can have a large amount of influence on each other. When apartheid was the official policy in South Africa, many sports people, particularly in rugby union, adopted the conscientious approach that they should not appear in competitive sports there. Some feel this was an effective contribution to the eventual demolition of the policy of apartheid, others feel that it may have prolonged and reinforced its worst effects.

The 1936 Summer Olympics held in Berlin was an illustration, perhaps best recognised in retrospect, where an ideology was developing which used the event to strengthen its spread through propaganda. In the history of Ireland, Gaelic sports were connected with cultural nationalism. Until the mid 20th century a person could have been banned from playing Gaelic football, hurling, or other sports administered by the Gaelic Athletic Association (GAA) if she/he played or supported soccer, or other games seen to be of British origin. Until recently the GAA continued to ban the playing of soccer and rugby union at Gaelic venues.

This ban is still enforced, but has been modified to allow football and rugby be played in Croke Park while Lansdowne Road is being redeveloped. Until recently, under Rule 21, the GAA also banned members of the British security forces and members of the RUC from playing Gaelic games, but the advent of the Good Friday Agreement in 1998 led to the eventual removal of the ban. Nationalism is often evident in the pursuit of sports, or in its reporting: people compete in national teams, or commentators and audiences can adopt a partisan view. On occasion, such tensions can lead to violent confrontation among players or spectators within and beyond the sporting venue. These trends are seen by many as contrary to the fundamental ethos of sports being carried on for its own sake and for the enjoyment of its participants.

As a Physical Art

Sports have many affinities with art. Ice skating and Tai chi, and Dancesport for example, are sports that come close to artistic spectacles in themselves. Similarly, there are other activities that have elements of sport and art in their execution, such as artistic gymnastics, Bodybuilding, Parkour, performance art, Yoga, bossaball, dressage, culinary arts, etc. Perhaps the best example is Bull-fighting, which in Spain is reported in the arts pages of newspapers.

The fact that art is so close to sports in some situations is probably related to the nature of sports. The definition of "sports" above put forward the idea of an activity pursued not just for the usual purposes, for example, running not simply to get places, but running for its own sake, running as well as we can.

This is similar to a common view of aesthetic value, which is seen as something over and above the strictly functional value coming from an object's normal use. So an aesthetically pleasing car is one which doesn't just get from A to B, but which impresses us with its grace, poise, and charisma. In the same way, a sporting performance such as jumping doesn't just impress us as being an effective way to avoid obstacles or to get across streams. It impresses us because of the ability, skill, and style which is shown. Art and sports were probably more clearly linked at the time of Ancient Greece, when gymnastics and calisthenics invoked admiration and aesthetic appreciation for the physical build, prowess and 'arete' displayed by participants.

The modern term 'art' as skill, is related to this ancient Greek term 'arete'. The closeness of art and sport in these times was revealed by the nature of the Olympic Games which, as we have seen, were celebrations of both sporting and artistic achievements, poetry, sculpture and architecture.

Technology

Technology has an important role in sports, whether applied to an athlete's health, the athlete's technique, or equipment's characteristics.

Equipment As sports have grown more competitive, the need for better equipment has arisen. Golf clubs, football helmets, tennis racquets, baseball bats, soccer balls, hockey skates, and other equipment have all seen considerable changes when new technologies have been applied.

Health Ranging from nutrition to the treatment of injuries, as the knowledge of the human body has deepened over time, an athlete's potential has been increased. Athletes are now able to play to an older age, recover more quickly from injuries, and train more effectively than previous generations of athletes.

Instruction Advancing technology created new opportunities for research into sports. It is now possible to analyse aspects of sports that were previously out of the reach of comprehension. Being able to use motion capture to capture an athlete's movement, or advanced computer simulations to model physical scenarios has greatly increased an athlete's ability to understand what they are doing and how they can improve themselves.

Spectator Sport

As well as being a form of recreation for the participants, much sport is played in front of an audience. Most professional sport is played in a 'theatre' of some kind; be it a stadium, arena, golf course, race track, or the open road, with provision for the (often paying) public.

HISTORY OF SPORT

The history of sport probably extends as far back as the existence of people as purposive sportive and active beings. Sport has been a useful way for people to increase their mastery of nature and the environment. The history of sport can teach us a great deal about social changes and about the nature of sport itself. Sport seems to involve basic human skills being developed and exercised for their own sake, in parallel with being exercised for their usefulness. It also shows how society has changed its beliefs and therefore there are changes in the rules.

Of course, as we go further back in history the dwindling evidence makes the theories of the origins and purposes of sport difficult to support. Nonetheless, its importance in human history is undeniable.

Sports that are at least two and a half thousand years old include hurling (similar to field hockey) in Ireland, harpastum (similar to rugby) in Rome, cuju (similar to association football) in China, and polo in Persia. The Mesoamerican ballgame originated over three thousand years ago. There are artifacts and structures that suggest that the Chinese engaged in sporting activities as early as 4000 BC. Gymnastics appears to have been a popular sport in China's ancient past. Monuments to the Pharaohs indicate that a number of sports, including swimming and fishing, were well-developed and regulated several thousands of years ago in ancient Egypt. Other Egyptian sports included javelin throwing, high jump, and wrestling. Ancient Persian sports such as the traditional Iranian martial art of Zourkhaneh had a close connection to the warfare skills. Among other sports that originate in Persia are polo and jousting.

Depictions of ritual sporting events are seen in the Minoan art of Bronze Age Crete (from approximately 2700 to 1450 BC), mainly involving religious bull-leaping and possibly bullfighting. Homer tells us that sport was practised in Mycenaean times, between 1600 BC and ca. 1100 BC. In the Iliad there are extensive descriptions of funeral sports games held in honour of deceased warriors, and engaging in sports is described as the occupation of the noble and wealthy, who have no need to do manual labour themselves. In the Odyssey, king Odysseus of Ithaca proves his royal status to king Alkinoös of the Phaiakes by showing his proficiency in throwing the javelin. It was predictably in Greece that sports were first instituted formally, with the first Olympics recorded in 776 BC in Olympia, where they were celebrated until 393 AD.

Initially a single sprinting event, the Olympics gradually expanded to include several footraces, run in the nude or in armor, boxing, wrestling, *pankration*, chariot racing, long jump, javelin throw, and discus throw. A variety of informal and formal games were popular in Ancient Greece, with the most prestigious ones achieving Panhellenic status.

Some games, e.g. the Panathenaia of Athens, included musical, reading and other non-athletic contests in addition to regular sports events. High-profile athletes were major celebrities in Ancient Greece. City walls were torn down when victors returned home, as a city of such men was said to be in no need for walls to defend itself. They were often granted lifetime pensions or dining rights at public expense. Regardless of such material rewards granted afterwards, the most prestigious games were strictly *stephanítai* (from the Greek: óôÝöáíïò, *stéphanos*, a wreath or crown of plant branches), i.e. the only prize awarded was a wreath and the athletes competed for glory alone.

For at least seven hundred years, entire villages have competed with each other in rough, and sometimes violent, ballgames in England (Shrovetide football) and Ireland (caid). In contrast, the game of calcio Fiorentino, in Florence, Italy, was originally reserved for the aristocracy. The aristocracy throughout Europe favoured sports as patrons. Horse racing, in particular, was a favourite of the upper class in Great Britain, with Queen Anne founding the Ascot Racecourse.

Modern Sport

Writing about cricket in particular, John Leach (2005a) have explained the role of Puritan power, the Civil War, and the Restoration of the monarchy in England. The Long Parliament in 1642 "banned theatres, which had met with Puritan disapproval. Although similar action would be taken against certain sports, it is not clear if cricket was in any way prohibited, except that players must not break the Sabbath.

In 1660, "the Restoration of the monarchy in England was immediately followed by the reopening of the theatres and so any sanctions that had been imposed by the Puritans on cricket would also have been lifted." He goes on to make the very important point that political, social and economic conditions in the aftermath of the Restoration encouraged excessive gambling, so much so that a Gambling Act was necessary in 1664.

It is certain that cricket, horse racing and boxing (i.e., prizefighting) were financed by gambling interests. Leach explains that it was the habit of cricket patrons, all of whom were gamblers, to form strong teams through the 18th century to represent their interests. He defines a strong team as one representative of more than one parish and he is certain that such teams were first assembled in or immediately after 1660.

Prior to the English Civil War and the Commonwealth, all available evidence concludes that cricket had evolved to the level of village cricket only where teams that are strictly representative of individual parishes compete. The "strong teams" of the post-Restoration mark the evolution of cricket (and, indeed of professional team sport, for cricket is the oldest professional team sport) from the parish standard to the county standard. As he rightly says, this was the point of origin for major, or first-class, cricket.1660 also marks the origin of *professional team sport.*

A number of the English Public Schools, such as Winchester and Eton, introduced sports for their pupils, particularly variants of football. These were described at the time as "innocent and lawful," certainly in comparison with the rural games.With the coming of the Industrial Revolution and the movement of the populace from the country to the cities, the rural games moved to the new urban centres and came under the influence of the middle and upper classes. The rules and regulations devised at English public schools began to be applied to the wider game, with governing bodies in England being set up for a number of sports by the end of the 19th century. The rising influence of the upper class also produced an emphasis of the amateur, and the spirit of 'fair play'.

The industrial revolution also brought with it increasing mobility, and created the opportunity for English public schools, and universities in Britain and elsewhere, to compete with each other. This sparked increasing attempts to unify and reconcile various public school games in England, leading to the establishment of the Football Association in London, the first official governing body in football.

The influence of British sports and their codified rules began to spread across the world in the late 19th and early 20th century, particularly association football. A number of major teams elsewhere in the world still show these British origins in their names, such as AC Milan in Italy, Corinthians in Brazil, and Athletic Bilbao in Spain. Cricket became popular in several of the nations of the then British Empire, such as Australia, South Africa and India. The revival of the Olympic Games by Baron Pierre de Coubertin was also heavily influenced by the amateur ethos of the English public schools. Baseball became established in the urban Northeastern United States, with the first rules being codified in the 1840s, while American football was very popular in the south-east. With baseball spreading to the south, and American football spreading to the north after the Civil War.

In the 1870s the game split between the professionals and amateurs; the professional game rapidly gained dominance, and marked a shift in the focus from the player to the club. The rise of baseball also helped squeeze out other sports such as Cricket, which had been popular in Philadelphia prior to the rise of Baseball.American football also has its origins in the English variants of the game, with the first set of intercollegiate football rules based directly on the rules of the Football Association in London. However, Harvard chose to play a game based on the rules of Rugby football. Walter Camp would then heavily modify this variant in the 1880s, with the modifications also heavily influencing the rules of Canadian football.Some historians—notably Bernard Lewis—claim that team sports are primarily an invention of Western cultures. The traditional teams sports, according to these authors, springs from Europe, primarily England. This ignores some of the ancient games of cooperation from Central America and the Indian subcontinent.

The Industrial Revolution and mass production brought increased leisure which allowed increases in spectator sports, less elitism in sports, and greater accessibility. With the advent of mass media and global communication, professionalism became prevalent in sports.

This further sports popularity in general. Perhaps in a reaction to the demands of contemporary life, there have been developments in sport that are best described as post-modern: extreme ironing being a notable example. There is also a move towards adventure sports as a form of escaping or transcending the routines of life, examples being white water rafting, paragliding, canyoning, BASE jumping, Parkour and more genteelly, orienteering. The history of sport education is an important topic of the political history.

Women's Sport

Women's competition in sports has been frowned upon by many societies in the past. The English public-school background of organised sport in the 19th and early 20th century led to a paternalism that tended to discourage women's involvement in sports, with, for example, no women officially competing in the 1896 Olympic Games.The 20th century saw major advances in the participation of women in sports, although women's participation as fans, administrators, officials, coaches, journalists, and athletes remains in general less than men's. Mass involvement tends to favour sports such as swimming and aerobics, and tends to stress the competitive aspects less than men.

The increase has been partly related to the drive for more women's rights. In the United States, female students participation in sports was significantly boosted by the Title 9 Act in 1972, preventing gender discrimination and equal opportunity for women to participate in sport at all levels.Pressure from sports funding bodies has also improved gender equality in sports.

GAMESMANSHIP

Gamesmanship is the use of dubious (although not technically illegal) methods to win a game, such as golf or snooker. "Pushing the rules to the limit without getting caught, using whatever dubious methods possible to achieve the desired end." (Lumpkin, Stoll and Beller, 1994:92). As opposed to sportsmanship, it may be inferred that the term derives from playing for the game (to win at any cost) as opposed to playing for sport.

Stephen Potter cites the origin of gamesmanship to be a tennis match in which he and the philosopher C. E. M. Joad competed against two younger and fitter men who were outplaying them fairly comfortably. On returning a serve, Joad hit the ball straight into the back-netting twelve feet behind the back-line. While the opponents were preparing for the next serve Joad queried whether the ball had landed in, or out. Being young, polite university students, their opponents offered to replay the point, but Joad declined. Because they were young and polite, the slight suggestion by Joad that their etiquette and sportsmanship was in question was extremely off-putting. Potter and Joad went on to win the match.

Techniques

The most common techniques of gamesmanship are the following.

1. Breaking the flow of an opponent's play.
2. Causing an opponent to take the game less seriously or to overthink his or her position.
3. Intentionally making a "mistake" which gains an advantage over an opponent.

While the first method is more common at higher levels of sports, the last two are more powerful in amateur games.

Breaking the Flow

Examples of "flow-breaking" methods include:

- In darts, the player intentionally takes a long time to take their darts out of the dartboard. (Peter Manley has been widely accused of this.)
- Feigning injury to delay the game, or to imply you won't be playing at your best. The skilled gamesman can counter this tactic by waiting until the game has been in play for some time, before revealing that he or she suffers from a far more serious condition, such as a heart defect.
- In billiards or snooker, intentionally standing in your opponent's line of sight, and then suddenly moving when you "realise" you're in the wrong place.
- Distracting your opponent by complaining about other people who might be (but weren't) distracting your opponent. Potter, who always insisted that the good gamesman must give the appearance of being a good sportsman, recommended this approach. For example, if an opponent is about to take a shot at billiards, it is bad gamesmanship to fidget and whistle but good gamesmanship to distract him by loudly requesting silence from spectators.
- When winning a point you should look directly at the opponent, but when losing one always avoid eye contact.
- In cricket, coming out to bat with two right-handed gloves and then wasting time sorting it out.

- In baseball, a batter can disrupt a pitcher's flow by calling time just before he delivers the pitch.
- When losing an outdoor game, feigning a deep, informed and more than amateur interest in e.g. botany or ornithology, in order to convey the breadth of your interests and suggest to opponent that you are not really concerned about losing. This can cause them to relax their attention, or at any rate rob them of the satisfaction of beating you.
- In amateur hockey, types of "flow-breaking" include intentionally icing the puck, lining up at the wrong face-off dot, or shooting the puck over the glass (in professional hockey, the team that ices the puck is not allowed a line change, while shooting the puck over the glass leads to a two-minute penalty).

Causing your Opponent to Overthink

Examples of methods designed to cause your opponent to overthink or to not take the game seriously enough include:

- Giving intentionally vague advice in the hope of making your opponent focus on his play.
- Asking one's opponent's advice for a (fictitious) match the following day, against an implied stronger opponent.
- Claiming that the game you are playing "just isn't my sport", or claiming less expertise than you actually possess (a mild form of hustling).
- In American football, the very common practice of taking one or more timeouts to give an opposing kicker an excessive amount of time to think about a critical kick; most often a field goal or extra point

but sometimes a potential on-side kick. The intent is to cause the kicker to get overly stressed about making a mistake and hopefully create a self-fulfilling prophecy. This is commonly referred to as "icing the kicker".

- The converse approach, suggesting a level of expertise far higher than you actually possess, can also be effective. For example, although gamesmanship frowns on simple distractions like whistling loudly while an opponent takes a shot, it is good gamesmanship to do so when taking a shot oneself, suggesting as it does a level of carefree detachment which your opponent does not possess.

PROFESSIONAL SPORTS

Most sports played professionally also have amateur players far outnumbering the professionals. Professional athleticism is seen by some as a contradiction of the central ethos of sport, competition performed for its own sake and pure enjoyment, rather than as a means of earning a living. Consequently, many organisations and commentators have resisted the growth of professional athleticism, saying that it was so incredible that he has impeded the development of sport. For example, rugby union was for many years a part-time sport engaged in by amateurs, and English cricket has allegedly suffered in quality because of a "non-professional" approach.

Professional sports, as opposed to amateur sports, are sports in which athletes receive payment for their performance. Professional athleticism has come to the fore through a combination of developments. Mass media and increased leisure have brought larger audiences, so that sports organizations or teams can command large incomes.

As a result, more sportspeople can afford to make athleticism their primary career, devoting the training time necessary to increase skills, physical condition, and experience to modern levels of achievement. This proficiency has also helped boost the popularity of sports.

Public schools had a deep involvement in the development many team sports had codes of football as well as cricket and hockey. Moreover, the ethos of English public schools greatly influenced Pierre de Coubertin. The International Olympic Committee (IOC) invited a representative of the Headmasters' Conference (HC, the association of headmasters of the English public schools) to attend their early meetings. The Headmasters' Conference chose the Reverend Robert Laffan, the headmaster of Cheltenham College, as their representative to the IOC meetings. He was made a Member of the IOC in 1897 and, following the first visit of the IOC to London in 1904, he was central to the founding of the British Olympic Association a year later.

Until recent times professional athletes in English sport, particularly cricket, were unthinkable and hence most players were amateurs. The EPS subscribed to the Ancient Greek and Roman belief that sport formed an important part of education, an attitude summed up in the saying: *mens sana in corpore sano* – a sound mind in a healthy body. In this ethos, taking part has more importance than winning, because society expected gentlemen to become all-rounders and not the best at everything. Class prejudice against "trade" reinforced this attitude.

The house of a typical EPS boy would have a tradesman's entrance, because tradesmen did not rank as the social equals of gentlemen. Within this class view it follows that if a person played a sport as a paid "professional", that would make the person a member of a trade. How could a club function when expectations demanded that some of the players enter through a side entrance? How would the social side of the club flourish if some of the members did not rank as gentlemen? How could a club of gentlemen which played a club of professionals possibly entertain their social inferiors? Another prejudice which existed amongst late Victorian and Edwardian gentlemen held that the all-round abilities of British gentlemen allegedly meant that, if they put their minds to something, they would perform better than anyone else. This included the other British classes. The British attempts under Scott to reach the South Pole illustrate this prejudice.

In the Scott expeditions, gentlemen refused to take the instructions of Canadian dog-handlers seriously, or to learn from Scandinavians how to use cross-country skis properly. To compensate for their failures to master dog and ski they persuaded themselves (and their contemporaries) that walking and to man-hauling sledges to the South Pole made the process more of an achievement. If professional teams were to beat gentlemen amateur teams consistently, that might burst the illusion of social superiority, and that could lead to social instability, something not in the perceived interests of the British upper classes of the time.

Olympic Games

Until the late 20th century the Olympic Games nominally only accepted amateur athletes. However, successful Olympians from Western countries often had endorsement contracts from sponsors. Complex rules involving the payment of the athlete's earnings into trust funds rather than directly to the athletes themselves, were developed in an attempt to work around this issue, but the intellectual evasion involved was considered embarrassing to the Olympic movement and the key Olympic sports by some. In the same era, the nations of the Communist bloc entered teams of Olympians who were all nominally students or working in a profession, but many of whom were in reality paid by the state to train on a full time basis. In 1982 Adidas was paying British Olympic athletes to wear their gear. The first Olympics to officially accept professional athletes was 1988 in selected sports and 1992 in the remainder.

Sports Salaries

Professional sportspeople can earn a great deal of money. For instance, the highest-paid team in professional baseball is New York Yankees. Tiger Woods is the highest paid athlete totaling $127,902,706, including his endorsement income, which massively exceeds what he earns from tournament golf. Tiger recently became the world's first athlete to earn a billion dollars from prize money and endorsements. It would have taken the salary of 2,000 1980s professional golfers each making $58,500 to match up with Tiger Woods' current salary. The top ten tennis players make about $3 million a year on average. Much of the growth in income for sports and athletes has come from broadcasting rights. For example, the 2011-2013 NFL broadcast contract has been valued at $20.4 billion.

Now we come to the important aspect of sports i.e. sports diplomacy.

SPORTS DIPLOMACY

Sports Diplomacy is when sport is used as a political tool to enhance diplomatic relations between two entities. The intention is sometimes to bring about radical change. While the Olympics is often the biggest political example of using sports for diplomatic means, cricket and association football, as well as other sports in the global arena, have also been used in this regard. In the case of Apartheid, sport was used to isolate South Africa and bring about a major overhaul in the country's social structure.

Table Tennis

In the 1970s an exchange of table tennis players from the United States and the People's Republic of China led to a thaw in Sino-American relations that eventually led to U.S. President Richard Nixon's rapprochement with China.

Olympics

Going as far back as the 1936 Olympics, Adolf Hitler used this as a stage to promote Aryan superiority for Germany with his ideological belief of racial supremacy. The Olympics were used as a method of hardening the German spirit and instilling unity among German youth. It was also believed that sport was a "way to weed out the weak, Jewish, and other undesirables." As a result, many Jews and Gypsies were banned from participating in sporting events. While Germany did top the medal table, the Nazi depiction of ethnic Africans as inferior was dispelled by Jesse Owens' gold medals in the 100m, 200m, 4x100m relay and long jump events.

Once again, in 1968, the global stage of the Olympics was used to show the world the plight of the African-American struggle during the civil rights movement in their home country. The famous Black Power salute was performed by Tommie Smith and John Carlos during the medal ceremony in Mexico City.

In 1972, the Israeli Olympic Team were massacred in an attack by Palestinian gunmen that started at the Olympic village and eventually resulted in the deaths of 17. In 1980, the Soviet invasion of Afghanistan led to a boycott of the Moscow games by a large part of the Western powers and their allies in protest of Russian actions. In the 1984 Los Angeles Olympics the Soviet Bloc led a retaliatory boycott of the games in response to the American-led Moscow games boycott.

Cricket

Cricket has also had a hand to play in sporting diplomacy. Following the Soviet invasion of Afghanistan, and Soviet pressure on India to deflect the tension they faced, in 1987 Pakistan's president at the time, General Zia ul-Haq, attended a test match between India and Pakistan in Jaipur - a visit that apparently helped cool a flare-up in tensions. Furthermore, following a fifteen year lull in test matches, cricket tours between India and Pakistan were revived in 2004 in the wake of diplomatic initiatives to bury half a century of mutual hostility. Both sides relaxed their tough visa regulations for each other, allowing thousands of fans to travel across the border. In an attempt to replicate the cricket diplomacy of the past General Pervez Musharraf came to India in 2005 ostensibly for a cricket match. The trip, however, quickly took on the air of a summit as the sides were urged "to seize a historic chance to end their dispute over Kashmir." Often this rivalry has been tinged with a religious-political bent to it. A Pakistani fan in Karachi ran onto the pitch to attack the Indian captain, and fans threw stones at the Indian players during the match in Karachi. In 2000 right-wing Hindus dug up the cricket pitch in New Delhi to protest against the Pakistani team's visit.

China have also gotten in on the cricket diplomacy act. Cross-Strait relations have once again been the impetus for doing so. During the buildup to the 2007 World Cup, Antigua received a $55 million grant to build the Sir Vivian Richards Stadium, while Jamaica received $30 million for a new Trelawny stadium. St. Lucia have also got both a cricket and a football stadium courtesy of China. China spent a remarkable $132 million on cricket facilities in the West Indies over the past few years, a massive amount compared to the International Cricket Council's paltry 10-year budget of $70 million to promote cricket *globally*.

It is said that the motive for China's generosity is because "Most of the remaining countries that recognize Taiwan are located in the Caribbean and Latin America." The diplomacy paid off in the end as Grenada and Dominica derecognized Taiwan as an independent country. Further, "Of the remaining 24 countries that recognize Taiwan, four are in the Caribbean and two of these play cricket." Grenada previously had a stadium built by Taiwan, but saw it flattened by a hurricane. To join the action, China quickly came in to erect another stadium. Consequently, Taiwan took Grenada to a New York City court to force the latter to return the original loan.

Put on the back foot, a beleaguered Taiwan also used the World Cup to shore up its position among its shrinking West Indian support base. It doled out $21 million to St. Kitts and Nevis and $12 million to the even smaller St. Vincent and the Grenadines for cricket grounds. China's aggressive ambitions have benefited the Caribbean Islands as "Strategic analysts say China is laying out more money than is needed to just isolate Taiwan. China, which has built large embassies in each of the islands, now has a bigger diplomatic presence in the Caribbean than the United

States, the superpower next door." And that "Mainland China's long-term strategy coincides with its foreign policy."

Remarkably, in 2008, the England and Wales Cricket Board cancelled Zimbabwe's 2009 tour of England and suspended all bilateral relations between the two states in response to the situation regarding the 2008 Zimbabwean presidential election.

Association Football

The most infamous declaration of politics and sport was the Football War between El Salvador and Honduras. Though the build up to the war had to do with more socio-economic issues like immigration and land reform, the impetus for war was an inflammation of tensions set off by rioters during the second North American qualifying round for the 1970 FIFA World Cup. Disturbances broke out during the first game in Tegucigalpa, but the second leg saw the situation get considerably worse in San Salvador. Honduran fans were roughed up, the Honduran flag and national anthem were insulted, and the emotions of both nations became considerably agitated. In retaliation, violence against Salvadoran residents in Honduras, including several Vice Consuls, increased. An unknown number of Salvadorans were killed or brutalized, and tens of thousands began fleeing the country. The press of both nations contributed to a growing climate of near-hysteria, and on June 27, 1969, twelve days after the second-leg game, Honduras broke diplomatic relations with El Salvador. On July 14, 1969, the Salvadoran army launched an attack against Honduras. The Organization of American States negotiated a cease-fire which took effect on July 20, with the Salvadoran troops withdrawn in early August. Athletic Bilbao are famous for the cantera policy of signing only Basque players. Along with fellow Basque side Real Sociedad, Bilbao raised the still banned Basque flag in a game shortly after the death of General Francisco Franco.

In the 1986 Mexico World Cup, following the Falklands War between Argentina and the United Kingdom, Diego Maradona scored a goal via the "Hand of God" to fuel the flames between the two sides. To make matters worse, this was an unrecognized foul using the hand to score a goal.

At the 1998 FIFA World Cup, held in France, Iran recorded their first World Cup victory in the second game, beating the United States 2-1, with Estili and Mahdavikia scoring goals for Iran. The match was preheated with much excitement because of each country's political stance after the Iranian revolution. However, in an act of defiance against all forms of hatred or politics in sports, both sides presented one another with gifts and flowers and stood together for a picture before the match kickoff.

The 2004 AFC Asian Cup held in China made headlines due to events that took place during the final between China and Japan, apparently due to historical relations dating back to World War II (see Second Sino-Japanese War and Nanjing Massacre). As the Japanese national athem was being played, the home fans expressed their anti-Japanese sentiment by drowning out the national anthem with their chants. The Chinese home fans continually booed at the players and visiting fans as they watched Japan rout China 3-1. After the match, some Chinese fans rioted outside the Beijing Worker's Stadium.

The 2007 AFC Asian Cup was another facet of sporting politics. The victorious Iraqi team came out despite ethnic factionalism in their country and an invasion by the american military to win the biggest tournament in Asian football.

Following a previous round win, Iraqi Military spokesman Brigadier General Qassim Moussawi said they wanted to stop "terrorists, Sunni extremists and criminals from targeting the joy of the people." There was controversy as the Iraqi captain said he "dared not return to his homeland because of the conditions created by the US occupation." President Jalal Talabani said it was disappointing they couldn't celebrate at home with the fans. Yet many hailed the victory as a show of unity. Iraq's Brazilian coach Jorvan Vieira signified they importance of the win, "This is not just about football... this is more important than that...This has brought great happiness to a whole country. This is not about a team, this is about human beings."

Likewise, Saudi coach Helio Cesar dos Anjos chimed in that "Iraq deserved to win today...They were very motivated and we knew the whole world was supporting this team." Likewise, the American leadership also came out in praise. However, Iraqi midfielder Ahmed Manajid said that if wasn't playing for his country he would have fought in his native Fallujah against U.S. forces. He was one of several players who criticized then-U.S. president George W. Bush for using the team's success in his campaign speeches.

Once again, on September 6, 2008, Armenia and Turkey faced each other in a 2010 FIFA World Cup qualification match in Yerevan. In an unprecedented step, Turkish president Abdullah Gul was invited to watch the match, where the presidents of Turkey and Armenia sat together, albeit behind bullet-proof glass. However, the Turkish national anthem was almost drowned out by booing from 35,000 Armenian fans, showing there is still a lot of mistrust between the two countries. However, the gesture "between the presidents showed that they believed 'football diplomacy' had achieved the most important result." This was a first for the two countries divided by the legacy of the 20th century's first genocide.

In 2010 relations between Iran and the UAE took a turn for the worse when the Football Federation of the Islamic Republic of Iran sent a letter to the AFC complaining about the misuse of the *Persian Gulf* name. "The move was made after the UAE misrepresented the name *Persian Gulf* during a match between Iran's Sepahan and the UAE's Al Ain. The Emirate television displayed various banners showing a fictitious name for the Persian Gulf during the match between Iran's Sepahan and the UAE's Al Ain. The AFC must take serious measures to deal with UAE actions of the sort," Taj added. "The UAE side must be fined for showing a fictitious name for the Persian Gulf during the live broadcast of the match." In addition to official comments from the UAE in regards to comparing the three disputed islands of Greater Tunb, the Lesser Tunb and Abu Musa, held by Iran, to the occupation of Palestine calls were made for a downgrade of ties. This also comes after the Islamic Solidarity Games, to be held in Iran, were canceled over the dispute of the *Persian Gulf* label.

Nationalist Sports

In the history of Ireland, Gaelic sports were clearly carried on with nationalist overtones: for example, for most of the last century a person could have been banned from playing Gaelic football, hurling, or other sport, if the person was seen to have played soccer, cricket, rugby or any other game which was perceived to be of British origin. Furthermore, the Old Firm derby in Glasgow featuring Celtic, historically linked to the city's Catholic community, and Rangers, similarly linked to the city's Protestant community, have also historically seen trends along religio-political lines.

The nationalistic Italian fascists also created Volata as their own home-grown alternative to soccer and rugby. It was intended to be a replacement for the popular games perceived to be of British origin that would be of a more local character, tracing its heritage back to the earlier Italian games of Harpastum and Calcio Fiorentino. However, unlike its Gaelic equivalents, Volata was short-lived and is no longer played.

The policy of Spanish football team Athletic Bilbao of picking only Basque players is strongly linked to Basque nationalism.

REFERENCES

Andy Miah *Sport & the Extreme Spectacle: Technological Dependence and Human Limits* (PDF) Unpublished manuscript, 1998

Leach (2005a) is a heavily annotated chronology of cricket 1300-1730 and the source for numerous entries here.

Making the Rugby World: Race, Gender, Commerce edited by Timothy J L Chandler and John Nauright (ISBN 0-7146-4853-1). See especially pages 92-94. Book page:

Mayr, Walter. How a Proud Basque Team Is Resisting Globalization. *Der Spiegel.* April 11, 2008

Mckinley, James C., Jr (1999-03-26). "Baseball; Clash of Cultures, Pride and Passion". *The New York Times.*

"Mr Ahmed D. Touny (EGY), IOC Member". http://www.ioa.leeds.ac.uk/1980s/84085.htm.

Nagy, Peter Tibor, "To the history of sport politics and physical education in Hungary between the world wars 1920-1944".

"Persian warriors". http://www.kuwait-info.com/newsnew/NewsDetails1.asp?id=78319&dt=10/13/2006&ntype=World.

See James A. Mangan, *Athleticism in the Victorian and Edwardian Public School. The emergence and consolidation of an educational ideology*, Cambridge University Press, 1981, Revised Edition: Routledge 2000

"Sports History in China". http://chineseculture.about.com/library/weekly/aa032301a.htm.

Steve Baily *A Noble Ally and Olympic Disciple: The Reverend Robert S. de Courcy Laffan, Coubertin's 'man' in England* (PDF) Steve Bailey is Director of Sports, Winchester College, Winchester, England

Steve Baily *The Reverend Robert S. de Courcy Laffan: Baron Pierre de Coubertin and the Olympic Movement*

The Department of Education (UK) (1996) A National Survey of Involvement in Sport and Physical Activity, Health Promotion Unit,Department of Education.

3

Commonwealth Games: An Overview

> "Wild animals never kill for sport. Man is the only one to whom the torture and death of his fellow creatures is amusing in itself."
>
> —*James Anthony Froude*

After having been acquainted with the history of Commonwealth of Nations' and sport in the preceding chapters now we come to the main theme of Commonwealth games. Here we shall elucidate an overview of themes in historical perspective.

Basically Commonwealth Games is a multinational, multi-sport event which features competitions involving thousands of elite athletes from members of the Commonwealth of Nations. Organised every four years, they are the third-largest multi-sport event in the world, after the Summer Olympic Games and the Asian Games.

As well as many Olympic sports, the Games also include some sports that are played mainly in Commonwealth countries, such as lawn bowls, rugby sevens and netball. The Games are overseen by the Commonwealth Games Federation (CGF), which also controls the sporting programme and selects the host cities. The host city is selected from across the Commonwealth, with eighteen cities in seven countries having hosted it.

History

First it is remarkable to note that sporting competition bringing together the members of the British Empire was first proposed by the Reverend Astley Cooper in 1891 when he wrote an article in *The Times* suggesting a "Pan-Britannic-Pan-Anglican Contest and Festival every four years as a means of increasing the goodwill and good understanding of the British Empire".

In 1911, the Festival of the Empire was held in London to celebrate the coronation of King George V. As part of the festival an Inter-Empire Championships was held in which teams from Australia, Canada, South Africa and the United Kingdom competed in events such as boxing, wrestling, swimming and athletics.

Further, in 1928, Melville Marks Robinson of Canada was asked to organise the first ever British Empire Games which were held in Hamilton, Ontario two years later.

Remarkably, the first Games were held in 1930 in Hamilton, Ontario, Canada. The name changed to British Empire and Commonwealth Games in 1954, to British Commonwealth Games in 1970 and assumed the current name of the Commonwealth Games in 1978.

As a significant development at the 1930 games, women competed in the swimming events only. From 1934, women also competed in some athletics events.

The Empire Games flag was donated in 1931 by the British Empire Games Association of Canada. The year and location of subsequent games were added until the 1950 games. The name of the event was changed to the British Empire and Commonwealth Games and the flag was retired as a result.

The event was first held in 1930 under the title of the British Empire Games. The event was renamed as the British Empire and Commonwealth Games in 1954, the British Commonwealth Games in 1970, and gained its current title in 1978. Only six teams have attended every Commonwealth Games: Australia, Canada, England, New Zealand, Scotland and Wales. Australia has been the highest scoring team for ten games, England for seven and Canada for one.

As of now, there are 53 members of the Commonwealth of Nations, and 71 teams participate in the Games. The four Home Nations of the United Kingdom – England, Scotland, Wales and Northern Ireland – send separate teams to the Commonwealth Games (unlike at the Olympic Games, where the United Kingdom sends a single team), and individual teams are also sent from the British Crown dependencies – Guernsey, Jersey and the Isle of Man – and many of the British overseas territories. The Australian external territory of Norfolk Island also sends its own team, as do the Cook Islands and Niue, two states in free association with New Zealand.

The last games were in 2006 in Melbourne, Australia. The recent games are being hosted by India as Now Delhi being the venue. The games will start from October 2010.

Opening and Closing Ceremonies: Traditions

- From 1930 through 1950, the parade of nations was led by a single flagbearer carrying the Union Flag, symbolising Britain's leading role in the British Empire.
- Since 1958, there has been a relay of athletes carrying a baton from Buckingham Palace to the Opening Ceremony. This baton has within it the Queen's Message of Greeting to the athletes. The baton's final bearer is usually a famous sporting personage of the host nation.
- All other nations march in English alphabetical order, except that the first nation marching in the Parade of Athletes is the host nation of the previous games, and the host nation of the current games marches last. In 2006 countries marched in alphabetical order in geographical regions.
- Three national flags fly from the stadium on the poles that are used for medal ceremonies: Previous host nation, Current host nation, Next host nation.
- The military is more active in the Opening Ceremony than in the Olympic Games. This is to honour the British Military traditions of the Old Empire.

The first edition of the event was the 1930 British Empire Games and eleven nations took part. The quadrennial schedule of the games was interrupted by World War II and the 1942 Games (set to be held in Montreal, Canada) were abandoned. The games were continued in 1950 and underwent a name change four years later with the first British Empire and Commonwealth Games in 1954. Over 1000 athletes participated in the 1958 Games as over thirty teams took part for the first time.

The event was briefly known as the British Commonwealth Games for the 1970 and 1974 editions and the 1978 Games, held in Edmonton, Canada, were the first

Games	Year	Host	Dates	Sports	Events	Nations	Competitors			Officials
							Total	Men	Women	
			British Empire Games							
I	1930	Hamilton, Ontario, Canada	16 – 23 August	6	59	11	400	?	?	?
II	1934	London, England	4 – 11 August	6	68	16	500	?	?	?
III	1938	Sydney, Australia	5 – 12 February	7	71	15	464			
IV	1950	Auckland, New Zealand	4 – 11 February	9	88	12	590	495	95	
			British Empire and Commonwealth Games							
V	1954	Vancouver, Canada	30 July – 7 August	9	91	24	662			127
VI	1958	Cardiff, Wales	18 – 26 July	9	94	35	1122			228
VII	1962	Perth, Australia	22 November – 1 December	9	104	35	863			178
VIII	1966	Kingston, Jamaica	4 – 13 August	9	110	34	1050			266
			British Commonwealth Games							
IX	1970	Edinburgh, Scotland	16 – 25 July	9	121	42	1383			361
X	1974	Christchurch, New Zealand	24 January – 2 February	9	121	38	1276	977	299	372

Games	Year	Host	Dates	Sports	Events	Nations	Competitors			Officials
							Total	Men	Women	
				Commonwealth Games						
XI	1978	Edmonton, Canada	3 – 12 August	10	128	46	1474			
XII	1982	Brisbane, Australia	30 September – 9 October	10	142	46	1583			
XIII	1986	Edinburgh, Scotland	24 July – 2 August	10	163	26	1662			
XIV	1990	Auckland, New Zealand	24 January – 3 February	10	204	55	2073			
XV	1994	Victoria, Canada	18 – 28 August	10	217	63	2557			
XVI	1998	Kuala Lumpur, Malaysia	11 – 21 September	15	213	70	3633			
XVII	2002	Manchester, England	25 July – 4 August	17[1]	281	72	3679			
XVIII	2006	Melbourne, Australia	15 – 26 March	16[2]	245	71	4049			
XIX	2010	Delhi, India	3 – 14 October	17						
XX	2014	Glasgow, Scotland	23 July – 3 August							
XXI	2018	TBD	TBD							

Notes: 1. Includes 3 team sports. [2]Includes 4 team sports.

to be held under the title of the "Commonwealth Games". The Edmonton event marked a new high as almost 1500 athletes from 46 countries took part.

Participation at the 1986 Games was affected by a boycott over the United Kingdom's sporting relations with South Africa, but the Games rebounded and continued to grow thereafter. The 1998 Commonwealth Games in Kuala Lumpur, Malaysia saw the sporting programme grow from 10 to 15 sports as team sports were allowed for the first time. Participation also reached new levels as over 3500 athletes represented 70 teams at the event. At the most recent Games (in Melbourne, Australia in 2006), over 4000 athletes took part in sporting competitions.

The host cities of the Games have mostly come from four countries: Australia (4), Canada (4), New Zealand (3) and the United Kingdom (5). Two cities have held the games on multiple occasions: Auckland (1950 and 1990), and Edinburgh (1970 and 1986).

Approved Sports

There are a total of 31 sports (with two multi-disciplinary sports) and a further 7 para-sports which are approved by the Commonwealth Games Federation. They are categorised into three types. Core sports must be included on each programme. A number of optional sports may be picked by the host nation, which may include some team sports such as basketball. Recognised sports are sports which have been approved by the CGF but which are deemed to need expansion; host nations may not pick these sports for their programme until the CGF's requirements are fulfilled.

Sport	*Type*	*Years*
Archery	Optional	1982, *2010*
Athletics	Core	1930–present
Badminton	Core	1966–present
Basketball	Optional	2006
Billiards	Recognised	Never
Boxing	Core	1930–present
Canoeing	Recognised	Never
Cycling	Optional	1934–present
Diving	Optional	1930–present
Fencing	Recognised	1950–1970
Golf	Recognised	Never
Gymnastics (Artistic and Rhythmic)	Optional	1978, 1990–present
Handball	Recognised	Never
Field Hockey	Core	1998–present
Judo	Optional	1990, 2002, *2014*
Lawn bowls	Core	1930–present (except 1966)
Life saving	Recognised	Never
Netball	Core	1998–present
Rowing	Recognised	1930, 1938–62, 1986
Rugby sevens	Core	1998–present
Sailing	Recognised	Never
Shooting	Optional	1966, 1974–present
Softball	Recognised	Never
Squash	Core	1998–present
Swimming	Core	1930–present
Synchronized swimming	Optional	1986, 2006
Table tennis	Optional	2002–present
Tennis	Optional	*2010*
Tenpin bowling	Recognised	1998
Triathlon	Optional	2002, 2006, 2014
Volleyball	Recognised	Never
Water polo	Recognised	1950

Weightlifting	Core	1950–present
Wrestling	Optional	1930–present (except 1990 and 1998)

Participation

Nations/Dependencies that have Competed

Only six teams have attended every Commonwealth Games: Australia, Canada, England, New Zealand, Scotland and Wales. Australia has been the highest scoring team for ten games, England for seven and Canada for one.

- Aden[1] 1962
- Anguilla 1982, 1998–
- Antigua and Barbuda 1966–1970, 1978, 1994–
- Australia 1930–
- Bahamas 1954–1970, 1978–1982, 1990–
- Bangladesh 1978, 1990–
- Barbados 1954–1966, 1970–1982, 1990–
- Belize 1978, 1994–
- Bermuda 1930–1938, 1954–1982, 1990–
- Botswana 1974, 1982–
- British Guiana[2] 1930–1938, 1954–1962
- British Honduras[3] 1962–1966
- British Virgin Islands 1990–
- Brunei Darussalam 1958, 1990–
- Cameroon 1998–
- Canada 1930–
- Cayman Islands 1978–
- Ceylon[4] 1938–1950, 1958–1970

- Cook Islands 1974–1978, 1986–
- Cyprus 1978–1982, 1990–
- Dominica 1958–1962, 1970, 1994–
- England 1930–
- Falkland Islands 1982–
- Fiji[15] 1938, 1954–1986, 1998–2006
- The Gambia 1970–1982, 1990–
- Ghana 1958–1982, 1990–
- Gibraltar 1958–
- Gold Coast[5] 1954
- Grenada 1970–1974, 1994–
- Guernsey 1970–
- Guyana 1966–1970, 1978–1982, 1990–
- Hong Kong[6] 1934, 1954–1962, 1970–1994
- India 1934–1938, 1954–1958, 1966–1982, 1990–
- Ireland[7] 1930
- Irish Free State[7] 1934
- Isle of Man 1958–
- Jamaica 1934, 1954–1982, 1990–
- Jersey 1958–
- Kenya 1954–1982, 1990–
- Kiribati 1998–
- Lesotho 1974–
- Malawi[12] 1970–
- Malaya[8] 1950, 1958–1962
- Malaysia 1966–1982, 1990–

- Maldives 1986–
- Malta 1958–1962, 1970, 1982–
- Mauritius 1958, 1966–1982, 1990–
- Montserrat 1994–
- Mozambique 1998–
- Namibia 1994–
- Nauru 1990–
- Newfoundland[9] 1930–1934
- New Zealand 1930–
- Nigeria 1950–1958, 1966–1974, 1982, 1990–1994, 2002–
- Niue 2002–
- Norfolk Island 1986–
- North Borneo[8] 1958–1962
- Northern Ireland[7] 1934–1938, 1954–
- Northern Rhodesia[10] 1954
- Pakistan 1954–1970, 1990–
- Papua New Guinea 1962–1982, 1990–
- Rhodesia[11] 1934–1950
- Rhodesia and Nyasaland[10] 1958–1962
- Saint Helena 1982, 1998–
- Saint Kitts and Nevis (Saint Christopher-Nevis-Anguilla 1978), 1990–
- Saint Lucia 1962, 1970, 1978, 1994–
- Saint Vincent and the Grenadines 1958, 1966–1978, 1994–
- Samoa *and Western Samoa* 1974–

- Scotland 1930–
- Seychelles 1990–
- Sierra Leone 1966–1970, 1978, 1990–
- Singapore[8] 1958–
- Solomon Islands 1982, 1990–
- South Africa 1930–1958, 1994–
- South Arabia[1] 1966
- Southern Rhodesia[10] 1954
- Sri Lanka 1974–1982, 1990–
- Swaziland 1970–
- Tanganyika[13] 1962
- Tanzania 1966–1982, 1990–
- Tonga 1974, 1982, 1990–
- Trinidad and Tobago 1934–1982, 1990–
- Turks and Caicos Islands 1978, 1998–
- Tuvalu 1998–
- Uganda 1954–1982, 1990–
- Vanuatu 1982–
- Wales 1930–
- Zambia[12] 1970–1982, 1990–
- Zimbabwe[12,14] 1982, 1990–2002

Notes:

1: Aden became South Arabia which left the Commonwealth in 1968.

2: Became Guyana in 1966.

3: Became Belize in 1973.

4: Became Sri Lanka in 1972.

5: Became Ghana in 1957.

6: Left the Commonwealth when handed over to China in 1997.

7: Ireland was represented as a team from the whole of Ireland in 1930, and from the Irish Free State and Northern Ireland in 1934. The Irish Free State, renamed *Ireland* in 1937 (but also known by its name in the Irish *Eire*) formally left the Commonwealth when it declared that it was a Republic on 1 January 1949.

8: Malaya, North Borneo, Sarawak and Singapore federated as Malaysia in 1963. Singapore left the federation in 1965.

9: Joined Canada in 1949.

10: Southern Rhodesia and Northern Rhodesia federated with Nyasaland from 1953 as Rhodesia and Nyasaland which lasted till 1963.

11: Divided into Southern Rhodesia and Northern Rhodesia in 1953.

12: Competed from 1958–1962 as part of Rhodesia and Nyasaland.

13: Zanzibar and Tanganyika federated to form Tanzania in 1964.

14: Withdrew from the Commonwealth in 2003.

15: Suspended from the Commonwealth and Games in 2009.

Commonwealth Nations/Dependencies/Disputed Territories yet to Send Teams

Very few Commonwealth dependencies and nations have yet to take part.

- Tokelau is expected to take part in the 2010 Games in Delhi.
- The Turkish Republic of Northern Cyprus have made applications to the CGF to send teams.
- The Pitcairn Islands' tiny population (50 as of July 2009) would appear to prevent the overseas territory from competing. For the same reason Saint Helena's territories of Ascension Island and Tristan da Cunha are unlikely to ever send separate teams.

- The lack of a permanent population would seem to prevent the overseas territories of South Georgia and the South Sandwich Islands, British Antarctic Territory and British Indian Ocean Territory from competing
- Other states and territories with native populations within the Commonwealth that may be eligible include Christmas Island, the Cocos (Keeling) Islands, Rodrigues, and Zanzibar.
- It is also conceivable that any future members of the Commonwealth such as applicant Yemen may participate in future games.
- Rwanda may send a team due to becoming a member of the Commonwealth in November 2009.

Boycotts

The Commonwealth Games has suffered from political boycotts over its history, largely associated with apartheid-era South Africa. Nigeria boycotted the 1978 Games in protest of New Zealand's sporting contacts with South Africa, while 32 of 59 nations from Africa, Asia, and the Caribbean boycotted the 1986 Commonwealth Games due to the Thatcher government's attitude towards South African sporting contacts. Boycotts were also threatened in 1974, 1982, and 1990 because of South Africa.

Notable Competitors

Lawn bowler Willie Wood from Scotland is the first competitor to have competed in seven Commonwealth Games, from 1974 to 2002. Greg Yelavich a sports shooter from New Zealand has won 11 medals at 6 games, from 1986 to 2006.

FESTIVAL OF EMPIRE

The Festival of (the) Empire was held at The Crystal Palace in London in 1911, to celebrate the coronation of King George V. It opened on 12 May.

Exhibition

Exhibitions of products from the countries of the Empire were displayed in three-quarter size models of their Parliamentary buildings erected in the grounds.

Pageant

A pageant dramatising the history of London, England and the Empire was held.

Inter-Empire Championships

As part of the festival an Inter-Empire sports championship was held in which teams from Australia, Canada, New Zealand, South Africa and the United Kingdom competed in events such as boxing, wrestling, swimming and athletics. This is regarded as a forerunner of the British Empire (now Commonwealth) Games, held from 1930.

There were five athletics events (100 yards, 220 yards, 880 yards, 1 mile and 120 yards hurdles), two swimming events (100 yards and 1 mile), plus heavyweight boxing and middleweight wrestling.

QUEEN'S BATON RELAY

The Queen's Baton Relay, similar to the Olympic Torch Relay, is a relay around the world held prior to the beginning of the Commonwealth Games. The Baton carries a message from the Head of the Commonwealth, currently Her Majesty Queen Elizabeth II. The Relay traditionally begins at

Buckingham Palace in London as a part of the city's Commonwealth Day festivities. The Queen entrusts the baton to the first relay runner. At the Opening Ceremony of the Games, the final relay runner hands the baton back to the Queen or her representative, who reads the message aloud to officially open the Games.

The Relay was introduced at the 1958 British Empire and Commonwealth Games in Cardiff, Wales. Up until, and including, the 1994 Games, the Relay only went through England and the host nation. The Relay for the 1998 Games in Kuala Lumpur, Malaysia was the first to travel to other nations of the Commonwealth. The 2002 Relay covered over 100,000 kilometres and went through 23 nations. aluminium

Auckland, New Zealand 1990

This baton was a two-piece affair. Each piece went on its own individual relay run in the North and South Islands of New Zealand, only being joined back together in the final week before the Games began.

Victoria, British Columbia, Canada, 1994

The Baton was fashioned from sterling silver and was engraved with traditional symbols of the creative artists' families and cultures, including a wolf, a raven and an eagle with a frog in its mouth.

Kuala Lumpur, 1998

Malaysia placed their own flavour on the Games, with the Queen's Baton being carried into the stadium on an elephant. The baton was presented to Prince Edward by Malaysia's first ever Commonwealth medal winner Koh Eng Tong, a gold medallist in weightlifting in 1950.

The Baton design was inspired by a traditional Malay artifact, the 'Gobek', which is a unique cylindrical areca nut-pounder widely used and displayed in Malay homes.

Manchester, 2002

The baton has special significance as it marks the Golden Jubilee of Her Majesty The Queen and was designed to symbolise the uniqueness of the individual and the common rhythm of humanity.

Melbourne, 2006

The Melbourne 2006 Queen's Baton Relay was the world's longest, most inclusive relay, travelling more than 180,000 kilometres and visiting all 71 nations that send teams to the Commonwealth Games in one year and a day. The Queen's Baton Relay started, as it traditionally does, at Buckingham Palace and ended in Melbourne, Australia at the Melbourne Cricket Ground. It carried a message from the Queen to the Opening Ceremony of the Commonwealth Games.

The baton contained 71 lights on the front, representing the 71 member nations of the Commonwealth Games Federation. A video camera built into the front of the baton recorded continuously as the baton travelled, and a GPS tracker was fitted, so that the baton's location could be viewed live on the Commonwealth Games Website.

REFERENCES

A democratic country and therefore fulfilling the membership criteria now required since no colonial link is now required, e.g. Mozambique and Rwanda.

Crystal Palace Park.

Commonwealth Games Medallists.

Growth of the Commonwealth Games. Commonwealth Games Federation.

Harold, Perkin (September 1989). "Teaching the nations how to play: sport and society in the British Empire and Commonwealth". *International Journal of the History of Sport* 6 (2): pp. 145–155.

High Achievers. Australian Commonwealth Games Association.

Te Ara encyclopedia of New Zealand.

"1930 British Empire Games – Introduction". Commonwealth Games Federation.

4

Sports Competition

The Commonwealth Games sports comprise all the sports officially recognised and approved by the Commonwealth Games Federation (CGF). There are a total of 31 approved sports, two multi-disciplinary sports, and a further 7 para-sports. Not all sports are competed at each edition of the Games as programmes must be limited to a maximum of 17 sports and a maximum 15 para-sports events.

The precursor to the modern Games, at the 1930 British Empire Games, there were six sports: athletics, aquatics (swimming and diving), boxing, lawn bowls, rowing and wrestling.

If a number of activities are controlled by the same international federation then the Commonwealth Games Federation recognises each activity as a discipline, which belongs to the respective sport. For example, aquatics, which is organised by the International Swimming Federation, is a sport at the Commonwealth Games that comprises four disciplines: swimming, diving, synchronized swimming and water polo. Furthermore, the sport cycling also contains three separate disciplines: track, road, and mountain biking.

Sports and disciplines often feature separate events

for which athletes can received medals. For example, boxing has a number of weight divisions, gymnastics and diving have a number of styles, while athletics has numerous events based upon a wide range of activities.

Different Categories

The Commonwealth Games sports are divided into three main types: core sports, optional sports, and recognised sports. All ten core sports must be included in the Games programme, while the host nation may choose to include up to seven optional sports. Recognised sports are sports which have been approved by the CGF but are deemed to need further growth before their inclusion.

The host nation may also apply for the inclusion of a maximum of four team sports to the CGF General Assembly, as the Melbourne organising committee did with basketball for the 2006 Games. There is also a requirement to include some events for Elite Athletes with a Disability (EAD): there are four core para-sports and three optional para-sports.

Further, some optional sports, like billiards and sailing, have not yet been included in a Games programme. There have also been a number of exhibition sports. In 1958 there were exhibitions of polo and show jumping, and in 1978 lacrosse appeared as an exhibition sport. Cricket was included at the 1998 Commonwealth Games although it is not currently a recognised sport.

In fact, the CGF recognises Commonwealth Games records for a number of sports.

In 2002, the CGF introduced the David Dixon Award for the outstanding athlete of the Games.

On 18 November 2006, tennis and archery were added

to the list of disciplines for the 2010 Games in New Delhi, bringing the total number of sports to 17. Billiards and snooker were considered but not accepted.

Approved Sports

Sport	*Type*	*Years*
Archery (records)	Optional	1982, *2010*
Athletics (records)	Core	1930–present
Badminton (medallists)	Core	1966–present
Basketball	Optional	2006
Billiards	Recognised	Never
Boxing	Core	1930–present
Canoeing	Recognised	Never
Cycling (records)	Optional	1934–present
Diving	Optional	1930–present
Fencing	Recognised	1950–1970
Golf	Recognised	Never
Gymnastics (Artistic and Rhythmic)	Optional	1978, 1990–present
Handball	Recognised	Never
Hockey	Core	1998–present
Judo	Optional	1990, 2002, *2014*
Lawn bowls	Core	1930–present (except 1966)
Life saving	Recognised	Never
Sport	Type	Years
Netball	Core	1998–present
Rowing (records)	Recognised	1930, 1938–62, 1986, 1994
Rugby sevens	Core	1998–present
Sailing	Recognised	Never
Shooting (records)	Optional	1966, 1974–present
Softball	Recognised	Never
Squash	Core	1998–present
Swimming (records)	Core	1930–present
Synchronized swimming	Optional	1986, 2006
Table tennis	Optional	2002–present
Tennis	Optional	2010

Tenpin bowling (records)	Recognised	1998
Triathlon	Optional	2002, 2006, 2014
Volleyball	Recognised	Never
Water polo	Recognised	1950, 2002, 2006
Weightlifting (records)	Core	1950–present
Wrestling	Optional	1930–present (except 1990, 1998, 2006)

Approved Para-Sports

Sport	*Type*	*Years*
Athletics (records)	Core	2002–present
Cycling (records)	Optional	
Lawn bowls	Core	2002–present
Swimming (records)	Optional	2002
Table tennis	Optional	2002
Weightlifting (Powerlifting) (records)	Core	2002–present
Wheelchair basketball	Optional	

Commonwealth Championships

In addition to the sports at the Commonwealth Games, there are a number of related sporting championships in the Commonwealth of Nations, some of which are held in conjunction with the Commonwealth Games:

- Commonwealth Fencing Championships
- Commonwealth Karate Championships
- Commonwealth Korfball Championships
- Commonwealth Judo Championships
- Commonwealth Pool Lifesaving Championships
- Commonwealth Rowing Championships
- Commonwealth Rugby Sevens Championships
- Commonwealth Taekwondo Championships
- Commonwealth Tenpin Bowling Championships

COMMONWEALTH GAMES EVENTS

Now we will highlight the different sports competitions at different Commonwealth Games, individually.

1. Rugby Sevens

Rugby sevens, also known as seven-a-side and VIIs, is a variant of rugby union in which teams are made up of seven players, instead of the usual 15, with shorter matches. The game originated in Melrose, Scotland, where the Melrose Sevens tournament is still played annually. The game is popular at all levels, with amateur and club tournaments generally held in the summer months. Sevens is one of the most well distributed forms of rugby, and is popular in parts of Africa, Asia, Europe, and the Americas, and especially in the South Pacific.

Notable international competitions include the IRB Sevens World Series and the Rugby World Cup Sevens. Rugby sevens is also played at some multi-sport events such as the Commonwealth Games, taking place three times (1998 - Kuala Lumpur, Malaysia, 2002 - Manchester, England and 2006 - Melbourne, Australia), each time the gold medal being won by New Zealand.

Rugby sevens is now recognised as an Olympic sport and will make its debut in the 2016 Summer Olympics. This follows a vote by the executive board of the International Olympic Committee (IOC) to include the sport. That decision was backed at the 121st International Olympic Committee Session in Copenhagen on October 9, 2009.

Rugby sevens was initially conceived by Ned Haig and David Sanderson, who were butchers from Melrose, Scotland as a fund-raising event for his local club, Melrose RFC, in 1883. The first ever sevens match was played at the

Greenyards, the Melrose ground, where it was well received. Two years later, Tynedale was the first non-Scottish club to win one of the Borders Sevens titles at Gala in 1885.

Despite sevens' popularity in the Borders, it did not catch on elsewhere until after WWI, in the 1920s and 30s. The first sevens tournament outside Scotland was the Percy Park Sevens at North Shields in north east England in 1921. Because it was not far from the Scottish Borders, it attracted interest from the code's birthplace, and the final was contested between Selkirk (who won) and Melrose RFC (who were runners up).

In 1926, England's major tournament, the Middlesex Sevens was set up by Dr J.A. Russell-Cargill, a London based Scot. One of the key events in the spread of sevens to England was the Middlesex Sevens, which had some formidable figures on its subcommittee such as Wavell Wakefield and Bill Ramsay. The Middlesex Sevens were also a great fundraiser for charity, and in 1926, they raised £1,600 for King Edward Hospital, at a time when standard admission was a shilling, and stand seats coast five shillings.

A 1927 description of the game at the Middlesex Sevens (also for King Edward Hospital) gives an idea of the novelty of the game to English people:

> "You see the field is so open that if a man gets away with the ball a full sized gallop is required to catch him and very often it... wasn't there."

Whereas the Scottish Borders were a rural area, with a population in the tens of thousands, albeit near Edinburgh and Newcastle-upon-Tyne, the Middlesex Sevens were more or less in the suburbs of London, a densely populated area and transport hub, which was home to millions. As a result 10,000 spectators attended the second Middlesex tournament. And while the Border Sevens had honed the skills of players in the Scottish rugby heartland, the Middlesex Sevens did likewise for London rugby, with locally based players such as the aforementioned Wavell Wakefield, Carl Aarvold (later Recorder of the City of London) of Blackheath FC, Wick Powell of London Welsh RFC, and John Tallent, who would later become chairman of the Four Home Unions Tours Committee.

They rubbed shoulders with various invitation sides such as Sale RFC in 1936, which included such players as Wilf Wooller and Claud Davey of Wales and Ken Fyfe of Scotland amongst their backs; and in 1939, Cardiff RFC, which included players such as Wilf Wooller again, and Les Spence and "Wendy" Davis.

The first ever officially sanctioned international tournament occurred at Murrayfield as part of the "Scottish Rugby Union's Celebration of Rugby" centenary celebrations in 1973.

Due to the success of the format, the ongoing Hong Kong Sevens was launched three years later. In 1993, the Rugby World Cup Sevens, in which the *Melrose Cup* is contested, was launched. Three of the best known sevens competitions are the Hong Kong Sevens, Wellington Sevens, and the Dubai Sevens which now make up part of the IRB Sevens World Series. The Scottish connection continued in the foundation of the Hong Kong Sevens in the 1970s, founded largely by expats such as "Tokkie" Smith, and in England, London Scottish RFC was strongly involved in the Middlesex Sevens from the start. The Hong Kong Sevens were ahead of their time, and an influential force in the modernisation of rugby union, for example, the Hong Kong Sevens were one of the first rugby union tournaments to attract major sponsorship, when the airline Cathay Pacific sponsored the 1976 tournament.

They also provided a level of cosmopolitan international competition, which tended not to exist in rugby before the first Rugby World Cup in 1987, especially since Hong Kong was not seen as one of the "Big Eight", and other than some involvement with France, the British Commonwealth teams tended to be notoriously clannish. By 1986, the Hong Kong Sevens were held up as a positive example to others:

> "This Seven-a-Side international tournament is without a doubt the most spectacular, exotic, best organized Rugby competition of its kind in the world, and it has consistently produced the highest standard of Sevens Rugby seen anywhere.
>
> "I was not surprised on my first visit to see quality play from the Australian, New Zealand, Fijian, and British players, but I was staggered at the amazingly high quality play produced by countries I never even knew played Rugby. South Korea and Western Samoa were every bit as good as Japan and Tonga. Indonesia, Thailand and Singapore found their lack of sheer size and bulk an insuperable handicap, but against each other they displayed a range of running and handling skills which demanded unqualified praise. Papua New Guinea, Sri Lanka and the Solomon Islands were inevitably outgunned by the teams from the major Rugby-playing nations but they still have a remarkably high level of skill which promises well for the future of the game.
>
> "The week of the Hong Kong tournament allows 24 Rugby-playing nations to intermingle for several days, and the huge cross-fertilisation of ideas can only be beneficial in the long term for the emerging nations.

> After the first day of the play when the top eight seeded teams meet the smaller fish in a pool system, the second day is divided into three different competitions... The strength of this great tournament is that on the opening day the most famous players in the world share a pitch with unknown opponents from countries where Rugby is a minority sport... While tournaments like the Hong Kong Sevens continue to be played, Rugby administrators can be confident that the game will continue to thrive in over 100 countries worldwide."

However, despite this apparent diversity, some of the same old problems which had dogged international rugby were still manifest in the Hong Kong Sevens in the 1980s - for example, in a photograph of the Hong Kong vs Bahrain game at the tournament in 1984, the teams do not appear to include anyone who is ethnically Arabian or Chinese, instead both teams are quite clearly of northern European ethnic origin.

Rugby sevens continues to be popular in the Scottish Borders, where the ten most prestigious of these tournaments make up a league competition known as the "Radio Borders Kings of the Sevens". Sevens has also taken strong root in the South Sea island nations of Fiji, Tonga, and Samoa, as well as the African nation of Kenya.

Notably, in many minor rugby nations, such as the case of rugby union in Poland, development, has tended to concentrate on rugby sevens as a means of introducing the sport to people. Rugby sevens has become popular in places such as Hong Kong, Singapore and Dubai, which are not so successful in the full fifteen-a-side code. In honour of the role of Melrose RFC in the creation of rugby sevens, the club was inducted along with Haig to the IRB Hall of Fame in 2008.

Rugby sevens is sanctioned by the IRB, and is played under substantially the same laws and on a field of the same dimensions as the 15-player game. While a normal rugby union match lasts at least 80 minutes, a normal sevens match consists of two halves of seven minutes with a one-minute half-time break. The final of a competition can be played over two halves of ten minutes each, with a half-time break of two minutes. (In the IRB Sevens World Series, only the Cup final, which determines the overall winner of an event, is played with 10-minute halves; all finals for lower-level trophies are played with 7-minute halves.) This allows rugby tournaments to be completed in a day or a weekend. However, sevens scores are generally comparable to union scores; scoring occurs with much greater regularity in sevens, since the defenders are more spaced out.

Many sevens tournaments have a competition for a cup, a plate, a bowl, and a shield, allowing many teams of different standards to avoid leaving empty handed.

Sevens tournaments are traditionally known for having more of a relaxed atmosphere, than fifteen-a-side games, and are often known as "festivals". As The Encyclopedia of Rugby Union Football (1976) puts it, they gained their "popularity as an end of season diversion from the dourer and sterner stuff that provides the bulk of a normal season's watching."

Fans frequently attend in fancy dress, and entertainment is put on for them.

Playing Area

Sevens is played on a standard rugby union playing field as defined in the International Rugby Board's handbook.

Teams and Positions

Teams are composed of three forwards, one scrum half and three backs.

Scrums are composed of just three players from each team. Because of the speedy nature of the game, good sevens players are often backs or loose forwards in fifteens rugby.

Variations to the Laws of the Game

There are several variations in laws which apply to Rugby Sevens, primarily to speed up the game and to account for the reduced number of players. The main changes can be summarised as follows:

- Seven players per team on field (instead of 15).
- Five substitutes, with only three interchanges (instead of 7 and 7).
- Seven minute halves, though ten minute halves are allowed in the final of a competition (instead of forty minute halves).
- One minute half-time, two minutes in finals (instead of ten minutes).
- Matches drawn after regulation are continued into Extra Time, in 5-minute periods.
- All conversion attempts must be drop-kicked (instead of having the option to place-kick).
- Conversions must be taken within 40 seconds of scoring a try (instead of 60 seconds).
- Three player scrums (instead of eight players).
- Kick-offs: in sevens, the team which has just scored kicks off, rather than the conceding team, as in fifteen-a-side.

- Yellow cards net a 2-minute suspension (instead of 10 minutes).
    - Suspensions are more severe in Sevens than in Fifteens. The team plays a man down for 1/7th of the match instead of 1/8th, and losing 1 man out of 7 opens up more space than 1 man out of 15.
- Referees decide on advantage quickly (where one play usually ends advantage, not true in fifteens).
- In major competitions, there are additional officials present (in-goal touch judges) to judge success of kicks at goals and hence the game is not delayed waiting for touch judges to move into position to judge conversion attempts.

Major Tournaments

- Rugby World Cup Sevens — Sponsored by the IRB, and held every four years, this is the highest prize in the Sevens version of rugby union. However, due to the upcoming introduction of sevens to the Olympics in 2016, the next edition in 2013 will be the last.
- IRB Sevens World Series, which currently includes:
    - Adelaide Sevens (Australia Sevens)
    - Dubai Sevens
    - Edinburgh Sevens (also known as "Murrayfield Sevens" and "Scotland Sevens")
    - Hong Kong Sevens (Original event)
    - London Sevens
    - South Africa Sevens (Also known as "George Sevens", "Stellenbosch Sevens", etc.)

   - USA Sevens
   - Wellington Sevens (Original event; New Zealand International Sevens)
- Borders Sevens Circuit, including the Melrose Sevens
- New Zealand National Rugby Sevens Tournament, also known as the Pub Charity Rugby Sevens is held annually at Queenstown, New Zealand. The tournament features the top 16 Provincial Representative sides in the country who qualify for the tournament via 3 regional qualifying events. Of the 3 regions, the Northern and Central zones are both located in the North Island while the Southern zone encompasses the entire South Island.
- National Schools Sevens - held at Rosslyn Park, in England, the biggest sevens competition in the world. News, photos and up to the minute results can be found on the official website. Results can also be seen on The Schools' Rugby Website.

Other events (with alternative names in brackets):

- Aberystwyth Sevens
- Amsterdam Sevens
- Bangkok Sevens
- Barbados Sevens
- Benidorm Sevens (Spain)
- Bogota Sevens
- Bournemouth Sevens (England)
- Caldy Sevens (England)]]
- Cape Fear Sevens (USA)
- Caribbean Sevens

- Catania Sevens (Sicily, Italy)
- Cayman Sevens
- Cwmtawe Sevens (Wales)
- Hannover Sevens (Germany; European Sevens)
- Heidelberg Sevens
- Henley Sevens
- Denver Sevens (USA)
- Kiama Sevens
- Kinsale Sevens (Ireland)
- Kuala Lumpur Sevens
- Lisbon Sevens
- Madrid Sevens
- Mar Del Plata Sevens (Argentina)
- Middlesex Sevens (England)
- Neuchatel Sevens
- New York Sevens
- Northern Sevens
- Paris Sevens
- Pembroke Youth Sevens (Wales)
- Penryn Sevens
- Punta del Este Sevens (Uruguay)
- Ciudad de Quito Sevens
- Rome Sevens
- Safari Sevens (Kenya)
- Santa Teresa Sevens
- Scandinavian Sevens

- Shanghai Sevens
- Singapore Sevens
- Snelling Sevens (Wales; Welsh Sevens)
- Sri Lankan Sevens
- Sofia Sevens (Bulgarian Sevens)
- SPAC Lions Sevens (Brazil)
- Suva Sevens (Fiji Sevens)
- Tokyo Sevens
- Victoria Falls Sevens (Zimbabwe)

Rugby Sevens at Multisport Competitions

- Asian Games (both sevens and fifteen-a-side are played.)
- Pacific Games (sevens and fifteen-a-side have been played, as well as touch rugby, and rugby league sevens)
- World Games
- 2016 Summer Olympics
- Doxbridge invitational sevens

Rugby sevens has been played at three Commonwealth Games since its first appearance, at the 1998 Commonwealth Games, in Kuala Lumpur, Malaysia. Appearing in 2002 and 2006, it is now considered a 'Core' sport by the Commonwealth Games Federation, necessitating its appearance at all future games, including the upcoming 2010 Games. It is one of the two male-only sports at the Commonwealth Games, the other being boxing.

The 16th Commonwealth Games in Kuala Lumpur, Malaysia saw the introduction of rugby sevens along with cricket, field hockey and netball. New Zealand has never lost a match at the Commonwealth Games, winning gold in all three Games at which the sport has been played.

Editions

Games	*Year*	*Host city*	*Host country*	*Medallists*		
				Gold	*Silver*	*Bronze*
XVI	1998	Kuala Lumpur	Malaysia	New Zealand	Fiji	Australia
XVII	2002	Manchester	England	New Zealand	Fiji	South Africa
XVIII	2006	Melbourne, Victoria	Australia	New Zealand	England	Fiji
XIX	*2010*	Delhi	India			
XX	*2014*	Glasgow	Scotland			

Winners

1998 - Kuala Lumpur, Malaysia

Event	*Gold*	*Silver*	*Bronze*
Men's Rugby Sevens	New Zealand	Fiji	Australia

In front of 20,000 fans at the Petaling Jaya Stadium, Rugby sevens was an enormous success with New Zealand collecting its 100th Commonwealth Games medal with a 21-12 win over the plucky Fiji (the reigning world champions). Man of the match was the giant Jonah Lomu who had worked tirelessly during the 10-minutes each way final. Led by veteran star David Campese, Australia took the bronze beating Samoa 33-12.

2002 - Manchester, England

Event	*Gold*	*Silver*	*Bronze*
Men's Rugby Sevens	New Zealand	Fiji	South Africa

Rugby sevens events were held at the City of Manchester Stadium, purpose built for the Games.

2006 - Melbourne, Victoria, Australia

Event	*Gold*	*Silver*	*Bronze*
Men's Rugby Sevens	New Zealand	England	Fiji

The venue for the rugby sevens was the Telstra Dome, on the western edge of Melbourne's Central Business District. Preliminary matches were held on 16 March, with the finals the following day.

The gold medal was won by New Zealand who defeated England 29-21 in the final on 17 March 2006. Fiji won the bronze medal, defeating Australia 24-17 in the 3rd place final. The game was overshadowed by a fit suffered by Australian Scott Fava after a legitimate tackle. Fortunately Fava recovered quickly and was released from hospital the following day.

Overall

Medals table for rugby sevens at the Commonwealth Games (first competed for in 1998).

Rank	*Nation*	*Gold*	*Silver*	*Bronze*	*Total*
1	New Zealand	3	0	0	3
2	Fiji	0	2	1	3
3	England	0	1	0	1
4	Australia	0	0	1	1
	South Africa	0	0	1	1

Summer Olympics

There have been proposals for sevens to be included in the Olympic Games (it has been in the Commonwealth Games since 1998). However, the International Olympic Committee (IOC) turned down the bid for the purposes of the 2012 Olympics to be held in London.

Oswald later confirmed that he had never in fact watched a game of sevens, or indeed, fifteens rugby. Although disappointed, the IRB responded by pointing out that in terms of the Olympic motto: *Citius, Altius, Fortius* (faster, higher, stronger), a rugby player was more likely to possess all of these attributes than competitors in some other Olympic events. The IRB has recently moved to counter criticisms that it only proposed for a male Olympic tournament, establishing a series of Sevens events for women; the 2009 Rugby World Cup Sevens included a women's championship for the first time. On the 13 August 2009, the executive board announced that rugby sevens would be recommended for inclusion in the 2016 Olympic Games. On 9 October 2009, IOC voted to include rugby sevens and golf on the program for the 2016 Olympic Games in Rio de Janeiro, Brazil. The other 26 sports were also confirmed with a big majority of the votes. The 2016 Summer Olympic program is scheduled to feature 28 sports and a total of 38 disciplines. There were two open spots for sports and initially seven sports began the bidding for inclusion in the 2016 program.

FIRA European Sevens

2005 FIRA European Sevens

Portugal defeated Russia 28-26 to the Grand Final of the 2005 FIRA European Sevens in Moscow to retain the trophy they have won for the last three years. Spain won the Plate with a 25-14 win over Germany, whilst Lithuania claimed the Bowl. Portugal topped their group on day one, recording four victories and a 7-7 draw, against Italy. In Pool B, Russia delighted the home fans with five wins out of five, including a 33-7 victory over France. They followed that up on day two by defeating Italy 17-0 in the Cup semi-finals, whilst Portugal beat France 22-7.

Women's Rugby Sevens

Women's rugby sevens has been dominated by New Zealand, with either the New Zealand team (1999-2001) or Aotearoa Maori Women's Rugby sevens team (playing as New Zealand) winning the annual Hong Kong Sevens tournament from 1997 until 2007. The United States won the Hong Kong Sevens in 2008 by defeating Canada in the final (New Zealand failed to send a team).

The inaugural Women's Rugby World Cup Sevens tournament took place in Dubai together with the men's tournament during the first weekend of March 2009. England defeated Canada 12-0 in the Bowl final while Australia edged New Zealand 15-10 in extra-time to become the first to win the Women's Rugby World Cup.

Women's rugby sevens was included in the IRB's successful bid to reintroduce rugby to the Olympics in 2016. It is also bidding for inclusion in the Commonwealth Games in 2018.

Rugby League Sevens

Rugby league may also be played under seven-a-side rules, though this is less common as an alternative when compared with rugby league nines. Rugby sevens originated some years before the split between rugby union and rugby league, but the game had not spread from Scotland at this stage, and it was not until the 1960s, that an RL version of sevens emerged.

Rugby league sevens is particularly popular with pub teams — formed from the regulars at a particular public house, the reason for this is that it is often difficult for a single pub to form a full squad of 13 players and four substitutes of willing players.

The game is substantially the same as full rugby league, however scrums involve only three players per team, and all kicks at goal must be made by drop-kicks. The major tournament was the World Sevens played prior to the start of the National Rugby League season in Sydney, but the tournament has been cancelled.

2. Badminton

For the first time, Badminton debuted at the 1966 Commonwealth Games.

Past Winners

Individual Competition

Year	*Host City*	*Country*
1966	Kingston	Jamaica
1970	Edinburgh	Scotland
1974	Christchurch	New Zealand
1978	Edmonton, Alberta	Canada
1982	Brisbane, Queensland	Australia
1986	Edinburgh	Scotland
1990	Auckland	New Zealand
1994	Victoria, British Columbia	Canada
1998	Kuala Lumpur	Malaysia
2002	Manchester	England
2006	Melbourne	Australia
2010	New Delhi	India

Year	*Men's singles*	*Women's singles*	*Men's doubles*	*Women's doubles*	*Mixed doubles*
1966	Tan Aik Huang	Angela Bairstow	Tan Aik Huang Yew Cheng Hoe	Helen Horton Ursula Smith	Roger Mills Angela Bairstow
1970	Jamie Paulson	Margaret Beck	Ng Boon Bee Punch Gunalan	Margaret Boxall Sue Whetnall	Derek Talbot Margaret Boxall
1974	Punch Gunalan	Gillian Gilks	Elliot Stuart Derek Talbot	Margaret Boxall Gillian Gilks	Derek Talbot Gillain Gilks

1978	Prakash Padukone	Sylvia Ng Meow Eng	Ray Stevens Mike Tredgett	Nora Perry Amme Statt	Mike Tredgett Nora Perry
1982	Syed Modi	Helen Troke	Ong Beng Teong Razif Sidek	Claire Backhouse Johanne Falardeau	Martin Dew Karen Chapman
1986	Steve Baddeley		Billy Gilliland Dan Travers	Gillian Clark Gillian Gowers	Mike Scandolera Audrey Tucker
1990	Rashid Sidek	Fiona Smith (Elliott)	Jalani Sidek Razif Sidek	Sara Sankey Fiona Smith (Elliott)	Chan Chi Choi Amy Chan
1994		Lisa Campbell	Cheah Soon Kit Soo Beng Kiang	Joanne Muggeridge Joanne Wright	Chris Hunt Gillian Clark
1998	Wong Cho-ong Hann	Kelly Morgan	Choong Tan Fook Lee Wan Wah	Joanne Wright Donna Kellogg	Simon Archer Joanne Goode
2002	Muhammad Hafiz Hashim	Li Li	Chan Chong Ming Chew Choon Eng	Ang Li Peng Lim Pek Siah	
2006	Lee Chong Wei	Tracey Hallam	Chan Chong Ming Koo Kien Keat	Chin Eei Hui Wong Pei Tty	Nathan Robertson Gail Emms

Medal Table

Rank	*Nation*	*Gold*	*Silver*	*Bronze*	*Total*
1	England	34	27	32	93
2	Malaysia	19	19	12	50
3	Canada	2	10	5	17
4	India	2	2	7	11
5	Australia	2	1	7	10
6	Singapore	1	2	1	4
7	Scotland	1	1	5	6
8	Hong Kong	1	0	2	3
9	Wales	1	0	1	2
10	New Zealand	0	2	8	10

3. Boxing

Boxing is one of the sports at the quadrennial Commonwealth Games competition. It has been a Commonwealth Games sport since the inaugural edition of the event's precursor, the 1930 British Empire Games. It is a core sport and must be included in the sporting programme of each edition of the Games.

Editions

Games	*Year*	*Host city*	*Host country*
I	1930	Hamilton, Ontario	Canada
II	1934	London	England
III	1938	Sydney, New South Wales	Australia
IV	1950	Auckland	New Zealand
V	1954	Vancouver, British Columbia	Canada
VI	1958	Cardiff	Wales
VII	1962	Perth, Western Australia	Australia
VIII	1966	Kingston	Jamaica
IX	1970	Edinburgh	Scotland
X	1974	Christchurch	New Zealand
XI	1978	Edmonton, Alberta	Canada
XII	1982	Brisbane, Queensland	Australia
XIII	1986	Edinburgh	Scotland
XIV	1990	Auckland	New Zealand
XV	1994	Victoria, British Columbia	Canada
XVI	1998	Kuala Lumpur	Malaysia
XVII	2002	Manchester	England
XVIII	2006	Melbourne, Victoria	Australia
XIX	*2010*	Delhi	India

4. Cricket at the Commonwealth Games

Though, Cricket is the most popular game watched by a largest number of audience the world over. But for the first time, one-day cricket made its debut at the 1998 Kuala Lumpur Commonwealth Games. This was a one-off event. The gold medal went to South Africa on 19 September 1998, after beating Australia by 4 wickets. Bronze medal went to New Zealand. This has been the only time this event was played at the commonwealth games.

5. Fencing

Fencing was featured in the Commonwealth Games official programme from 1950 to 1970.

Events

Event	*50*	*54*	*58*	*62*	*66*	*70*	*Years*
Men's Foil, Individual	•	•	•	•	•	•	6
Men's Foil, Team	•	•	•	•	•	•	6
Women's Foil, Individual	•	•	•	•	•	•	6
Women's Foil, Team					•	•	2
Épée, Individual	•	•	•	•	•	•	25
Épée, Team	•	•	•	•	•	•	6
Sabre, Individual	•	•	•	•	•	•	26
Sabre, Team	•	•	•	•	•	•	23
Total Events	6	6	6	6	7	7	

6. Diving

Diving is one of the sports at the quadrennial Commonwealth Games competition. It has been a Commonwealth Games sport since the inaugural edition of the event's precursor, the 1930 British Empire Games. It is an optional sport and may or may not be included in the sporting programme of each edition of the Games.

Editions

Games	*Year*	*Host city*	*Host country*
I	1930	Hamilton, Ontario	Canada
II	1934	London	England
III	1938	Sydney, New South Wales	Australia
IV	1950	Auckland	New Zealand
V	1954	Vancouver, British Columbia	Canada
VI	1958	Cardiff	Wales
VII	1962	Perth, Western Australia	Australia

VIII	1966	Kingston	Jamaica
IX	1970	Edinburgh	Scotland
X	1974	Christchurch	New Zealand
XI	1978	Edmonton, Alberta	Canada
XII	1982	Brisbane, Queensland	Australia
XIII	1986	Edinburgh	Scotland
XIV	1990	Auckland	New Zealand
XV	1994	Victoria, British Columbia	Canada
XVI	1998	Kuala Lumpur	Malaysia
XVII	2002	Manchester	England
XVIII	2006	Melbourne, Victoria	Australia
XIX	*2010*	Delhi	India

7. Gymnastics

Gymnastics is one of the sports at the quadrennial Commonwealth Games competition. It has been a Commonwealth Games sport since 1978. It is an optional sport and may, or may not, be included in the sporting programme of each edition of the Games.

Editions

Games	*Year*	*Host city*	*Host country*
XI	1978	Edmonton, Alberta	Canada
XII	1982 (Not included)	Brisbane, Queensland	Australia
XIII	1986 (Not included)	Edinburgh	Scotland
XIV	1990	Auckland	New Zealand
XV	1994	Victoria, British Columbia	Canada
XVI	1998	Kuala Lumpur	Malaysia
XVII	2002	Manchester	England
XVIII	2006	Melbourne, Victoria	Australia
XIX	*2010*	Delhi	India

8. Hockey

Field hockey became a permanent sport in the Commonwealth Games with its introduction in 1998 Games in Kuala Lumpur.

Men

Summaries

Year	*Host*	*Final*			*Third Place Match*		
		Gold Medal	*Score*	*Silver Medal*	*Bronze Medal*	*Score*	*Fourth Place*
1998	Kuala Lumpur, Malaysia	Australia	4–0	Malaysia	England	1–1 (4–2) Penalty strokes	India
2002	Manchester, England	Australia	5–2	New Zealand	Pakistan	10–2	South Africa
2006	Melbourne, Australia	Australia	3–0	Pakistan	Malaysia	2–0	England
2010	Delhi, India					–	

Medalists

Team	*Gold*	*Silver*	*Bronze*
Australia	3 (1998, 2002, 2006*)		
Malaysia		1 (1998)	1 (2002)
Pakistan		1 (2006)	1 (2002)
New Zealand		1 (2002)	
England			1 (1998)

Women

Summaries

Year	*Host*	*Final*			*Third Place Match*		
		Gold Medal	*Score*	*Silver Medal*	*Bronze Medal*	*Score*	*Fourth Place*
1998	Kuala Lumpur, Malaysia	Australia	8–1	England	New Zealand	3–0	India

2002	Manchester, England	India	3–2 after extra time	England	Australia	4–3	New Zealand
2006	Melbourne, Australia	Australia	1–0	India	England	0–0 (3–1) Penalty strokes	New Zealand
2010	Delhi, India		–			–	

Medalists

Team	*Gold*	*Silver*	*Bronze*
Australia	2 (1998, 2006*)	1 (2002)	
India	1 (2002)	1 (2006)	
England		2 (1998, 2002*)	1 (2006)
New Zealand			1 (1998)

10. Judo

Judo is one of the sports at the quadrennial Commonwealth Games competition. It has been a Commonwealth Games sport since the 1990. It is an optional sport and may or may not be included in the sporting programme of each edition of the Games. It will be included in the forthcoming 2014 Commonwealth Games.

Games	*Year*	*Host city*	*Host country*
XIV	1990	Auckland	New Zealand
XV	1994 (Not included)	Victoria, British Columbia	Canada
XVI	1998 (Not included)	Kuala Lumpur	Malaysia
XVII	2002	Manchester	England
XVIII	2006 (Not included)	Melbourne, Victoria	Australia
XIX	2010 (Not included)	Delhi	India
XX	*2014*	Glasgow	Scotland

9. Netball

Netball is one of the sports at the quadrennial Commonwealth Games competition. It has been a Commonwealth Games sport since the 1998. It is a core sport and must be included in the sporting programme of each edition of the Games.

Editions

Games	*Year*	*Host city*	*Host country*	*Madallists*		
				Gold	*Silver*	*Bronze*
XVI	1998	Kuala Lumpur	Malaysia	Australia	New Zealand	England
XVII	2002	Manchester	England	Australia	New Zealand	Jamaica
XVIII	2006	Melbourne, Victoria	Australia	New Zealand	Australia	England
XIX	*2010*	Delhi	India	?	?	?

All-Time Medal Table

Rank	*Nation*	*Gold*	*Silver*	*Bronze*	*Total*
1	Australia	2	1	0	3
2	New Zealand	1	2	0	3
3	England	0	0	2	2
4	Jamaica	0	0	1	1

11. Squash

Squash is one of the sports at the quadrennial Commonwealth Games competition. It has been a Commonwealth Games sport since 1998. It is a core sport and must be included in the sporting programme of each edition of the Games.

Editions

Games	*Year*	*Host city*	*Host country*
Games	Year	Host city	Host country
XVI	1998	Kuala Lumpur	Malaysia
XVII	2002	Manchester	England
XVIII	2006	Melbourne, Victoria	Australia
XIX	*2010*	Delhi	India

12. Table tennis

Table tennis competition has been in the Commonwealth Games since 2002, with singles and doubles events for both men and women.

Events

Event	*02*	*06*
Men's singles	•	•
Men's doubles	•	•
Men's team	•	•
Women's singles	•	•
Women's doubles	•	•
Mixed doubles	•	•
Women's team	•	•
Events	7	7

13. Triathlon

Triathlon is one of the sports at the quadrennial Commonwealth Games competition. It was first granted Commonwealth Games sport status in 2002. It is an optional sport which may, or may not, be included in each competition's sporting programme.

At the 1990 Commonwealth Games at Auckland, the Triathlon was a demonstration event; won by Erin Baker (women) and Rick Wells (men), both from New Zealand.

Editions

Games	*Year*	*Host city*	*Host country*
XVII	2002	Manchester	England
XVIII	2006	Melbourne, Victoria	Australia
XIX	2010 (Not included)	Delhi	India
XIX	*2014*	Glasgow	Scotland

REFERENCES

Bath, Richard (ed.) *The Complete Book of Rugby* (Seven Oaks Ltd, 1997.

Bath, Richard (ed.) *The Scotland Rugby Miscellany* (Vision Sports Publishing Ltd, 2007.

Jones, J.R. *Encyclopedia of Rugby Union Football* (Robert Hale, London, 1976.

McLaren, Bill *Talking of Rugby* (1991, Stanley Paul, London.

Massie, Allan *A Portrait of Scottish Rugby* (Polygon, Edinburgh;.

Richards, Huw (2007). *A Game for Hooligans: The History of Rugby Union*. Edinburgh: Mainstream Publishing.

"Rugby sevens and golf get Olympic spot in 2016". BBC. 2009-08-13.

Sevens World Series Media Guide" (PDF). International Rugby Board.

Starmer-Smith, Nigel (ed) *Rugby - A Way of Life, An Illustrated History of Rugby* (Lennard Books, 1986.

Stubbs, Ray (2009). *The Sports Book*. Dorling Kindersley.

The Spread of the Sevens, Melrose Sevens official site, retrieved 25th February, 2010

PART - II

HIGHLIGHTS OF GAMES FROM BEGINNING TO 2006

5

1930 British Empire Games

The 1930 British Empire Games were the first of what later become known as the Commonwealth Games, and were held in Hamilton, in the province of Ontario in Canada from August 16-23 1930.

The events included Athletics, Boxing, Lawn Bowls, Rowing, Swimming, and Wrestling. The opening ceremonies and many events were held at the Civic Stadium (now Ivor Wynne Stadium) in east Hamilton.

Participating Teams

There were 11 teams participating in these first British Empire Games:

1. Australia
2. Bermuda
3. British Guiana
4. Canada
5. England
6. Ireland
7. Newfoundland
8. New Zealand

9. Scotland
10. South Africa
11. Wales

Medals Won (Country-wise)

Rank	*Nation*	*Gold*	*Silver*	*Bronze*	*Total*
1	England	25	22	13	60
2	Canada	20	16	18	54
3	South Africa	6	4	8	18
4	New Zealand	3	4	2	9
5	Australia	3	4	1	8
6	Scotland	2	3	5	10
7	Wales	0	2	1	3
8	British Guiana	0	1	1	2
9	Ireland	0	1	0	1
	Total	59	57	49	165

Medals (Event-wise)

Athletics

Remarkably, all events were for men only.

Event	Gold		Silver		Bronze	
100 yards	Percy Williams (CAN)	9.9	Ernie Page (ENG)	10.2e	Johnny Fitzpatrick (CAN)	10.2e
220 yards	Stanley Engelhart (ENG)	21.8	Johnny Fitzpatrick (CAN)		Willie Walters (SAF)	
440 yards	Alex Wilson (CAN)	48.8	Willie Walters (SAF)	48.9e	George Golding (AUS)	
880 yards	Tommy Hampson (ENG)	1:52	Reg Thomas (ENG)	1:55.5e	Alex Wilson (CAN)	1:55.6e
1 mile	Reg Thomas (ENG)	04:14	William Whyte (AUS)	4:17.0e	Jerry Cornes (ENG)	
3 miles	Stan Tomlin (ENG)	14:27	Alex Hillhouse (AUS)	14:27.6e	Jack Winfield (ENG)	14:28e
6 miles	Billy Savidan (NZL)	30:50	Ernie Harper (ENG)	31:01.6e	Tom Evenson (ENG)	

Event	Gold		Silver		Bronze	
Marathon	Dunky Wright (SCO)	2'43:43	Samuel Ferris (ENG)	2'47.13e	Johnny Miles (CAN)	2'48:23e
2 Mile steeplechase	George Bailey (ENG)	9:52	Alex Hillhouse (AUS)		Vernon Morgan (ENG)	
120 yards hurdles	David Burghley (ENG)	14.6	Howard Davies (SAF)	14.7e	Fred Gaby (ENG)	
440 yards hurdles	David Burghley (ENG)	54.4	Roger Leigh-Wood (ENG)	55.9e	Douglas Neame (ENG)	
High jump	Johannes Viljoen (SAF)	1.90	Colin Gordon (BGU)	1.88	William Stargratt (CAN)	1.85
Pole vault	Vic Pickard (CAN)	3.73	Howard Ford (ENG)	3.73	Robert Stoddard (CAN)	3.66
Long jump	Len Hutton (CAN)	7.20	Reg Revans (ENG)	6.96	Johannes Viljoen (SAF)	6.86
Triple jump	Gordon Smallacombe (CAN)	14.76	Reg Revans (ENG)	14.29	Len Hutton (CAN)	13.90
Shot put	Harry Hart (SAF)	14.58	Robert Howland (ENG)	13.46	Charlie Herman (CAN)	12.98
Discus throw	Harry Hart (SAF)	41.43	Charlie Herman (CAN)	41.22	Abe Zvonkin (CAN)	41.17
Hammer throw	Malcolm Nokes (ENG)	47.13	Bill Britton (IRL)	46.89	John Cameron (CAN)	44.45
Javelin throw	Stan Lay (NZL)	63.13	Doral Pilling (CAN)	55.93	Harry Hart (SAF)	53.21
4×110 yards relay	Canada Jim Brown Johnny Fitzpatrick Leigh Miller Ralph Adams	42.2	England James Cohen John Heap John Hanlon Stanley Engelhart	42.7e	South Africa Howard Davies Werner Gerhardt Willie Legg Willie Waiters	
4×440 yards relay	England David Burghley Stuart Townend Kenneth Brangwin Roger Leigh-Wood	3:19	Canada Alex Wilson Art Scott Jimmy Ball Stanley Glover	3:19.8e	South Africa John Chandler Werner Gerhardt Willie Legg Willie Walters	

Boxing

All events were for men only.

Event	*Gold*	*Silver*	*Bronze*
Flyweight	Jacob Smith (SAF)	Thomas Pardoe (ENG)	Ross Galloway (CAN)
Bantamweight	Harry Mizler (ENG)	Tommy Holt (SCO)	John Keller (CAN)
Featherweight	Freddie Meachem (ENG)	Lawrence Stevens (SAF)	Alex Lyons (SCO)
Lightweight	James Rolland (SCO)	Cosmos Canzano (CAN)	Albert Love (ENG)
Welterweight	Leonard Hall (SAF)	Howard Williams (CAN)	Frank Brooman (ENG)
Middleweight	Fred Mallin (ENG)	Dudley Gallagher (AUS)	Ernest Peirce (SAF)

Light heavyweight	Joe Goyder (ENG)	Al Pitcher (CAN)	Joey Basson (SAF)
Heavyweight	Vincent Stuart (ENG)	William Skimming (CAN)	*none awarded*

Diving

Men's Events

Event	*Gold*		*Silver*		*Bronze*	
3 m springboard	Alfred Phillips (CAN)	147	Cyril Kennett (CAN)	138	Arthur Stott (CAN)	127
10 m platform	Alfred Phillips (CAN)	90.6	Samuel Walker (CAN)	83.3	Thomas Scott (ENG)	82.3

Women's Events

Event	*Gold*		*Silver*		*Bronze*	
3 m springboard	Oonagh Whitsett (SAF)	90.1	Doris Ogilvie (CAN)	89.7	Mollie Bailey (CAN)	88.7
10 m platform	Pearl Stoneham (CAN)	39.3	Helen McCormack (CAN)	38.3	*none awarded*	

Lawn Bowls

All events were for men only.

Event	*Gold*	*Silver*	*Bronze*
Singles	Robert Colquhoun (ENG)	J.G. Thomas (SAF)	William Fielding (NZL)
Pairs	Tommy Hills and George Wright (ENG)	William Fielding and Percy McWhannell (NZL)	W.H. Moore and Arthur Reid (CAN)
Fours	England Ernie Gudgeon James Edney Jack Frith Albert Hough	Canada Harry Allen Jimmy Campbell Mitch Thomas Billy Rae	Scotland David Fraser John Orr Tom Chambers (*)William Campbell

(*) Tom Chambers was Canadian. As one of the original team members died on the journey to Canada and the other teams agreed that Chambers could be a substitute even though he was not Scottish.

Rowing

All events were for men only. In the double sculls

event, only Canada was represented, so the organisers simply invited a couple of crews from the United States to provide some opposition.

Event	*Gold*		*Silver*		*Bronze*	
Single sculls	Bobby Pearce (AUS)	8:04	Jack Beresford (ENG)		Fred Bradley (ENG)	
Double sculls	Elswood Bole and Bob Richards (CAN)	7:48	*none awarded*		*none awarded*	
Coxless fours	England F.M.L Fitzwilliams A.J. Halby Hugh Edwards Humphrey Boardman	7:05	Canada J. Gayner J. Fleming O.G. Bellew Henry Pelham	+2 lgths	New Zealand Berry Johnson Vic Olsson Alex Ross Charley Saunders	
Coxed fours	New Zealand Mick Brough John MacDonald Ben Waters Bert Sandos Arthur Eastwood	8:02	Canada B.L. Gales R.S. Evans J.A. Butler H.R. McCuaig A. Miles	+2 lgths	British Guiana J.I. Matthews F.O. Gomes, B.P. Bagley E.M. Gonsa-lves J. Jardine	
Eights	England A.J. Halby D.E.L. Howitt F.M.L Fitzwilliams Humphrey Boardman Hugh Edwards J. A. Brown J. H. Crawford R. Close-Brooke Terence O'Brien	6:37	New Zealand Arthur Eastwood Bert Sandos Charley Saunders Ben Waters Mick Brough Fred Thompson John Gilby John MacDonald Vic Olsson	+0.75 lgths	Canada Albert Taylor Don Boal Earl Eastwood Harry Fry Joseph Zabinsky Joseph Bowkes Leslie MacDonald William Moore William Thoburn	+4 lgths

Swimming

Men's Events

Event	*Gold*		*Silver*		*Bronze*	
100 yd freestyle	Munroe Bourne (CAN)	56.0	Norman Brooks (ENG)	56.1	Bert Gibson (CAN)	
400 yd freestyle	Noel Ryan (AUS)	4.39.8	Gordon Bridson (NZL)	4.45.8	George Burleigh (CAN)	
1500 yd freestyle	Noel Ryan (AUS)	18:55.4	Gordon Bridson (NZL)	19:41	George Burleigh (CAN)	
100 yd backstroke	Bill Trippett (ENG)	1:05.4	Willie Francis (SCO)	1:06	John Besford (ENG)	1:07
200 yd breaststroke	Jack Aubin (CAN)	2.38.4	Stanley Bell (ENG)	2.39.6	Reginald Flint (ENG)	2:45

4×200 yd freestyle relay	Canada Bert Gibson MunroeBourne George Burleigh James Thompson	8:42.4	England Freddie Milton Norman Brooks Arthur Watts Joseph Whiteside	8:43	*none awarded*

Women's Events

Event	*Gold*		*Silver*		*Bronze*	
100 yd freestyle	Joyce Cooper (ENG)	1:03.0	Ellen King (SCO)	1:07	Valerie Davies (WAL)	
400 yd freestyle	Joyce Cooper (ENG)	5:25	Valerie Davies (WAL)	5:28	Cissie Stewart (SCO)	
100 yd backstroke	Joyce Cooper (ENG)	1:15	Valerie Davies (WAL)	1:17	Phyllis Harding (ENG)	1:18
200 yd breaststroke	Cecelia Wolstenholme (ENG)	3:06.3	Margery Hinton (ENG)		Ellen King (SCO)	
4×100 yd freestyle relay	England Joyce Cooper Doreen Cooper Olive Joynes Phyllis Harding	4:32.8	Canada Betty Edwards Irene Pirie Marjorie Linton Peggy Bailey	4:33.0	Scotland Cissie Stewart Ellen King Jean McDowell Jessie McVey	4:37.0

Wrestling

All events were for men only.

Event	*Gold*	*Silver*	*Bronze*
Bantamweight	Jim Trifunov (CAN)	Joseph Reid (ENG)	*none awarded*
Featherweight	Cliff Chilcott (CAN)	*none awarded*	*none awarded*
Lightweight	Howard Thomas (CAN)	Harold Angus (ENG)	*none awarded*
Welterweight	Reg Priestley (CAN)	Harry Johnson (ENG)	*none awarded*
Middleweight	Mike Chepwick (CAN)	Stanley Bissell (ENG)	Max Thiel (SAF)
Light heavyweight	Bill McIntyre (CAN)	Edgar Bacon (ENG)	*none awarded*
Heavyweight	Earl McCready (CAN)	Albert Sangwine (ENG)	*none awarded*

REFERENCE

The Hamilton Spectator-Memory Project (Souvenir Edition) page MP56 (10 June 2006). "Tigertown Triumphs". Press release.

6

1934 British Empire Games

The 1934 British Empire Games were the second of what we now know of as the Commonwealth Games. They were held at the White City Stadium in London, England from August 4-11 1934, apart from the cycling at Fallowfield Stadium, Manchester, and the swimming, which took place at the Empire Pool in Wembley. Seventeen national teams took part, including the Irish Free State (the only Games in which they participated, although at the 1930 Games a team representing the whole of Ireland competed).

The 1934 Games had originally been awarded to Johannesburg, South Africa, but were changed to London because of concerns (particularly from Canada) about the way South Africa would treat black and Asian athletes.

In fact, six sports were featured in the Games: athletics, boxing, cycling, lawn bowls, swimming and diving, and wrestling. A highlight of the 1934 Games was the inclusion of events for women in athletics, with careful consideration given not to include events that were considered 'too exhaustive'.

The running events were restricted to the short sprints and a shortened 4 x 220 yard relay instead of the 4 x 440 yard relay as per the men's program. Nevertheless this was a breakthrough for women in sport that would one day lead to full recognition and programming for women's athletics on the international stage.

Participants

- Australia
- Bermuda
- British Guiana
- Canada
- England
- India
- Irish Free State
- Jamaica
- New Zealand
- Newfoundland
- Northern Ireland
- Southern Rhodesia
- Scotland
- South Africa
- Wales

Medals (Country-wise)

Rank	*Nation*	*Gold*	*Silver*	*Bronze*	*Total*
1	England	29	20	24	73
2	Canada	17	25	9	51
3	Australia	8	4	2	14
4	South Africa	7	10	5	22
5	Scotland	5	4	17	26
6	New Zealand	1	0	2	3

7	British Guiana	1	0	0	1
8	Wales	0	3	3	6
9	Northern Ireland	0	1	2	3
10	Jamaica	0	1	1	2
11	Southern Rhodesia	0	0	2	2
12	India	0	0	1	1
	Total	68	68	68	204

Medals by Event

Athletics

Men's Events

Event	*Gold*		*Silver*		*Bronze*	
100 yards	Arthur Sweeney (ENG)	10.0	Marthinus Theunissen (SAF)	10.1e	Ian Young (SCO)	10.1e
220 yards	Arthur Sweeney (ENG)	21.9	Marthinus Theunissen (SAF)	22.0e	Walter Rangeley (ENG)	22.1e
440 yards	Godfrey Rampling (ENG)	48.0	William Roberts (ENG)	48.5e	Crew Stoneley (ENG)	48.6e
880 yards	Phil Edwards (BGU)	1:54	Willie Botha (SAF)	1:55.5e	Hamish Stothard (SCO)	1:55.6e
1 mile	Jack Lovelock (NZL)	4:13	Sydney Wooderson (ENG)	4:13.4e	Jerry Cornes (ENG)	4:16.6e
3 miles	Wally Beavers (ENG)	14:33	Cyril Allen (ENG)	14:38	Alec Burns (ENG)	14:45
6 miles	Arthur Penny (ENG)	31:01	Scotty Rankine (CAN)	31:03e	Arthur Furze (ENG)	31:04e
Marathon	Harold Webster (CAN)	2'40:36	Donald Robertson (SCO)	2'45:08	Dunky Wright (SCO)	2'56:20
2 mi steeplechase	Stanley Scarsbrook (ENG)	10:23	Tom Evenson (ENG)	10:25.8e	George Bailey (ENG)	
120 yards hurdles	Donald Finlay (ENG)	15.2	James Worrall (CAN)	15.5e	Ashleigh Pilbrow (ENG)	15.7e
440 yards hurdles	Alan Hunter (SCO)	55.2	Charles Reilly (AUS)	55.8e	Ralph Brown (ENG)	56.0e
High jump	Edwin Thacker (SAF)	1.90	Joe Haley (CAN)	1.90	John Michie (SCO)	1.90
Pole vault	Syl Apps (CAN)	3.88	Alf Gilbert (CAN)	3.81	Fred Woodhouse (AUS)	3.66
Long jump	Sam Richardson (CAN)	7.17	Johann Luckhoff (SAF)	7.10	Jack Metcalfe (AUS)	6.93

Triple jump	Jack Metcalfe (AUS)	15.63	Sam Richardson (CAN)	14.65	Harold Brainsby (NZL)	14.62
Shot put	Harry Hart (SAF)	14.67	Robert Howland (ENG)	13.53	Kenneth Pridie (ENG)	13.43
Discus throw	Harry Hart (SAF)	41.53	Douglas Bell (ENG)	40.44	Bernard Prendergast (JAM)	40.23
Hammer throw	Malcolm Nokes (ENG)	48.25	George Sutherland (CAN)	46.24	William Mackenzie (SCO)	42.49
Javelin throw	Bob Dixon (CAN)	60.02	Harry Hart (SAF)	58.27	Johann Luckhoff (SAF)	56.49
4×110 yards relay	England Arthur Sweeney Everard Davis George Saunders Walter Rangeley	42.2	Canada Allan Poole Bert Pearson Frank Nicks Bill Christie	42.5e	Scotland Archie Turner David Brown Ian Young Bob Murdoch	43.0e
4×440 yards relay	England Crew Stoneley Denis Rathbone Geoffrey Blake Godfrey Rampling	3:16.8	Canada Art Scott John Addison Ray Lewis Bill Fritz	3:17.2e	Scotland Alan Hunter Hamish Stothard Robert Wallace Ronald Wylde	

Women's Events

Event	*Gold*		*Silver*		*Bronze*	
100 yards	Eileen Hiscock (ENG)	11.3	Hilda Strike (CAN)	11.5	Lillian Chalmers (ENG)	11.6
220 yards	Eileen Hiscock (ENG)	25.0	Aileen Meagher (CAN)	25.4	Nellie Halstead (ENG)	25.6
880 yards	Gladys Lunn (ENG)	2:19	Ida Jones (ENG)	2:21.0	Dorothy Butterfield (ENG)	2:21.4
80 metre hurdles	Marjorie Clark (SAF)	11.8	Betty Taylor (CAN)	11.9	Elsie Green (ENG)	12.2
High jump	Marjorie Clark (SAF)	1.60	Eva Dawes (CAN)	1.57	Margaret Bell (CAN)	1.52
Long jump	Phyllis Bartholomew (ENG)	5.47	Evelyn Goshawk (CAN)	5.41	Violet Webb (ENG)	5.23
Javelin throw	Gladys Lunn (ENG)	32.19	Edith Halstead(*) (ENG)	30.94	Margaret Cox (ENG)	30.08
110-220-110 yards relay	England Eileen Hiscock Nellie Halstead Elsie Maguire	49.4	Canada Audrey Dearnley Aileen Meagher Hilda Strike	50.2e	Southern Rhodesia Cynthia Keay Dorothy Ballantyne Mollie Bragg	52.0e
220-110-220-110 yards relay	Canada Audrey Dearnley Betty White	1:14.4	England Eileen Hiscock Nellie Halstead		Scotland Cathie Jackson Joan Cunningham	

Aileen Meagher	Ethel Johnson	Margaret Mackenzie
Lillian Palmer	Ivy Walker	Sheena Dobbie

(*) "Edith" Eddie Halstead was later discovered to have been male.

Boxing

Event	*Gold*	*Silver*	*Bronze*
Flyweight	Patrick Palmer (ENG)	Maxie Berger (CAN)	Jackie Pottinger (WAL)
Bantamweight	Freddy Ryan (ENG)	Albert Barnes (WAL)	Thomas Wells (SCO)
Featherweight	Charles Catterall (SAF)	J.D. Jones (WAL)	William Fulton (RHO)
Lightweight	Leslie Cook (AUS)	Frank Taylor (WAL)	Harry Moy (ENG)
Welterweight	Dave McCleave (ENG)	Dick Barton (SAF)	William Duncan (NIR)
Middleweight	Alf Shawyer (ENG)	Leonard Wadsworth (CAN)	Jimmy Magill (NIR)
Light heavyweight	George Brennan (ENG)	George Holton (SCO)	Robey Leibbrandt (SAF)
Heavyweight	Pat Floyd (ENG)	Jan van Rensburg (SAF)	David Douglas Hamilton (SCO)

Cycling

Track

Event	*Gold*		*Silver*		*Bronze*	
Time Trial	Dunc Gray (AUS)	1:16.4	Bob McLeod (CAN)	1:18.0	Ted Clayton (SAF)	1:18.4
Sprint 1000 yd	Ernest Higgins (ENG)		Horace Pethybridge (AUS)		Ted Clayton (SAF)	
10 mile Scratch	Bob McLeod (CAN)	24:26.2	Ted Clayton (SAF)		William Harvell (ENG)	

Diving

Men's Events

Event	*Gold*		*Silver*		*Bronze*	
3 m spring-board	J. Briscoe Ray (ENG)	117.12	Doug Tomalin (ENG)	110.50	Harry Class (CAN)	106.57
10 m platform	Tommy Mather (ENG)	83.83	Doug Tomalin (ENG)	83.63	Louis Marchant (ENG)	70.64

Women's Events

Event	*Gold*		*Silver*		*Bronze*	
3 m spring-board	Judith Moss (CAN)	62.27	Lesley Thompson (AUS)	60.49	Doris Ogilvie (CAN)	57.00
10 m platform	Elizabeth MacReady (ENG)	30.74	Lesley Thompson (AUS)	27.64	Cecily Cousens (ENG)	27.36

Lawn Bowls

All events were for men only.

Event	*Gold*	*Silver*	*Bronze*
Singles	Robert Sprot (SCO)	W. S. MacDonald (CAN)	Andrew Harvey (SAF)
Pairs	Tommy Hillsand George Wright (ENG)	W. G. Hutchinsonand A. A. Langford (CAN)	Thomas Daviesand Stan Weaver (WAL)
Fours	England Fred Biggin Ernie Gudgeon Percy Thom-linson` Robert Slater	Northern Ireland Percy Watson Charlie Clawson George Watson Cecil Curran	Scotland William Lowe Charles Tait James Morrison James Brown

Swimming

Men's Events

Event	*Gold*		*Silver*		*Bronze*	
100 yd freestyle	George Burleigh (CAN)	55.0	George Larson (CAN)	55.6	Noel Crump (NZL)	56.2
440 yd freestyle	Noel Ryan (AUS)	5:03.0	Norman Wainwright (ENG)	5:07.8	Bob Pirie (CAN)	5:14.8
1500 yd freestyle	Noel Ryan (AUS)	18:25.4	Bob Pirie (CAN)	18:28.4	Norman Wainwright (ENG)	18:33.[illegible]

100 yd backstroke	Willie Francis (SCO)	01:05.2	John Besford (ENG)	1:05.6	Ben Gazell (CAN)	1:06.6
200 yd breaststroke	Norman Hamilton (SCO)	2:41.4	William McCarty (JAM)	2:42.4	Bill Puddy (CAN)	2:42.8
4×200 yd freestyle relay	Canada George Larson George Burleigh Robert Hooper Bob Pirie	8:40.6	England Mostyn Ffrench-Williams Norman Wainwright Reginald Sutton Bob Leivers	8:52.8	Scotland George Anderson Henry Cunningham Merilees Chassels William Burns	9:23.4
3×110 yd medley relay	Canada Ben Gazell George Burleigh Albert Puddy	3:11.2	Scotland Merilees Chassels Norman Hamilton Willie Francis	3:15.2	England Alan Summers John Besford Mostyn Ffrench Williams	3:16.0

Women's Events

Event	*Gold*		*Silver*		*Bronze*	
100 yd freestyle	Phyllis Dewar (CAN)	1:03.0	Irene Pirie (CAN)	1:03.6	Jean Mc-Dowell (SCO)	1:05.8
440 yd freestyle	Phyllis Dewar (CAN)	5:45.6	Jenny Maakal (SAF)	5:53.0	Irene Pirie (CAN)	5:54.4
100 yd backstroke	Phyllis Harding (ENG)	1:13.8	Margot Hamilton (SCO)	1:15.0	Valerie Davies (WAL)	1:18.2
200 yd breaststroke	Clare Dennis (AUS)	2:50.2	Phyllis Haslam (CAN)	2:55.4	Margery Hinton (ENG)	2:58.6
4×110 yd freestyle relay	Canada Phyllis Dewar Florence Humble Margaret Hutton Irene Pirie	4:21.8	South Africa Jenny Maakal Enid Hayward Kathleen Russell Molly Ryde	4:34.0	England Edna Hughes Beatrice Wolstenholme Olive Bartle Margery Hinton	4:34.4
3×110 yd medley relay	Canada Margaret Hutton Phyllis Haslam Phyllis Dewar	3:42.0	England Phyllis Harding Vera Kingston Edna Hughes	3:43.0	Scotland Jean McDowell Margot Hamilton Margaret McCullum	3:50.0

Wrestling

All events were for men only.

Event	*Gold*	*Silver*	*Bronze*
Bantamweight	Edward Melrose (SCO)	Ted McKinley (CAN)	Joseph Reid (ENG)
Featherweight	Robert McNab (CAN)	Joe Nelson (ENG)	Murdoch White (SCO)
Lightweight	Dick Garrard (AUS)	G. E. North (ENG)	Howard Thomas (CAN)
Welterweight	Joe Schleimer (CAN)	William Fox (ENG)	Rashid Anwar (IND)
Middleweight	Terry Evans (CAN)	Stanley Bissell (ENG)	Robert Harcus (SCO)
Light heavyweight	Mick Cubbin (SAF)	Bernard Rowe (ENG)	Alex Watt (CAN)
Heavyweight	Jack Knight (AUS)	Pat Meehan (CAN)	Archie Dudgeon (SCO)

7

British Empire Games 1938

The 1938 British Empire Games was the third British Empire Games, the Commonwealth Games being the modern-day equivalent. Held in Sydney, New South Wales, Australia from February 5-12 1938, they were timed to coincide with Sydney's sesqui-centenary (150 years since the foundation of British settlement in Australia). Venues included the Sydney Cricket Ground (the main stadium), the Sydney Sports Ground, North Sydney Pool and Henson Park. An estimated 40,000 people attended the opening ceremony. A competitors' residential village was established within the grounds of the Sydney Showground.

The star of the games was the Australian athlete Decima Norman, who won five gold medals in track and field. Margaret Dovey, the future wife of the former Australian prime minister Gough Whitlam, finished sixth in the 200 yards breaststroke.

Participating Teams

- Australia
- Bermuda
- British Guiana

- Canada
- Ceylon
- England
- Fiji
- India
- New Zealand
- Northern Ireland
- Southern Rhodesia
- Scotland
- South Africa
- Trinidad and Tobago
- Wales

Medals by Country

Rank	*Nation*	*Gold*	*Silver*	*Bronze*	*Total*
1	Australia	25	19	22	66
2	England	15	15	10	40
3	Canada	13	16	15	44
4	South Africa	10	10	6	26
5	New Zealand	5	7	13	25
6	Wales	2	1	0	3
7	Ceylon	1	0	0	1
8	Scotland	0	2	3	5
9	British Guiana	0	1	0	1
10	Southern Rhodesia	0	0	2	2
	Total	71	71	71	213

Medals by Event

Athletics

Men's Events

Event	*Gold*		*Silver*		*Bronze*	
100 yards	Cyril Holmes (ENG)	9.7	John Mumford (AUS)	9.8e	Ted Best (AUS)	9.9e
220 yards	Cyril Holmes (ENG)	21.2	John Mumford (AUS)	21.3e	Ted Best (AUS)	21.4e
440 yards	William Roberts (ENG)	47.9	Bill Fritz (CAN)	47.9e	Denis Shore (SAF)	48.1e
880 yards	Pat Boot (NZL)	1:51.2	Frank Handley (ENG)	1:54.0e	Bill Dale (CAN)	1:54.2e
1 mile	James Alford (WAL)	4:11.6	Gerald Backhouse (AUS)	4:12.2e	Pat Boot (NZL)	4:12.6e
3 miles	Cecil Matthews (NZL)	13.59.6	Peter Ward (ENG)	14:05.4	Scotty Rankine (CAN)	14:24.0e
6 miles	Cecil Matthews (NZL)	30:14.5	Scotty Rankine (CAN)	+180 yd	Wally Hayward (SAF)	+250 yd
Marathon	Johannes Coleman (SAF)	2'30:15	Bert Norris (ENG)	2'37:57	Jackie Gibson (SAF)	2'38:20
120 yards hurdles	Tom Lavery (SAF)	14.0w	Larry O'Connor (CAN)	14.2ew	Sid Stenner (AUS)	14.4ew
440 yards hurdles	John Loaring (CAN)	52.9	John Park (AUS)	54.6e	Alan McDougall (AUS)	55.2e
High jump	Edwin Thacker (SAF)	1.96	Robert Heffernan (AUS)	1.88	Doug Shetliffe (AUS)	1.88
Pole vault	Andries du Plessis (SAF)	4.11	Les Fletcher (AUS)	3.97	Stuart Frid (CAN)	3.88
Long jump	Harold Brown (CAN)	7.43	Jim Panton (CAN)	7.25	Basil Dickinson (AUS)	7.15
Triple jump	Jack Metcalfe (AUS)	15.49	Lloyd Miller (AUS)	15.41	Basil Dickinson (AUS)	15.28
Shot put	Louis Fouché (SAF)	14.47	Eric Coy (CAN)	13.96	Francis Drew (AUS)	13.8
Discus throw	Eric Coy (CAN)	44.75	David Young (SCO)	43.04	George Sutherland (CAN)	41.47
Hammer throw	George Sutherland (CAN)	48.71	Keith Pardon (AUS)	45.11	James Leckie (NZL)	44.21

Javelin throw	Jim M. Courtright (CAN)	62.8	Stan Lay (NZL)	62.21	Jack Metcalfe (AUS)	55.5
4×110 yards relay	Canada Jack Brown John Loaring Larry O'Connor Pat Haley	41.6	England Cyril Holmes Ken Richardson Sandy Duncan Lawrence Wallace	41.8e	Australia Alf Watson Teddy Hampson Ted Best Howard Yates	41.9e
4×440 yards relay	Canada John Loaring Lee Orr Bill Dale Bill Fritz	3:16.9	England Brian MacCabe Frank Handley Henry Pack William Roberts	3:19.2	New Zealand Alan Sayers Arnold Anderson Graham Quinn Harold Tyrie	3:22.0

Women's Events

Event	*Gold*		*Silver*		*Bronze*	
100 yards	Decima Norman (AUS)	11.1	Joyce Walker (AUS)	11.3e	Jeanette Dolson (CAN)	11.4e
220 yards	Decima Norman (AUS)	24.7	Jean Coleman (AUS)	25.1e	Eileen Wearne (AUS)	25.3e
80 metre hurdles	Barbara Burke (SAF)	11.7w	Isabel Grant (AUS)	11.7ew	Rona Tong (NZL)	11.8ew
High jump	Dorothy Odam (ENG)	1.60	Dora Gardner (ENG)	1.57	Elizabeth Forbes (NZL)	1.57
Long jump	Decima Norman (AUS)	5.80	Ethel Raby (ENG)	5.65	Thelma Peake (AUS)	5.55
Javelin throw	Robina Higgins (CAN)	38.28	Antonia Robertson (SAF)	36.98	Gladys Lunn (ENG)	36.41
110-220-110 yards relay	Australia Eileen Wearne Decima Norman Jean Coleman	49.1	Canada Barbara Howard Aileen Meagher Jeanette Dolson	49.9e	England Dorothy Saunders Kate Stokes Winnifred Jeffrey	51.3e
220-110-220-110 yards relay	Australia Decima Norman Jean Coleman Joan Woodland Thelma Peake	1:15.2	England Dorothy Saunders Ethel Raby Kate Stokes Winnifred Jeffrey	1:17.2e	Canada Barbara Howard Aileen Meagher Jeanette Dolson Violet Montgomery	1:19.0e

Boxing

Event	*Gold*	*Silver*	*Bronze*
Flyweight	Johnny Joubert (SAF)	Joe Gagnon (CAN)	Hugh Cameron (SCO)
Bantamweight	William Butler (ENG)	Hendrik Knoesen (SAF)	Jack Dillon (AUS)

Featherweight	Ceylon Barney Henricus (CEY)	James Watson (SCO)	Kenneth Moran (NZL)
Lightweight	Harry Groves (ENG)	Harry Hurst (CAN)	William Fulton (RHO)
Welterweight	Bill Smith (AUS)	Arthur Heeney (NZL)	Andrew Tsirindonis (RHO)
Middleweight	Denis Reardon (WAL)	Maurice Dennis (ENG)	Rex Carey (CAN)
Light heavyweight	Nick Wolmarans (SAF)	Cecil Overell (AUS)	Joseph Wilby (ENG)
Heavyweight	Thomas Osborne (CAN)	Claude Sterley (SAF)	Leslie Harley (AUS)

Cycling

Track

Event	*Gold*		*Silver*		*Bronze*	
Time Trial	Bob Porter (AUS)	1:15.2	Tasman Johnson (AUS)	1:15.7	Ernest Mills (ENG)	1:15.9
Sprint 1000 yd	Dunc Gray (AUS)		Bob Porter (AUS)		George Giles (NZL)	
10 mile Scratch	William Maxfield (ENG)	24:44.0	Ray Hicks (ENG)		Syd Rose (SAF)	

Road

Event	*Gold*		*Silver*		*Bronze*	
Time Trial	Hennie Binneman (SAF)	2'53:29.6	John Brown (NZL)	s.t.	Ray Jones (ENG)	s.t.

Diving

Men's Events

Event	*Gold*		*Silver*		*Bronze*	
3 m springboard	Ron Masters (AUS)	126.36	Doug Tomalin (ENG)	124.78	George Athans (CAN)	117.90
10 m platform	Doug Tomalin (ENG)	108.74	Ron Masters (AUS)	102.87	George Athans (CAN)	98.93

Women's Events

Event	*Gold*		*Silver*		*Bronze*	
3 m spring-board	Irene Donnett (AUS)	91.18	Lynda Adams (CAN)	88.27	Marie Sharkey (CAN)	81.66
10 m platform	Lurline Hook (AUS)	36.47	Lynda Adams (CAN)	36.39	Irene Donnett (AUS)	34.57

Lawn Bowls

All events were for men only.

Event	*Gold*	*Silver*	*Bronze*
Singles	Horace Harvey (SAF)	Frank Livingstone (NZL)	Jack Low (AUS)
Pairs	Walter Denison and Lance Macey (NZL)	Percy Hutton and Howard Mildren (AUS)	D.A. Adamson and J.R. Appleford (SAF)
	NZL	South Africa	Australia
Fours	Alec Robertson Ernie Jury Bill Bremner Bill Whittaker	F. Stevenson J. G. Donaldson Norman Walker T. H. Samson	Aub Murray Charlie H. McNeill Frank Murray Tom Kinder

Rowing

All events were for men only. The double sculls competition was an invitation event and originally no medals were awarded nevertheless these medals were counted nowadays. The bronze medal is listed as won by New Zealand.

Event	*Gold*		*Silver*		*Bronze*	
Single sculls	Herb Turner (AUS)	8:24	Peter Jackson (ENG)		Robert Smith (NZL)	
Double sculls	Cecil Pearce and William Bradley (AUS)	7:29.4	Jack Offer and Dick Offer (ENG)		Gus Jackson and Robert Smith (NZL)	
Coxed fours	Australia Don Fraser Gordon Freeth Harry Kerr Jack Fisher Stewart Elder	7:16.8	New Zealand Albert Hope George Burns John Rigby Kenneth Boswell Jim Clayton	+1.25 lgths	Canada Donald Davis James Temple James Mac- Donald Kenneth Jaggard Max Winkler	+0.75 lgths

Eights	England Basil Beazley Desmond Kingsford John Sturrock John Burrough John Turnbull Peter Jackson Rhodes Hambridge J.T. Turner Thomas Reeve	6:29	Australia Joe Gould Alfred Gregory Edward Bromley Frank le Souef Gordon Yewers Richard Paramor William Thomas Bill Dixon` Doug Bowden	+0.75 lgths	New Zealand Gus Jackson Cyril Stiles Fred Thompson Howard Benge John Charters Leslie Pithie Oswald Denison James Gould William Stodart	+2 lgths

Swimming

Men's Events

Event	*Gold*		*Silver*		*Bronze*	
110 yd freestyle	Bob Pirie (CAN)	59.6	Terry Collard (SAF)	60.8	Bill Fleming (AUS)	61.0
440 yd freestyle	Bob Pirie (CAN)	4:54.6	Bob Leivers (ENG)	4:55.4	Robin Biddulph (AUS)	4:55.5
1650 yd freestyle	Bob Leivers (ENG)	19:46.4	Bob Pirie (CAN)	19:59.2	Norman Wain-wright (ENG)	20:17.4
110 yd backstroke	Percy Oliver (AUS)	01:07.9	Gordon Kerr (CAN)	1:09.0	Micky Taylor (ENG)	1:09.3
220 yd bre-aststroke	John Davies (ENG)	2:51.9	Walter Spence (BGU)	3:00.5	Jimmy Prentice (CAN)	3:00.8
4×220 yd freestyle relay	England Frederick Dove Mostyn Ffrench-Williams Norman Wainwright Bob Leivers	9:19.0	Canada George Burleigh Gordon Devlin Robert Hooper Bob Pirie	9:20.2	Australia Robert Wilshire Noel Ryan Robin Biddulph Bill Fleming	9:32.9
3×110 yd medley relay	England Frederick Dove John Davies Micky Taylor	3:28.2	Canada Gordon Kerr Jimmy Prentice Bob Pirie	3:30.5	Australia Ernest Hobbs Percy Oliver Bill Fleming	3:31.8

Women's Events

Event	*Gold*		*Silver*		*Bronze*	
110 yd freestyle	Evelyn de Lacy (AUS)	1:10.1	Dorothy Green (AUS)	1:11.1	Dorothy Lyon (CAN)	1:12.1
440 yd freestyle	Dorothy Green (AUS)	5:39.7	Margaret Jeffrey (ENG)	5:40.2	Móna Leydon (NZL)	5:42.0

110 yd backstroke	Pat Norton (AUS)	1:19.5	Jeanne Greenland (WAL)	1:22.5	Margot Hamilton (SCO)	1:23.2
220 yd breaststroke	Doris Storey (ENG)	3:06.3	Carla Gerke (SAF)	3:12.1	Joan Langdon (CAN)	3:22.2
4×110 yd freestyle relay	Canada Noel Oxenbury Dorothy Lyon Mary Baggaley Phyllis Dewar	4:48.3	Australia Dorothy Green Evelyn de Lacy Margaret Rawson Pat Norton	4:49.0	England Edna Hughes Joyce Harrowby Margery Hinton Zilpha Grant	4:50.1
3×110 yd medley relay	England Doris Storey Lorna Frampton Margery Hinton	3:57.7	South Africa Carla Gerke Hazel Holmes Molly Ryde	4:07.5	Australia Evelyn de Lacy Pat Norton Valerie George	4:10.0

Wrestling

All events were for men only.

Event	*Gold*	*Silver*	*Bronze*
Bantamweight	Ted Purcell (AUS)	Vernon Blake (CAN)	Ray Cazaux (ENG)
Featherweight	Roy Purchase (ENG)	Larry Clarke (CAN)	Joseph Genet (NZL)
Lightweight	Dick Garrard (AUS)	Vernon Thomas (NZL)	Alfred Harding (SAF)
Welterweight	Tom Trevaskis (AUS)	Felix Stander (SAF)	Jeremiah Podjursky (NZL)
Middleweight	Terry Evans (CAN)	Peter Sheasby (SAF)	Leslie Jeffers (ENG)
Light heavyweight	Eddie Scarf (AUS)	Sidney Greenspan (SAF)	Thomas Ward (SCO)
Heavyweight	Jack Knight (AUS)	James Dryden (NZL)	John Whelan (CAN)

8

1950 British Empire Games

The 1950 British Empire Games was the fourth edition of what is now called the Commonwealth Games. It was held in Auckland, New Zealand between the 4th and 11th of February 1950, after a 12 year gap from the 3rd edition of the games. The main venue was Eden Park, although the closing ceremonies were held at Western Springs Stadium.

Participants

- Australia
- Canada
- Ceylon
- England
- Fiji
- Malaya
- New Zealand
- Nigeria
- Southern Rhodesia
- Scotland
- South Africa
- Wales

Medals by Country

At the 1950 British Empire Games all the teams won at least one medal.

Rank	Nation	Gold	Silver	Bronze	Total
1	Australia	34	27	19	80
2	England	19	16	13	48
3	New Zealand	10	22	22	54
4	Canada	8	9	14	31
5	South Africa	8	4	8	20
6	Scotland	5	3	2	10
7	Malaya	2	1	1	4
8	Fiji	1	2	2	5
9	Ceylon	1	2	1	4
10	Nigeria	0	1	0	1
11	Wales	0	1	0	1
12	Southern Rhodesia	0	1	0	1
	Total	88	89	80	257

Medals by Event

Athletics

Men's Events

Event	Gold		Silver		Bronze	
100 yards	John Treloar (AUS)	9.7	Bill de Gruchy (AUS)	9.8	Don Pettie (CAN)	9.9
220 yards	John Treloar (AUS)	21.5	David Johnson (AUS)	21.8	Don Jowett (NZL)	21.8
440 yards	Edwin Carr (AUS)	47.9	Les Lewis (ENG)	48.0	David Batten (NZL)	48.8
880 yards	John Parlett (ENG)	1:53.1	Jack Hutchins (CAN)	1:53.4	Bill Parnell (CAN)	1:53.4
1 mile	Bill Parnell (CAN)	4:11.0	Len Eyre (ENG)	4:11.8	Maurice Marshall (NZL)	4:13.2

3 miles	Len Eyre (ENG)	14:23.6	Harold Nelson (NZL)	14:27.8	Anthony Chivers (ENG)	14:28.1
6 miles	Harold Nelson (NZL)	30:29.6	Andrew Forbes (SCO)	30:31.9	Noel Taylor (NZL)	30:31.9
Marathon	Jack Holden (ENG)	2'32:57	Syd Luyt (SAF)	2'37:03	John Clarke (NZL)	2'39:27
120 yards hurdles	Peter Gardner (AUS)	14.3	Ray Weinberg (AUS)	14.4	Tom Lavery (SAF)	14.6
440 yards hurdles	Duncan White (CEY)	52.5	John Holland (NZL)	52.7	Geoff Goodacre (AUS)	53.1
High jump	John Winter (AUS)	1.98	Josiah Majekodunmi (NGR) 1.95 Alan Paterson (SCO)		*none awarded*	
Pole vault	Tim Anderson (ENG)	3.97	Stan Egerton (CAN)	3.97	Peter Denton (AUS)	3.88
Long jump	Neville Price (SAF)	7.31	Bevan Hough (NZL)	7.2	David Dephoff (NZL)	7.08
Triple jump	Brian Oliver (AUS)	15.61	Les McKeand (AUS)	15.28	Ian Polmear (AUS)	14.67
Shot put	Mataika Tuicakau (FIJ)	14.64	Harold Moody (ENG)	13.92	Leo Roininen (CAN)	13.68
Discus throw	Ian Reed (AUS)	47.72	Mataika Tuicakau (FIJ)	44	Svein Sigfusson (CAN)	43.48
Hammer throw	Duncan Clark (SCO)	49.94	Keith Pardon (AUS)	47.83	Herb Barker (AUS)	45.62
Javelin throw	Leo Roininen (CAN)	57.11	Luke Tunabuna (FIJ)	56.02	Doug Robinson (CAN)	55.6
4×110 yards relay	Australia Scotchy Gordon David Johnson John Treloar Bill de Gruchy	42.2	England Brian Shenton John Archer Les Lewis Nick Stacey	42.5	New Zealand Arthur Eustace Clem Parker Keith Beardsley Peter Henderson	42.6
4×440 yards relay	Australia Edwin Carr George Gedge James Humphreys Ross Price	3:17.8	England Derek Pugh Harold Parlett Les Lewis Terry Higgins	3:19.3	New Zealand David Batten Derek Steward John Holland Jack Sutherland	3:20.0

Women's Events

Event	*Gold*		*Silver*		*Bronze*	
100 yards	Marjorie Jackson (AUS)	10.8	Shirley Strickland (AUS)	11.0	Verna Johnston (AUS)	11.1

220 yards	Marjorie Jackson (AUS)	24.3	Shirley Strickland (AUS)	24.5	Daphne Robb (SAF)	24.7
80 metre hurdles	Shirley Strickland (AUS)	11.6	June Schoch (NZL)	11.6	Janet Shackleton (NZL)	11.7
High jump	Dorothy Odam (ENG)	1.6	Bertha Crowther (ENG)	1.6	Noeline Swinton (NZL)	1.55
Long jump	Yvette Williams (NZL)	5.90	Judy Canty (AUS)	5.78	Ruth Dowman (NZL)	5.74
Javelin throw	Charlotte Mac-Gibbon (AUS)	38.84	Yvette Williams (NZL)	37.96	Cleone Rivett-Carnac (NZL	34.43
110-220-110 yards relay	Australia Marjorie Jackson Shirley Strickland Verna Johnston	47.9	New Zealand Lesley Rowe Dorothea Parker Shirley Hardman	48.7	England Dorothy Hall Margaret Walker Sylvia Cheeseman	50.0
220-110-220-110 yards relay	Australia Ann Shanley Marjorie Jackson Shirley Strickland Verna Johnston	1:13.4	England Doris Batter Dorothy Hall Margaret Walker Sylvia Cheeseman	1:17.5	Canada Elaine Silburn Eleanor McKenzie Gerry Bemister Patricia Jones	

Boxing

Event	*Gold*	*Silver*	*Bronze*
Flyweight	Hugh Riley (SCO)	K. Edwin (CEY)	Marcus Temple (SAF)
Bantamweight	Jan van Rensburg (SAF)	Albert Percra (CEY)	Len Walters (CAN)
Featherweight	Henry Gilliland (SCO)	Andy Verceuil (RHO)	Peter Brander (ENG)
Lightweight	Ronny Latham (ENG)	Billy Barber (AUS)	Eddie Haddad (CAN)
Welterweight	Terry Ratcliffe (ENG)	Bill Seewitz (AUS)	Alex Obeyesekera (CEY)
Middleweight	Theunis van Schalkwyk (SAF)	James Beal (NZL)	Bill Pinkus (CAN)
Light heavyweight	Don Scott (ENG)	Chris Rollinson (NZL)	Jack Taylor (AUS)
Heavyweight	Frank Creagh (NZL)	Sid Cousins (AUS)	*none awarded*

Cycling

Track

Event	*Gold*		*Silver*		*Bronze*	
Time Trial	Russell Mockridge (AUS)	1:13.4	Sid Patterson (AUS)	1:13.5	Tommy Godwin (ENG)	1:13.6
Sprint 1000 m	Russell Mockridge (AUS)	2 - 0	Sid Patterson (AUS)	0 - 2	Graham Avery (NZL)	2 - 1

4000 m Ind. Pursuit	Cyril Cartwright (ENG)	5:16.3	Russell Mockridge (AUS)	5:27.0	Les Lock (NZL)	5:26.7
10 mile Scratch	William Heseltine (ENG)	23:23.4	Les Lock (NZL)		Ken Caves (AUS)	

Road

Event	Gold		Silver		Bronze	
Road race	Hector Sutherland (AUS)	3'13:06.4	Nick Carter (NZL)	3'13:06.5	Jack Fowler (AUS)	3'13:06.6

Diving

Men's Events

Event	Gold		Silver		Bronze	
3 m spring board	George Athans (CAN)	169.21	Peter Heatly (SCO)	168.80	Jack Stewart (NZL)	168.17
10 m platform	Peter Heatly (SCO)	156.07	George Athans (CAN)	145.36	Frank Murphy (AUS)	129.40

Women's Events

Event	Gold		Silver		Bronze	
3 m spring board	Edna Child (ENG)	126.58	Noeline MacLean (AUS)	124.59	Lynda Hunt (CAN)	115.38
10 m platform	Edna Child (ENG)	70.89	Gwen Fawcett (AUS)	65.64	Noeline MacLean (AUS)	59.93

Fencing

Men's Events

Event	Gold		Silver		Bronze	
Foil	René Paul (ENG)	7 wins	John Fethers (AUS)	6 wins	George Pouliot (CAN)	4 wins
Foil team	England Arthur Pilbrow Robert Anderson René Paul	20 wins	New Zealand Austin Gittos Gordon Dearing Murray Gittos Malcolm Millar	13 wins	Canada George Pouliot Robert Desjar- lais Edward Brooke	12 win
Épée	Charles de Beaumont (ENG)	7 wins	Robert Anderson (ENG)	6 wins	Ivan Lund (AUS)	5 wins

Event	Gold		Silver		Bronze	
Épée team	Australia Allan Jay Ivan Lund Charles Stanmore	3 wins	England René Paul Charles de Beaumont Robert Anderson	2 wins	Canada George Pouliot Robert Desjarlais Edward Brooke	1 win
Sabre	Arthur Pilbrow (ENG)		Robert Anderson (ENG)		George Pouliot (CAN)	
Sabre team	England Charles de Beaumont Arthur Pilbrow Robert Anderson	4 wins	Canada George Pouliot Robert Desjarlais Edward Brooke	2 wins	Australia Norman Booth Leslie Chillug Edwin Dean Jock Gibson	1 win

Women's Events

Event	*Gold*		*Silver*		*Bronze*	
Foil	Mary Glen-Haig (ENG)	7 wins	Patricia Woodroffe (NZL)	6 wins	Catherine Pym (AUS)	5 wins

Lawn Bowls

All events were for men only.

Event	*Gold*		*Silver*		*Bronze*	
Singles	James Pirrett (NZL)	101 points	Albert Newton (AUS)	93 points	Lionel Garnett (FIJ)	90 points
Pairs	Evan Exelbyand Robert Henry (NZL)	93 points	W. Gibb and H. J. van Zyl (SAF)	50 points	Leslie Brownand James Poulton (FIJ)	41 points
Fours	South Africa Alfred Blumberg H. Currer Harry Atkinson Norman Walker	4 wins	Australia Charles Cordaiy James Cobley John Cobley Len Knight	2 wins	New Zealand Fred Russell John Englebretson Noel Jolly Pete Skoglund	1 win

Rowing

All events were for men only.

Event	*Gold*		*Silver*		*Bronze*	
Single sculls	Mervyn Wood (AUS)	7:46.8	Tony Rowe (ENG)	7:54.0	Ian Stephen (SAF)	8:04.0
Double	Mervyn		Joe Schneider		Ken	

sculls	Wood and Murray Riley (AUS)	7:22	and Des Simonson (NZL)	7:32	Tinegate and Jack Brown (ENG)	7:39
Coxless pairs	Wal Lambert and Jack Webster (AUS)	7:58	David Gould and Humphrey Gould (NZL)	8:10	*none awarded*	
Coxed fours	New Zealand Ted Johnson John O'Brien Bill James Bill Carroll Colin Johnstone	7:17.2	Australia Leslie Montgomery Erwin Elder Cecil Winkworth Kenneth Gee Kevin Fox	7:24.0	*none awarded*	
Eights	Australia Alan Brown Bruce Goswell Edward Pain Eric Longley James Barnes Peter Holmes Phil Cayzer Bob Tinning Ross Selman	6:27	New Zealand Bruce Culpan Donald Adam Don Rowlands Edwin Smith Graham Jarratt Kerry Ashby Murray Ashby Thomas Engel William Tinnock	6:27.5	England Tony Butcher Hank Rushmere Michael Lapage Patrick Bradley Peter de Giles Peter Kirkpatrick Dickie Burnell Bill Windham Jack Dearlove	6:40

Swimming

Men's Events

Event	*Gold*		*Silver*		*Bronze*	
110 yd freestyle	Peter Salmon (CAN)	1:00.4	Frank O'Neill (AUS)	1:00.6	Pat Kendall (ENG)	1:01.8
440 yd freestyle	Garrick Agnew (AUS)	4:54.6	Graham Johnston (SAF)	60.8	Buddy Lucas (NZL)	4:55.5
1650 yd freestyle	Graham Johnston (SAF)	19:55.7	Jim Portelance (CAN)	20:08.3	Buddy Lucas (NZL)	20:10.1
110 yd backstroke	Jackie Wiid (SAF)	1:07.7	John Brockway (WAL)	1:08.0	Bert Kinnear (SCO)	1:10.8
220 yd breaststroke	David Hawkins (AUS)	2:54.1	Roy Romain (ENG)	2:54.2	Ron Sharpe (AUS)	2:56.0
4×220 yd freestyle relay	New Zealand Fred Lucas Lyall Barry Michael Amos Colin Chambers	9:27.7	Australia Barrie Kellaway Garrick Agnew Frank O'Neill James Beard	9:34.5	England Donald Bland Jack Hale Pat Kendall Ray Legg	9:36.8
3×110 yd medley relay	England Jack Hale Pat Kendall Roy Romain	3:26.6	Canada Allan Gilchrist Lucien Beaumont Peter Salmon	3:29.4	New Zealand John Shana-han Lyall Barry Peter Mathieson	3:30.1

Women's Events

Event	*Gold*		*Silver*		*Bronze*	
110 yd freestyle	Marjorie McQuade (AUS)	1:09.0	Margaret Wellington (ENG)	1:09.6	Joan Harrison (SAF)	1:10.7
440 yd freestyle	Joan Harrison (SAF)	5:26.4	Margaret Wellington (ENG)	5:33.7	Denise Norton (AUS)	5:33.8
110 yd backstroke	Judy-Joy Davies (AUS)	1:18.6	Jean Stewart (NZL)	1:19.1	Helen Yate (ENG)	1:20.5
220 yd breaststroke	Elenor Gordon (SCO)	3:01.7	Nancy Lyons (AUS)	3:03.6	Elizbeth Church (ENG)	3:10.3
4×110 yd freestyle relay	Australia Denise Spencer Denise Norton Judy-Joy Davies Marjorie McQuade	4:44.9	New Zealand Joan Hastings Kristin Jacobi Norma Bridson Winifred Griffin	4:48.7	England Grace Wood Helen Yate Lillian Preece Margaret Wellington	4:56.0
3×110 yd medley relay	Australia Judy-Joy Davies Marjorie McQuade Nancy Lyons	3:53.8	England Elizbeth Church Helen Yate Margaret Wellington	3:56.6	Scotland Elizabeth Turner Elenor Gordon Margaret Girvan	3:58.9

Weightlifting

All events were for men only.

Event	*Gold*		*Silver*		*Bronze*	
Bantam-weight	Tho Fook Hung (MAL)	655 lb	Rosaire Smith (CAN)	615 lb	Keith Caple (AUS)	600 lb
Feather-weight	Koh Eng Tong (MAL)	685 lb	Julian Creus (ENG)	670 lb	Barrie Engel brecht (SAF)	640 lb
Light-weight	Jim Halliday (ENG)	760 lb	Thong Saw Pak (MAL)	735 lb	Vern Barberis (AUS)	730 lb
Middle-weight	Gerry Gratton (CAN)	795 lb	Bruce George (NZL)	740 lb	Fred Griffin (AUS)	720 lb
Light Heavy weight	Jim Varaleau (CAN)	815 lb	Issy Bloomberg (SAF)	815 lb	Tan Kim Bee (MAL)	765 lb
Heavy weight	Harold Cleghorn (NZL)	900 lb	Ray Magee (AUS)	830 lb	*none awarded*	

Wrestling

All events were for men only.

Event	*Gold*		*Silver*		*Bronze*	
Fly-weight	Bert Harris (AUS)	1 win	Eric Matthews (NZL)	1 loss	*none awarded*	
Bantam-weight	Douglas Mudgway (NZL)	1 win	Jim Chapman (AUS)	1 loss	*none awarded*	
Feather-weight	John Armitt (NZL)	3 wins	Roland Milord (CAN)	2 w - 1 l	Arnold Parsons (ENG)	1 w - 2 l
Light-weight	Dick Garrard (AUS)	3 wins	Morgan Plumb (CAN)	2 wins	George Hobson (NZL)	1 win
Welter-weight	Henry Hudson (CAN)	3 wins	Jack Little (AUS)	3 w - 1 l	Martin Jooste (SAF)	1 win
Middle weight	Maurice Vachon (CAN)	3 wins	Bruce Arthur (AUS)	3 w - 1 l	Carel Reitz (SAF)	2 w - 2 l
Light heavy weight	Patrick Morton (SAF)	2 wins	Arthur Sneddon (NZL)	1 win	Tom Trevaskis (AUS)	
Heavy-weight	Jim Armstrong (AUS)	3 wins	Pat O' Connor (NZL)	2 wins	Kenneth Richmond (ENG)	1 win

9

British Empire and Commonwealth Games, 1954

The 1954 British Empire and Commonwealth Games were held in Vancouver, in the province of British Columbia in Canada, from 30 July-7 August 1954. These were the first games since the name change from British Empire Games took effect in 1952.

It was at these games that the "Miracle Mile" took place between Roger Bannister and John Landy at Empire Stadium. This was the first time these two (and at that time the only two) sub-four minute mile runners appeared in the same race, and also the first time two runners broke four minutes in the same race.

On the same afternoon, Jim Peters, the holder of the world best for the marathon, entered the stadium 17 minutes ahead of his nearest rival, but collapsed on his final lap, and never completed the race.

Participating Teams

24 teams were represented at the 1954 British Empire and Commonwealth Games. Those competing for the first time are shown in bold

- Australia
- Bahamas
- Barbados
- Bermuda
- British Guiana
- Canada
- England
- Fiji
- Gold Coast
- Hong Kong
- India
- Jamaica
- Kenya
- New Zealand
- Nigeria
- Northern Ireland
- Northern Rhodesia
- Pakistan
- Scotland
- South Africa
- Southern Rhodesia
- Trinidad and Tobago
- Uganda
- Wales

Country-wise Medal

Rank	*Nation*	*Gold*	*Silver*	*Bronze*	*Total*
1	England	23	24	20	67
2	Australia	20	11	17	48
3	South Africa	16	6	13	35
4	Canada	9	20	14	43
5	New Zealand	7	7	5	19
6	Scotland	6	2	5	13
7	Southern Rhodesia	3	6	3	12
8	Trinidad and Tobago	2	2	0	4
9	Northern Ireland	2	1	0	3
10	Nigeria	1	3	3	7
11	Pakistan	1	3	2	6
12	Wales	1	1	5	7
13	Jamaica	1	0	0	1
14	Barbados	0	1	0	1
	Hong Kong	0	1	0	1
	Uganda	0	1	0	1
17	British Guiana	0	0	1	1
	Northern Rhodesia	0	0	1	1
	Total	92	89	89	270

Medal Winners

Athletics

Women

Event	*Gold*		*Silver*		*Bronze*	
100 Yards	Marjorie Nelson (Jackson) (AUS)	10.7w	Winsome Cripps (AUS)	10.8w	Edna Maskell (NRH)	10.8w
220 Yards	Marjorie Nelson (Jackson) (AUS)	24.0	Winsome Cripps (AUS)	24.5	Shirley Hampton (ENG)	25.0
80 Metres Hurdles	Edna Maskell (NRH)	10.9w	Gwen Hobbins (CAN)	11.2w	Jean Desforges (ENG)	11.2w

High Jump	Thelma Hopkins (NIR)	1.67	Dorothy Tyler (ENG)	1.60	Alice Whitty (CAN)	1.60
Long Jump	Yvette Williams (NZL)	6.08	Thelma Hopkins (NIR)	5.84	Jean Desforges (ENG)	5.84
Shot	Yvette Williams (NZL)	13.96	Jackie MacDonald (CAN)	12.98	Magdalena Swanepoel (SAF)	12.81
Discus	Yvette Williams (NZL)	45.01	Suzanne Allday (ENG)	40.02	Marie Depree (CAN)	38.66
Javelin	Magdalena Swanepoel (SAF)	43.83	Pearl Fisher (NRH)	41.97	Shirley Couzens (CAN)	38.98
4 x 110 Yards Relay	Australia (AUS)	46.8	England (ENG)	46.9	Canada (CAN)	47.8

Men

Event	*Gold*		*Silver*		*Bronze*	
100 Yards	Mike Agostini (TRI)	9.6	Don McFarlane (CAN)	9.7	Hector Hogan (AUS)	9.7
220 Yards	Don Jowett (NZL)	21.5	Brian Shenton (ENG)	21.5	Ken Jones (WAL)	21.9
440 Yards	Kevan Gosper (AUS)	47.2	Don Jowett (NZL)	47.4	Terry Tobacco (CAN)	47.8
880 Yards	Derek Johnson (ENG)	1:51	Brian Hewson (ENG)	1:51	Ian Boyd (ENG)	1:52
1 Mile	Roger Bannister (ENG)	3:58.8	John Landy (AUS)	3:59.6	Rich Ferguson (CAN)	4:05
3 Miles	Chris Chataway (ENG)	13:35	Fred Green (ENG)	13:37	Frank Sando (ENG)	13:37
6 Miles	Peter Driver (ENG)	29:09	Frank Sando (ENG)	29:10	Jim Peters (ENG)	29:20
Marathon	Joseph McGhee (SCO)	2:39:36	Jack Mekler (SAF)	2:40:57	Johannes Barnard (SAF)	2:51:50
120 Yards Hurdles	Keith Gardner (JAM)	14.2	Chris Higham (ENG)	14.9	Norman Williams (CAN)	14.9
440 Yards Hurdles	David Lean (AUS)	52.4	Harry Kane (ENG)	53.3	Bob Shaw (WAL)	53.3
High Jump	Emmanuel Ifeajuna (NGR)	2.03	Patrick Etolu (UGA)	1.99	Nafio Osagie (NGR)	1.99
Pole Vault	Geoff Elliott (ENG)	4.26	Ron Miller (CAN)	4.2	Andries Burger (SAF)	4.13
Long Jump	Ken Wilmshurst (ENG)	7.54	Karim Oluwu (NGR)	7.39	Sylvanus Williams (NGR)	7.22
Triple	Ken		Peter		Brian	

Jump	Wilmshurst (ENG)	15.28	Esiri (NGR)	15.25	Oliver (AUS)	15.14
Shot	John Savidge (ENG)	16.77	John Pavelich (CAN)	14.95	Stephanus du Plessis (SAF)	14.93
Discus	Stephanus du Plessis (SAF)	51.70	Roy Pella (CAN)	49.53	Mark Pharaoh (ENG)	47.84
Hammer	Muhammad Iqbal (PAK)	55.37	Jakobus Dreyer (SAF)	54.75	Ewan Douglas (SCO)	52.81
Javelin	James Achurch (AUS)	68.52	Muhammad Nawaz (PAK)	68.09	Khan Jalal (PAK)	67.50
4 x 110 Yards Relay	Canada (CAN)	41.3	Nigeria (NGR)	41.3	Australia (AUS)	41.7
4 x 440 Yards Relay	England (ENG)	3:11	Canada (CAN)	3:12	Australia (AUS)	3:16

Bowls

Event		*Gold*	*Silver*	*Bronze*
Singles	Men	Ralph Hodges (SRH)	James Pirrett (NZL)	Arthur Saunders (SAF)
Pairs	Men	William Rosbotham & Percy Watson (NIR)	Sam Gardiner & Richard Williams (CAN)	George Budge & John Carswell (SCO)
Fours	Men	South Africa (SAF)	Hong Kong (HKG)	Southern Rhodesia (SRH)

Boxing

Event		*Gold*	*Silver*	*Bronze*
Fly-weight	Men	Dick Currie (SCO)	Abe Bekker (NRH)	Warner Batchelor (AUS)
Bantam-weight	Men	John Smillie (SCO)	Gordon Smith (SRH)	Abubakar Idi Garuba (NGR)
Feathe-rweight	Men	Leonard Leisching (SAF)	Malcolm Collins (WAL)	Dave Charnley (ENG)
Light-weight	Men	Piet van Staden (SRH)	Frank McQuillan (SCO)	Brian Cahill (AUS)
Light Wel-terweight	Men	Mickey Bergin (CAN)	Aubrey Harris (SRH)	Des Duguid (AUS)
Welter-weight	Men	Nicholas Gargano (ENG)	Rodney Litzow (AUS)	Hendrik van der Linde (SAF)

Light Middleweight	Men	Wilf Greaves (CAN)	Freddy Wright (SRH)	Bruce Wells (ENG)
Middleweight	Men	Johannes van der Kolff (SAF)	Arthur Crawford (SRH)	Marcel Piau (CAN)
Light Heavyweight	Men	Piet van Vuuren (SAF)	Tony Madigan (AUS)	Bill Misselbrooke (CAN)
Heavy weight	Men	Brian Harper (ENG)	Gerry Buchanan (CAN)	George Jenkins (SAF)

Cycling

Track

Event		*Gold*		*Silver*		*Bronze*	
Time Trial	Men	Dick Ploog (AUS)	00:01:12			Keith Harrison (ENG)	00:01:13
		Alfred Swift (SAF)	00:01:12				
Sprint	Men	Cyril Peacock (ENG)				Tom Shardelow (SAF)	
Individual Pursuit	Men	Norman Sheil (ENG)	00:05:03	Peter Brotherton (ENG)	00:05:09	Robert Fowler (SAF)	00:05:07
10 Miles Scratch	Men	Lindsay Cocks (AUS)	00:21:59	Keith Harrison (ENG)		Don Skene (WAL)	

Road

Event		*Gold*		*Silver*		*Bronze*
Road Race	Men	Eric Thompson (ENG)	02:44:08	John Baird (NZL)	NTT	Bernard Pusey (ENG)

Fencing

Event		*Gold*	*Silver*	*Bronze*
Foil	Men	René Paul (ENG)	John Fethers (AUS)	Allan Jay (ENG)
Foil–Team	Men	England (ENG)	Australia (AUS)	Canada (CAN)
Épée	Men	Ivan Lund (AUS)	René Paul wende (ENG)	Carl Sch- (CAN)
Épée – Team	Men	England (ENG)	Canada (CAN)	Australia (AUS)
Sabre	Men	Mike Amberg (ENG)	Ralph Cooperman (ENG)	John Fethers (AUS)

Sabre-Team	Men	Canada (CAN)	England (ENG)	Australia (AUS)
Foil	Women	Marry Glen-Haig (ENG)	Gillian Sheen (ENG)	Aileen Harding (WAL)

Rowing

Event		*Gold*		*Silver*		*Bronze*	
Single Sculls	Men	Don Rowlands (NZL)	00:08:28	Sidney Rand (ENG)	00:08:43	Bobby Williams (CAN)	00:08:51
Double Sculls	Men	Mervyn Wood & Murray Riley (AUS)	00:07:55	Bob Parker & Reg Douglas (NZL)	00:08:05	Donald Guest & Lawrence Stéphan (CAN)	00:08:29
Coxless Pairs	Men	Bob Parker (rower) & Reg Douglas (NZL)	00:08:24	Tom Christie & Nicholas Clack (ENG)	00:08:24	Dave Anderson & Geoff Williamson (AUS)	00:08:30
Coxed Fours	Men	Lionel Robberds, Dave Anderson, Peter Evatt, Geoff Williamson & Mervyn Wood (AUS)	00:07:58	Bruce Culpan, Kerry Ashby, Murray Ashby, Bill Tinnock & Stanley Gallagher (NZL)	00:08:04	Geoffrey Page, Roderick Macmillan, Alastair Davidson, Maurice Legg & David Glynne-Jones (ENG)	00:08:05
Eights	Men	Canada (CAN)	00:06:59	England (ENG)	00:07:11		

Swimming

Men's Events

Event	*Gold*		*Silver*		*Bronze*	
110 yd freestyle	Jon Henricks (AUS)	56.5	Cyrus Weld (AUS)	58.5	Rex Aubrey (AUS)	58.7
440 yd freestyle	Gary Chapman (AUS)	4:39.8	Jack Wardrop (SCO)	4:41.5	Graham Johnston (SAF)	4:43.3
1650 yd freestyle	Graham Johnston (SAF)	19:01.4	Peter Duncan (SAF)	19:22.1	Gary Chapman (AUS)	19:28.4
110 yd backstroke	John Brockway (WAL)	1:06.5	Lincoln Hurring (NZL)	1:06.9	Cyrus Weld (AUS)	1:08.6
220 yd breaststroke	Jack Doms (NZL)	2:52.6	Peter Jervis (ENG)	2:52.6	Alan Hime (ENG)	2:52.8
4×220 yd	Australia David Hawkins		Canada Allan Gilchrist		South Africa Dennis Ford	

freestyle relay	Gary Chapman Jon Henricks Rex Aubrey	8:47.6	George Park Gerald McNamee Ted Simpson	8:56.0	Graham John-ston Peter Duncan William Steuart	8:56.3
3×110 yd medley relay	Australia Cyrus James Weld David Hawkins Jon Henricks	3:22.0	New Zealand Frederick Lucas Jack Doms Lincoln Hurring	3:26.6	Scotland Jack Wardrop John Service Robert Wardrop	3:27.3

Women's Events

Event	*Gold*		*Silver*		*Bronze*	
110 yd freestyle	Lorraine Crapp (AUS)	1:05.8	Virginia Grant (CAN)	1:06.3	Joan Harrison (SAF)	1:08.2
440 yd freestyle	Lorraine Crapp (AUS)	5:11.4	Gladys Pristley (CAN)	5:19.6	Margaret Girvan (SCO)	5:21.4
110 yd backstroke	Joan Harrison (SAF)	1:15.2	Pat Symons (ENG)	1:17.4	Jean Stewart (NZL)	1:17.5
220 yd breaststroke	Elenor Gordon (SCO)	2:59.2	Mary Morgan (SAF)	3:03.3	Margaret Grundy (ENG)	3:04.5
4×110 yd freestyle relay	South Africa Felicity Loveday Joan Harrison Machduldt Petzer Natalie Myburgh	4:33.9	Canada Beth Whittall Gladys Priestley Helen Stewart Virginia Grant	4:37.0	England Diana Wilkinson Fearne Ewart Jean Botham Valerie Nares-Pillow	4:41.8
3×110 yd medley relay	Scotland Helen Gordon Mar-garet McDowell Margaret Girvan	3:51.0	South Africa Joan Harrison Machduldt Petzer Mary Morgan	3:52.7	Australia Jann Grier Judith Knight Lorraine Crapp	3:55.6

Diving

Event		*Gold*		*Silver*		*Bronze*	
3 Metres Spring board Diving	Men	Peter Heatly (SCO)	146.76	Tony Turner (ENG)	145.27	Jack Stewart (NZL)	144.98
10 Metres Highboard [Platform] Diving	Men	Bill Patrick (CAN)	142.7	Kevin Newell (AUS)	142.06	Peter Heatly (SCO)	141.32
3 Metres Springbo-ard Diving	Women	Ann Long (ENG)	128.26 (AUS)	Barbara McAulay	127.74	Irene MacDonald (CAN)	126.19

10 Metres Highboard [Platform] Diving	Women	Barbara Mc Aulay (AUS)	86.55	Eunice Miller (ENG)	79.86	Ann Long (ENG)	79.53

Weightlifting

Event		*Gold*		*Silver*		*Bronze*	
Bantamweight - Overall	Men	Maurice Megennis (ENG)	281	Frank Cope (ENG)	276.5	Keith Caple (AUS)	274
Featherweight - Overall	Men	Rodney Wilkes (TRI)	313	Jules Sylvain (CAN)	297	Ron Jenkins (WAL)	279
Lightweight Overall	Men	Vern Barberis (AUS)	347	George Nicholls (BAR)	344.5	Jan Pieterse (SAF)	333
Middleweight Overall	Men	Jim Halliday (ENG)	362.5	Lionel de Freitas (TRI)	342	Julius Park (BGU)	338
Light Heavy-weight Overall	Men	Gerry Gratton (CAN)	403.5	Louis Greeff (SAF)	367	Bruce George (NZL)	353.5
Middle Heavy-weight Overall	Men	Keevil Daly (CAN)	399	Lennox Kilgour (TRI)	392	Joseph Barnett (ENG)	376.5
Heavyweight Overall	Men	Doug Hepburn (CAN)	471.5	Dave Baillie (CAN)	453.5	Harold Cleg-horn (NZL)	421.5

Wrestling

Event		*Gold*	*Silver*	*Bronze*
Flyweight	Men	Louis Baise (SAF)	Fred Flannery (AUS)	Muhammad Din (PAK)
Bantamweight	Men	Geoff Jameson (AUS)	Muhammad Amin (PAK)	Ian Epton (NRH)
Featherweight	Men	Abraham Geldenhuys (SAF)	Herb Hall (ENG)	John Armitt (NZL)
Lightweight	Men	Godfrey Pienaar (SAF)	Ruby Leobovitch (CAN)	Dick Garrard (AUS)
Welterweight	Men	Nick Loubscher (SAF)	Abdul Rashid (PAK)	Ray Myland (ENG)
Middleweight	Men	Hermanus van Zyl (SAF)	Jim Christie (CAN)	Harry Kendall (ENG)
Light Heavy-weight	Men	Jacob Theron (SAF)	Bob Steckle (CAN)	Dan van Staden (NRH)
Heavyweight	Men	Ken Richmond (ENG)	Keith Maltman (CAN)	

10

British Empire and Commonwealth Games, 1958

The 1958 British Empire and Commonwealth Games were held in Cardiff, capital of Wales from 18-26 July 1958.

Thirty-five nations sent a total of 1,130 athletes and 228 officials to the Cardiff Games and 23 countries and dependencies won medals, including, for the first time, Singapore, Ghana, Kenya and the Isle of Man.

The Cardiff Games introduced the Queen's Baton Relay, which has been conducted as a prelude to every British Empire and Commonwealth Games ever since.

Participant

35 teams were represented, being the largest number to date, with a significant amount of teams competing for the first time.

- Australia
- Bahamas
- Barbados
- British Guiana
- Brunei

- Canada
- Ceylon
- Dominica
- England
- Fiji
- Ghana
- Gibraltar
- Hong Kong
- India
- Isle of Man
- Jamaica
- Jersey
- Kenya
- Malaya
- Malta
- New Zealand
- Nigeria
- North Borneo
- Northern Ireland
- Northern Rhodesia
- Pakistan
- Penang
- Sarawak
- Scotland
- Singapore
- South Africa

- Southern Rhodesia
- St Vincent
- Trinidad & Tobago
- Uganda
- Wales

Medals (Country-wise)

Rank	*Nation*	*Gold*	*Silver*	*Bronze*	*Total*
1	England	29	22	29	80
2	Australia	27	22	17	66
3	South Africa	13	10	8	31
4	Scotland	5	5	3	13
5	New Zealand	4	6	9	19
6	Jamaica	4	2	1	7
7	Pakistan	3	5	2	10
8	India	2	1	0	3
9	Singapore	2	0	0	2
10	Canada	1	10	16	27
11	Wales	1	3	7	11
12	Northern Ireland	1	1	3	5
13	Bahamas	1	1	0	2
14	Barbados	1	1	0	2
15	Malaya	0	2	0	2
16	Nigeria	0	1	1	2
17	Athletics British Guiana	0	1	0	1
18	Athletics Uganda	0	1	0	1
19	Southern Rhodesia	0	0	3	3
20	Kenya	0	0	2	2
21	Ghana	0	0	1	1

22	Isle of Man	0	0	1	1
23	Trinidad and Tobago	0	0	1	1
	Total	94	94	104	292

Medals (Event-wise)

Athletics

Event		*Gold*		*Silver*		*Bronze*	
100 Yards	Women	Marlene Willard (AUS)	10.7	Heather Young (ENG)	10.73	Madeleine Weston (ENG)	10.81
220 Yards	Women	Marlene Willard (AUS)	23.65	Betty Cuthbert (AUS)	23.77	Heather Young (ENG)	23.9
80 Metres Hurdles	Women	Norma Thrower (AUS)	10.72w	Carole Quinton (ENG)	10.77w	Gloria Wigney (AUS)	10.94w
High Jump	Women	Michele Mason (AUS)	1.7	Mary Donaghy (NZL)	1.7	Helen Frith (AUS)	1.65
Long Jump	Women	Sheila Hoskin (ENG)	6.02w	Mary Bignal (Rand) (ENG)	5.97w	Bev Watson (AUS)	5.97w
Shot	Women	Val Sloper (NZL)	15.54	Suzanne Allday (ENG)	14.44	Jackie Gelling (MacDonald) (CAN)	14.03
Discus	Women	Suzanne Allday (ENG)	45.91	Jennifer Thompson (NZL)	45.29	Val Sloper (NZL)	44.93
Javelin	Women	Anna Pazera (AUS)	57.41	Magdalena Swanepoel (SAF)	48.73	Averil Williams (ENG)	46.78
4 x 110 Yards Relay	Women	England (ENG	45.37	Australia (AUS)	46.12	Canada (CAN)	47.21
100 Yards	Men	Keith Gardner (JAM)	9.66	Tom Robinson (BAH)	9.69	Mike Agostini (CAN)	9.79
220 Yards	Men	Tom Robinson (BAH)	21.08	Keith Gardner (JAM)	21.11	Gordon Day (SAF)	21.15
440 Yards	Men	Milkha Singh (IND)	46.71	Malcolm Spence (SAF)	46.9	Terry Tobacco (CAN)	47.05
880 Yards	Men	Herb Elliott (AUS)	00:01:49	Brian Hewson (ENG)	00:01:49	Mike Rawson (ENG)	00:01:51
1 Mile	Men	Herb Elliott (AUS)	00:03:59	Merv Lincoln (AUS)	00:04:02	Albie Thomas (AUS)	00:04:03
3 Miles	Men	Murray Halberg (NZL)	00:13:15	Albie Thomas (AUS)	00:13:24	Neville Scott (NZL)	00:13:26
6 Miles	Men	Dave Power (AUS)	00:28:48	John Merriman (WAL)	00:28:49	Arere Anentia (KEN)	00:28:51
Marathon	Men	Dave Power (AUS)	02:22:46	Johannes Barnard (SAF)	02:22:58	Peter Wilkinson (ENG)	02:24:42

120 Yards Hurdles	Men	Keith Gardner (JAM)	14.20w	Jacobus Swart (SAF)	14.30w	Ghulam Raziq (PAK)	14.32w
440 Yards Hurdles	Men	Gert Potgieter (SAF)	49.73	David Lean (AUS)	50.59	Bartonjo Rotich (KEN)	51.75
High Jump	Men	Ernest Haisley (JAM)	2.06	Charles "Chilla" Porter (AUS)	2.03	Robert Kotei (GHA)	2
Pole Vault	Men	Geoff Elliott (ENG)	4.16	Robert Reid (CAN)	4.16	Merv Richards (NZL)	4.16
Long Jump	Men	Paul Foreman (JAM)	7.47	Deryck Taylor (JAM)	7.47	Muhammad Ramzan Ali (PAK)	7.33
Triple Jump	Men	Ian Tomlinson (AUS)	15.74w	Jack Smyth (CAN)	15.69	Dave Norris (NZL)	15.45
Shot	Men	Arthur Rowe (ENG)	17.57	Martyn Lucking (ENG)	16.5	Barry Donath (AUS)	15.79
Discus	Men	Fanie du Plessis (SAF)	55.94	Les Mills (NZL)	51.73	Gerry Carr (ENG)	51.63
Hammer	Men	Mike Ellis (ENG)	62.9	Muhammad Iqbal (PAK)	61.7	Peter Allday (ENG)	57.58
Javelin	Men	Colin Smith (ENG)	71.29	Jalal Khan (PAK)	70.83	Hans Moks (CAN)	70.41
4 x 110 Yards Relay	Men	England (ENG)	40.72	Nigeria (NGR)	41.05	Australia (AUS)	41.64
4 x 440 Yards Relay	Men	South Africa (SAF)	00:03:08.1	England (ENG)	00:03:09.6	Jamaica (JAM)	00:03:10.1

Bowls

Event		*Gold*	*Silver*	*Bronze*
Singles	Men	Phineas Danilowitz (SAF)	Percy Baker (ENG)	William Jackson (SRH)
Pairs	Men	John Morris & Richard Pilkington (NZL)	John Myrdal & Rudolph van Vuuren (SAF)	Hector Philp & William Yuill (SRH)
Fours	Men	England (ENG)	South Africa (SAF)	Northern Rhodesia (SRH)

Boxing

Event		*Gold*	*Silver*	*Bronze*
Flyweight	Men	Jackie Brown (SCO)	Tommy Bache (ENG)	Peter Lavery (NIR) Donald Braithwaite (WAL)
Bantamweight	Men	Howard Winstone (WAL)	Oliver "Frankie" Taylor (AUS)	Olfred Owen (SCO) Richard Hanna (NIR)
Featherweight	Men	Wally Taylor (AUS)	Malcolm Collins (WAL)	Gert Coetzee (SAF) John McClory (NIR)

Lightweight	Men	Dick Mc-Taggart (SCO)	James Jordan (NIR)	John Cooke (ENG) Thomas Donovan (NZL)
Light Welter weight	Men	Henry Loub-scher (SAF)	Robert Kane (SCO)	Joseph Jacobs (ENG) Raymond Galante (CAN)
Welter-weight	Men	Joseph Greyling (SAF)	Thomas Kawere (UGA)	Robert Dickson Scott (SCO) Brian Nancurvis (ENG)
Light Middle weight	Men	Grant Webster (SAF)	Stuart Pearson (ENG)	James Arthur Walters (CAN) Bill Brown (WAL)
Middle-weight	Men	Terry Milligan (NIR)	Philippus du Plessis (SAF)	Robert Piau (CAN) John Caiger (ENG)
Light Heavy-weight	Men	Tony Madigan (AUS)	Robert Higgins (WAL)	Gerhardus Jacobus De Bruyn (SAF) William Bannon (SCO)
Heavyweight	Men	Daniel Bekker (SAF)	David Thomas (ENG)	Roger Pleace (WAL) Gbadegesin Salawu (NGR)

Cycling

Track

Event		*Gold*		*Silver*		*Bronze*	
Time Trial	Men	Neville Tong (ENG)	00:01:12	Warren Scarfe (AUS)	00:01:12	Warwick Dalton (NZL)	00:01:13
Sprint	Men	Dick Ploog (AUS)		Karl Barton (ENG)		Lloyd Binch (ENG)	
Individual Pursuit	Men	Norman Sheil (ENG)	00:05:10	Tom Simpson (ENG)	00:05:11	Warwick Dalton (NZL)	00:05:15
10 Miles Scratch	Men	Ian Browne (AUS)	00:21:40	Warren Johnston (NZL)		Don Skene (WAL)	

Road

Event		*Gold*		*Silver*		*Bronze*	
Road Race	Men	Ray Booty (ENG)	05:16:34	Frank Brazier (AUS)	05:19:22	Stuart Slack (IOM)	05:19:22

Fencing

Event		*Gold*	*Silver*	*Bronze*
Foil	Men	Raymond Paul (ENG)	Ivan Lund (AUS)	René Paul (ENG)
Foil – Team	Men	England (ENG)	Australia (AUS)	Wales (WAL)
Épée	Men	Bill Hoskyns (ENG)	Mike Howard (ENG)	Allan Jay (ENG)
Épée - Team	Men	England (ENG)	Canada (CAN)	Australia (AUS)
Sabre	Men	Bill Hoskyns (ENG)	Ralph Cooperman (ENG)	Mike Amberg (ENG)
Sabre- Team	Men	England (ENG)	Australia (AUS)	Wales (WAL)
Foil	Women	Gillian Sheen (ENG)	Barbara McCreath (AUS)	Mary Glen-Haig (ENG)

Rowing

Event		*Gold*		*Silver*		*Bronze*	
Single Sculls	Men	Stuart Mackenzie (AUS)	00:07:20	James Hill (NZL)	00:07:24	Russell Carver (ENG)	00:07:27
Double Sculls	Men	Mike Spracklen & Geo ffrey Baker (ENG)	00:06:54	Mervyn Wood & Stuart Mackenzie (AUS)	00:07:01	Norman Suckling & James Hill (NZL)	+0.75 lgths
Coxless Pairs	Men	Bob Parker & Reginald Douglas (NZL)	00:07:11	Jonathan Hall & Stewart Douglas-Mann (ENG)	00:07:14	Stephen Roll & Kevin Webb (AUS)	00:07:33
Coxless Fours	Men	Roger Pope, Keith Shakell, David Young & Creighton Redman (ENG)	00:06:34	Glen Smith, Malcolm Turnbull, Richard McClure & John Madden (CAN)	00:06:39	David Edwards, John Fage, David Prichard & John Edwards (WAL)	00:06:48
Coxed Fours	Men	Colin Porter, John Vigurs, Simon Crosse, John Beresford & Richard Gabriel (ENG)	00:06:46	Donald Arnold, Walter D'Hondt, David Helliwell, Lawrence Stapleton & Sohen Biln (CAN)	00:06:53	Graeme Allen, Ralfe Currall, Kevin Evans, Lionel Robberds & Roland Waddington (AUS)	NTT
Eights	Men	Canada (CAN)	00:05:51	Australia (AUS)	00:05:56	England (ENG)	00:06:10

Swimming

Men's Events

Event	*Gold*		*Silver*		*Bronze*	
110 yd freestyle	John Devitt (AUS)	56.6 (AUS)	Gary Chapman man	56.6	Geoff Shipton (AUS)	57.0
440 yd freestyle	John Konrads (AUS)	4:25.9	Ian Black (SCO)	4:28.5	Gary Winram (AUS)	4:32.4
1650 yd freestyle	John Kon rads (AUS)	17:45.4	Gary Winram (AUS)	18:17.2	Murray Mc-Lachlan (SAF)	18:19.2
110 yd backstroke	John Monckton (AUS)	1:01.7	John Hayres (AUS)	1:03.5	Robert Wheaton (CAN)	1:06.5
220 yd breaststroke	Terry Gather-cole (AUS)	2:41.6	Peter Rocchi (SAF)	2:44.9	Chris Walkden (ENG)	2:47.3
220 yd butterfly	Ian Black (SCO)	2:22.6	Graham Symonds (ENG)	2:25.5	Brian Wil-kinson (AUS)	2:31.0
4×220 yd freestyle relay	Australia (AUS) Gary Chapman J. Wilkinson John Konrads John Devitt	8:33.4	Scotland (SCO) Athole Still Ian Black J.G. Leiper R.C. Sreenan	8:54.2	Canada (CAN) K. Williams P.W. Bell R.C. Grout W.G. Slater	9:01.8
4×110 yd medley relay	Australia (AUS) Gary Chapman John Monckton John Devitt Terry Gathercole	4:14.2	Canada (CAN) George Park K. Williams P.W. Bell R.J. Wheaton	4:26.3	England (ENG) C.Wal-kden G. Sykes G.H. Symonds N.G. McKechnie	4:26.4

Women's Events

Event	*Gold*		*Silver*		*Bronze*	
110 yd freestyle	Dawn Fraser (AUS)	1:01.4	Lorraine Crapp (AUS)	1:03.8	Colquhoun Alva (AUS)	1:04.0
440 yd freestyle	Ilsa Konrads (AUS)	4:49.4	Dawn Fraser (AUS)	5:00.8	Lorraine Crapp (AUS)	5:06.7
110 yd backstroke	Judy Grinham (ENG)	1:11.9	Margaret Edwards (ENG)	1:12.6	Philippa Gould (NZL)	1:13.7
220 yd bre-aststroke	Anita Lonsbrough (ENG)	2:53.5	Jackie Dyson (ENG)	2:58.2	Chris Gosden (ENG)	2:58.4
110 yd butterfly	Beverley Bain-bridge (AUS)	1:13.5	Tessa Staveley (NZL)	1:14.4	Margaret Iwasaki (CAN)	1:15.9
4×110 yd freestyle	Australia (AUS) Alva Colquhoun Dawn Fraser	4:17.4	Canada (CAN) Gladys Priestley M.H. Iwasaki	4:30.0	England (ENG) B.O. Noakes Diana Wilkin-	4:31.5

relay	Lorraine Crapp Sandra Morgan	S.J. Sangster Judy Grinham	son Sara Barber M.A. Marshall
4×110 yd medley relay	England (ENG) Anita Lonsbrough J. Oldroyd 4:54.0 M. Edwards M.A. Marshall	Australia (AUS) Alva Colquhoun Barbara Evans 4:55.1 Beverley Bainbridge Gergaynia Beckett	Canada (CAN) Gladys Priestley I.C.B. Service 5:01.6 M.H. Iwasaki Sara Barber

Diving

Event		*Gold*		*Silver*		*Bronze*	
3 Metres Spring-board Diving	Men	Keith Collin (ENG)	126.78	Bill Patrick (CAN)	124.62	David Tarsey (ENG)	118.81
10 Metres High-board [Plat-form] Diving	Men	Peter Heatly (SCO)	147.79	Brian Phelps (ENG)	144.49	Ray Cann (ENG)	138.5
3 Metres Spring-board Diving	Women	Charmian Welsh (ENG)	118.81	Irene Mac-Donald (CAN)	117.01	Liz Ferris (ENG)	113.3
10 Metres High-board [Plat-form] Diving	Women	Charmian Welsh (ENG)	77.23	Ann Long (ENG)	73.69	Molly Wieland (ENG)	65.82

Weightlifting

Event		*Gold*		*Silver*		*Bronze*	
Bantamweight - Overall	Men	Reginald Gaffley (SAF)	299	Ronald Bro-wnbill (ENG)	285.5	Marcel Gosse-lin (CAN)	274
Featherweight Overall	Men	Tan Ser Cher (SIN)	310.5	Chung Kum Weng (MAL)	306	Rodney Wilkes (TRI)	304
Lightweight Overall	Men	Tan Howe Liang (SIN)	358	Harry Webber (SAF)	340	Ben Helf-gott (ENG)	340
Middleweight Overall	Men	Blair Blen-man (BAR)	360.5	Winston Mc-Arthur (BGU)	360.5	Adrian Gilbert (CAN)	356
Light Heavy-weight Overall	Men	Caira Phil (SCO)	396.5	Sylvanus Blackman (BAR)	385.5	Jack Kes-tell (SAF)	385.5
Middle Heavy-weight Overall	Men	Manny Santos (AUS)	403.5	Tan Kim Bee (MAL)	392	Leonard Tre-ganowan (AUS)	378.5
Heavy-weight Overall	Men	Ken McDonald CAN (ENG)	455.5	Dave Baillie (CAN)	446.5	Arthur Shan-nos (AUS)	394.5

Wrestling

Event		*Gold*	*Silver*	*Bronze*
Flyweight	Men	Ian Epton (SAF)	Shujah-ud-Din (PAK)	Fred Flannery (CAN)
Bantamweight	Men	Muhammad Akhtar (PAK)	Geoff Jameson (AUS)	Daniel van der Walt (SAF)
Featherweight	Men	Abraham Gelden-huys (SAF)	Siraj-ud-Din (PAK)	Albert Aspen (ENG)
Lightweight	Men	Muhammad Ashraf (PAK)	Alastair Duncan (SCO)	Anthony Ries (SAF)
Welterweight	Men	Muhammad Bashir (PAK)	Lachmi Kant Pandey (IND)	Coenraad de Villiers (SAF)
Middleweight	Men	Hermanus van Zyl (SAF)	George Farquhar (SCO)	Ray Myland (ENG)
Light Heavy-weight	Men	Jacob Theron (SAF)	Muhammad Ali (PAK)	Bob Steckle (CAN)
Heavyweight	Men	Lila Ram (IND)	Jacobus Hanekom (SAF)	Ray Mitchell (AUS)

11

1962 British Empire and Commonwealth Games

The 1962 British Empire and Commonwealth Games were held in Perth, Western Australia, Australia from 22 November-1 December 1962. Athletic events were held at Perry Lakes Stadium in the suburb of Floreat and swimming events at Beatty Park in North Perth.

Participants

This time thirty five teams were represented at the Games.

- Aden
- Australia
- Bahamas
- Barbados
- British Guiana
- British Honduras
- Canada
- Ceylon
- Dominica

- England
- Fiji
- Ghana
- Gibraltar
- Hong Kong
- Isle of Man
- Jamaica
- Jersey
- Kenya
- Malaya
- Malta
- New Zealand
- North Borneo
- Northern Ireland
- Pakistan
- Papua & New Guinea
- Federation of Rhodesia and Nyasaland
- Sarawak
- Scotland
- Singapore
- St Lucia
- Tanganyika
- Trinidad & Tobago
- Uganda
- Wales

Medals (Country-wise) Medals

The medals used at these Games were the first to have a neck chain. All previous games had their medals in presentation boxes.

Rank	*Nation*	*Gold*	*Silver*	*Bronze*	*Total*
1	Australia	38	36	31	105
2	England	29	22	27	78
3	New Zealand	10	12	10	32
4	Pakistan	8	1	0	9
5	Canada	4	12	15	31
6	Scotland	4	7	3	14
7	Ghana	3	5	1	9
8	Jamaica	3	1	1	5
9	Kenya	2	2	1	5
10	Singapore	2	0	0	2
11	Uganda	1	1	4	6
12	Rhodesia and Nyasaland	0	2	5	7
13	Wales	0	2	4	6
14	Bahamas	0	1	0	1
15	Fiji	0	0	2	2
16	Trinidad and Tobago	0	0	2	2
17	Barbados	0	0	1	1
	Athletics British Guiana	0	0	1	1
	Jersey	0	0	1	1
	Malaya	0	0	1	1
	Northern Ireland	0	0	1	1
	Papua New Guinea	0	0	1	1
	Total	104	104	112	320

Medals by Event

Athletics

Event		*Gold*		*Silver*		*Bronze*	
100 Yards	Women	Dorothy Hyman (ENG)	11.2	Doreen Porter (NZL)	11.3	Brenda Cox (AUS)	11.4
220 Yards	Women	Dorothy Hyman (ENG)	24	Joyce Bennett (AUS)	24.21	Margaret Burvill (AUS)	24.42
880 Yards	Women	Dixie Willis (AUS)	00:02:04	Marise - Chamberlain (NZL)	00:02:06	Joy Jordan (ENG)	00:02:06
80 Metres Hurdles	Women	Pam Kilborn (AUS)	11.07	Betty Moore (ENG)	11.4	Avis McIn-tosh (NZL)	11.47
High Jump	Women	Robyn Wood-house (AUS)	1.78	Helen Frith (AUS)	1.73	Michele Mason (AUS)	1.73
Long Jump	Women	Pam Kilborn (AUS)	6.27w	Helen Frith (AUS)	6.24w	Janet Knee (AUS)	6.13w
Shot	Women	Val Young (Sloper) (NZL)	15.23	Jean Roberts (AUS)	14.51	Suzanne Allday (ENG)	13.56
Discus	Women	Val Young (Sloper) (NZL)	50.2	Rosslyn Williams (AUS)	46.66	Mary Mc-Donald (AUS)	46.23
Javelin	Women	Sue Platt (ENG)	50.26	Rosemary Morgan (ENG)	49.62	Anna Pazera (AUS)	48.68
4 x 110 Yards Relay	Women	Australia (AUS)	46.71	England (ENG)	46.81	New Zealand (NZL)	46.93
100 Yards	Men	Seraphino Antao (KEN)	9.5	Tom Robinson (BAH)	9.63	Michael Cleary (AUS)	9.78
220 Yards	Men	Seraphino Antao (KEN)	21.28	Dave Jones (ENG)	21.59	Johann du Preez (FRN)	21.7
440 Yards	Men	George Kerr (JAM)	46.74	Robbie Bri-ghtwell (ENG)	46.86	Amos Omolo (UGA)	46.88
880 Yards	Men	Peter Snell (NZL)	00:01:48	George Kerr (JAM)	00:01:48	Tony Blue (AUS)	00:01:49
1 Mile	Men	Peter Snell (NZL)	00:04:05	John Davies (NZL)	00:04:05	Terry Sulli-van (FRN)	00:04:07
3 Miles	Men	Murray Hal-berg (NZL)	00:13:34	Ron Clarke (AUS)	00:13:36	Bruce Kidd (CAN)	00:13:36
6 Miles	Men	Bruce Kidd (CAN)	00:28:26	Dave Power (AUS)	00:28:34	John Merri-man (WAL)	00:28:40
Marathon	Men	Brian Kilby (ENG)	02:21:17	Dave Power (AUS)	02:22:16	Rod Bo-nella (AUS)	02:24:07
3000 Metres Steeplechase	Men	Trevor Vin-cent (AUS)	00:08:43	Maurice Herriott (ENG)	00:08:45	Ron Blac-kney (AUS)	00:09:01
120 Yards Hurdles	Men	Ghulam Raziq (PAK)	14.34	Dave Prince (AUS)	14.48	Laurie Taitt (ENG)	14.81

440 Yards Hurdles	Men	Ken Roche (AUS)	51.5	Kimaru Songok (KEN)	51.9	Benson Ishiepai (UGA)	52.3
High Jump	Men	Percy Hobson (AUS)	2.11	Charles "Chilla" Porter (AUS)	2.08	Anton Norris (BAR)	2.03
Pole Vault	Men	Trevor Bickle (AUS)	4.49	Danie Burger (FRN)	4.42	Ross Filshie (AUS)	4.42
Long Jump	Men	Mike Ahey (GHA)	8.05w	Dave Norris (NZL)	7.75w	Wellesley Clayton (JAM)	7.73w
Triple Jump	Men	Ian Tomlinson (AUS)	16.2	John Baguley (AUS)	16.08	Fred Alsop (ENG)	16.03
Shot	Men	Martyn Lucking (ENG)	18.08	Mike Lindsay (SCO)	18.05	David Steen (CAN)	17.9
Discus	Men	Warwick Selvey (AUS)	56.48	Mike Lind say (SCO)	52.58	John Sheldrick (ENG)	50.67
Hammer	Men	Howard Payne (ENG)	61.65	Dick Leffler (AUS)	59.83	Robert Brown (AUS)	57.65
Javelin	Men	Alf Mitchell (AUS)	78.11	Colin Smith (ENG)	77.94	Nick Birks (AUS)	75.07
4 x 110 Yards Relay	Men	England (ENG)	40.62	Ghana (GHA)	40.74	Wales (WAL)	40.8
4 x 440 Yards Relay	Men	Jamaica (JAM)	00:03:10	England (ENG)	00:03:11	Ghana (GHA)	00:03:12

Bowls

Event		*Gold*	*Silver*	*Bronze*
Singles	Men	David Bryant (ENG)	Joseph Watson Black (SCO)	Alan Bradley (FRN)
Pairs	Men	Robert McDonald & Hugh Robson (NZL)	Thomas Hamill & Michael Purdon (SCO)	Charles Jackson & William Jackson (FRN)
Fours	Men	England (ENG) Skipperd	Scotland (SCO) by Sid Drysdale	Rhodesia & Nyasaland (FRN)

Boxing

Event		*Gold*	*Silver*	*Bronze*
Flyweight	Men	Robert Mallon (SCO)	Cassis Aryee (GHA)	Philip Warunige (KEN) Mike Pye (ENG)
Bantamweight	Men	Jeff Dynevor (AUS)	Sammy Abbey (GHA)	J. Sentongo (UGA) Peter Benneyworth (ENG)

Featherweight	Men	John McDermott (SCO)	Ali Juma (KEN)	Turori George (NZL) Ted Stone (AUS)
Lightweight	Men	Eddie Blay (GHA)	Kesi Odongo (UGA)	Thomas Donovan (NZL) Brian Whelan (ENG)
Light Welterweight	Men	Clement Quartey (GHA)	Dick McTaggart (SCO)	H. Reti (CAN) Brian Brazier (ENG)
Welterweight	Men	Wallace Coe (NZL)	John Pritchett (ENG)	Albert Turmel (JER)
Light Middleweight	Men	Harold Mann (CAN)	Brian Benson (FRN)	F. Nyangweso (UGA) Kenneth Hopkins (PNG)
Middleweight	Men	Cephas Colquhoun (JAM)	Thomas Arimi (GHA)	Moses Evans (FIJ)
Light Heavyweight	Men	Tony Madigan (AUS)	Jojo Miles (GHA)	Hans Christie (NIR) Tom Menzies (SCO)
Heavyweight	Men	George Oywello (UGA)	Bill Kini (NZL)	Holgar Johansen (FIJ) Graham Robinson (AUS)

Cycling

Track

Event		*Gold*		*Silver*		*Bronze*	
Time Trial	Men	Peter Bartels (AUS)	00:01:13	Ian Chapman (AUS)	00:01:13	Roger Whitfield (ENG)	00:01:14
Sprint	Men	Tom Harrison (AUS)		Karl Barton (ENG)		Ian Browne (AUS)	
Individual Pursuit	Men	Maxwell Langshaw (AUS)	00:05:08	Richard Hine (AUS)	00:05:13	Harry Jackson (ENG)	00:05:14
10 Miles Scratch	Men	Doug Adams (AUS)	00:22:11	Warren Johnston (NZL)		John Clarey (ENG)	

Road

Event		*Gold*		*Silver*		*Bronze*	
Road Race	Men	Wes Mason (ENG)	05:20:26	Anthony Walsh (NZL)	05:20:27	Laurie Byers (NZL)	05:20:27

Fencing

Event		*Gold*	*Silver*	*Bronze*
Foil	Men	Sandy Leckie (SCO)	Allan Jay (ENG)	Ralph Cooperman (ENG)
Foil–Team	Men	England (ENG)	Australia (AUS)	Canada (CAN)
Épée	Men	Ivan Lund (AUS)	John Pelling (ENG)	Peter Jacobs (ENG)
Épée–Team	Men	England (ENG)	Australia (AUS)	Canada (CAN)
Sabre	Men	Ralph Cooperman (ENG)	Benedek Simo (CAN)	John Andru (CAN)
Sabre- Team	Men	England (ENG)	Canada (CAN)	New Zealand (NZL)
Foil	Women	Melody Coleman (NZL)	Johanna Winter (AUS)	Janet Hopner (AUS)

Rowing

Event		*Gold*		*Silver*		*Bronze*	
Single Sculls	Men	James Hill (NZL)	00:07:40	Bill Barry (ENG)	00:07:45	Ian Tutty (AUS)	00:07:49
Double Sculls	Men	George Justicz & Nicholas Bir-kmyre (ENG)	00:06:52	Peter Watk-inson and Murray Wat-kinson (NZL)	00:06:54	Barclay Wade & Graeme Squires (AUS)	00:07:01
Coxless Pairs	Men	Stewart Farqu harson & Jim Lee-Nicholson (NZL)	00:07:04	Graham Lawrence & Murray Lawrence (ENG)	00:07:08	Rodger Ninham & William Hatfield (AUS)	00:07:10
Coxless Fours	Men	Chris Davidge, Michael Clay, John Beve-ridge & John Tilbury (ENG)	00:06:31	David Edw-ards, Jeremy Luke, Richard Luke & John Edwards (WAL)	00:06:32	Eldon Woro-bieff, Thomas Gray, Thomas Stokes & Ray McIntosh (CAN)	00:06:35
Coxed Fours	Men	Winston Step-hens, Keith Heselwood, Hugh Smedley, George Paterson & Douglas Pulman (NZL)	00:06:48	David Ramage, Derek Norwood, David Caithness, David John & Phillip Sarah (AUS)	00:06:49	John Russell, Richard Knight, John Vigurs, Colin Porter & Michael Howard-John ston (ENG)	00:07:05
Eights	Men	Australia (AUS)	00:05:53	New Zealand (NZL)	00:06:09	England (ENG)	00:05:54

Swimming

Men's Events

Event	*Gold*		*Silver*		*Bronze*	
110 yd freestyle	Dick Pound (CAN)	55.8	Bobby McGregor (SCO)	56.1	David Dickson (AUS)	56.1
440 yd freestyle	Murray Rose (AUS)	4:20.0	Allan Wood (AUS)	4:22.5	Robert Windle (AUS)	4:23.1
1650 yd freestyle	Murray Rose (AUS)	17:18.1	Robert Windle (AUS)	17:44.5	Allan Wood (AUS)	17:55.6
110 yd backstroke	Graham Sykes (ENG)	1.04.5	Julian Carroll (AUS)	1:05.4	Wayne Vincent (AUS)	1:06.2
220 yd backstroke	Julian Carroll (AUS)	2:20.9	Tony Fingleton (AUS)	2:21.0	Alan Robertson (NZL)	2:23.0
110 yd bre aststroke	Ian O'Brien (AUS)	1:11.4	William Burton (AUS)	1:13.9	Steve Rabino-vich (CAN)	1:14.1
220 yd brea ststroke	Ian O'Brien (AUS)	2:38.2	William Burton (AUS)	2:42.1	Neil Nicho-lson (ENG)	2:42.6
110 yd butterfly	Kevin Berry (AUS)	59.5	Neville Hayes (AUS)	1:02.3	Aldwin Mein-hardt (CAN)	1:02.6
220 yd butterfly	Kevin Berry (AUS)	2:10.8	Neville Hayes (AUS)	2:16.3	Brett Hill (AUS)	2:18.7
440 yd individual medley	Alex Alexander (AUS)	5:15.3	John Oravainen (AUS)	5:16.3	John Kelso (CAN)	5:16.5
4×110 yd freestyle relay	Australia (AUS) David Dickson Murray Rose Peter Doak Peter Phelps	3:43.9	Canada (CAN) A.W. Meinhardt J.A. Gilchrist J.G. Kelso Richard Pound	3:48.3	England (ENG) A. ClaydenJohn Martin-Dye P. Kendrew S.R. Clarke	3:51.3
4×220 yd freestyle relay	Australia (AUS) Allan Wood Anthony Strahan Murray Rose Robert Windle	8:13.4	Canada (CAN) A.W. Meinhardt J.A. Gilchrist J.G. Kelso Richard Pound	8:42.4	England (ENG) John Martin-Dye P. Kendrew R. Campion S.R. Clarke	8:46.0
4×110 yd medley relay	Australia (AUS) David Dickson Ian O'Brien Julian Carroll Kevin Berry	4:12.4	England (ENG) Graham Sykes Neil Nicholson P. Kendrew T.W. Glenville	4:19.9	Canada (CAN) Andrew Harro-wer F.C. Cowie I. Blyth Robert McGregor	4:19.9

Women's Events

Event	*Gold*		*Silver*		*Bronze*	
110 yd freestyle	Dawn Fraser (AUS)	59.5	Robin Thorn (AUS)	1:03.8	Mary Stewart (CAN)	1:04.4
440 yd freestyle	Dawn Fraser (AUS)	4:51.4	Ilsa Konrads (AUS)	4:55.0	Liz Long (ENG)	5:00.4
110 yd backstroke	Linda Ludgrove (ENG)	1:11.1	Pam Sergeant (AUS)	1:11.5	Syliva Lewis (ENG)	1:12.2
220 yd backstroke	Linda Ludgrove (ENG)	2:35.2	Sylvia Lewis (ENG)	2:36.7	Pam Sergeant (AUS)	2:37.5
110 yd bre-aststroke	Anita Lonsb-rough (ENG)	1:21.3	Vivien Haddon (NZL)	1:21.3	Dorinda Fraser (ENG)	1:21.7
220 yd bre-aststroke	Anita Lons-brough (ENG)	2:51.7	Jackie Enfield (ENG)	2:54.7	Vivien Haddon (NZL)	2:56.3
110 yd butterfly	Mary Stewart (CAN)	1:10.1	Anne Cotterill (ENG)	1:11.2	Linda McGill (AUS)	1:11.6
440 yd indi-vidual medley	Anita Lons-brough (ENG)	5:38.6	Linda McGill (AUS)	5:46.1	Jennifer Corish (AUS)	5:53.0
4×110 yd freestyle relay	Australia (AUS) Dawn Fraser Lynette Bell Robin Thorn Ruth Everuss	4:11.0	Canada (CAN) M. Sevigny M.P. Stewart Patricia Thompson Sara Barber	4:21.1	England (ENG) Diana Wilkinson Elizabeth Long L. Amos S. Keen	4:21.3
4×110 yd medley relay	Australia (AUS) Dawn Fraser Linda McGill Marguerite Ruygrok Pamela Sergeant	4:45.9	England (ENG) Anita Lonsbrough Diana Wilkinson Linda Ludgrove Mary Cotterill	4:47.9	Canada (CAN) A.J. Glendenning M.P. Stewart Patricia Thompson Sara Barber	4:48.1

Diving

Event		*Gold*		*Silver*		*Bronze*	
3 Metres Spring-board Diving	Men	Brian Phelps (ENG)	154.14	Thomas Dinsley (CAN)	147.22	Ernest Meissner (CAN)	145.03
10 Metres High-board [Plat-form] Diving	Men	Brian Phelps (ENG)	168.35	Graham Deuble (AUS)	151	Tony Kitcher (ENG)	150.81
3 Metres Spring-board Diving	Women	Susan Knight (AUS)	134.72	Liz Ferris (ENG)	132.74	Lorraine Mc-Arthur (AUS)	125.13
10 Metres High board [Plat-form] Diving	Women	Susan Knight (AUS)	101.15	Margaret Austen (ENG)	98.93	Patricia Plowman (AUS)	91.79

Weightlifting

Event		*Gold*		*Silver*		*Bronze*	
Bantamweight Overall	Men	Chua Phung Kim (SIN)	322	Allen Salter (CAN)	310.5	Martin Dias (BGU)	306
Featherweight Overall	Men	George Newton (ENG)	326.5	Ieuan Owen (WAL)	292.5	Cheong Kam Hong (MAL)	281
Lightweight Overall	Men	Carlton Goring (ENG)	351.5	Alan Oshyer (AUS)	340	Jimmy Moir (SCO)	340
Middleweight Overall	Men	Tan Howe Liang (SIN)	390	Pierre St. Jean (CAN)	376	Horace Johnson (WAL)	372
Light Heavy-weight Overall	Men	Phil Caira (SCO)	408	George Manners (ENG)	403.5	Peter Arthur (WAL)	392
Middle Heavy-weight Overall	Men	Louis Martin (ENG)	469.5	Cosford White (CAN)	408	Jackie Samuel (TRI)	399
Heavyweight Overall	Men	Arthur Shannos (AUS)	465	Don Oliver (NZL)	465	Brandon Bailey (TRI)	440

Wrestling

Event		*Gold*	*Silver*	*Bronze*
Flyweight	Men	Muhammad Niaz (PAK)	Peter Michienzi (CAN)	Warren Nisbet (NZL)
Bantamweight	Men	Siraj-ud-Din (PAK)	Walter Pilling (ENG)	James Turnbull (SCO)
Featherweight	Men	Ala-ud-Din (PAK)	Matti Jutila (CAN)	Albert Aspen (ENG)
Lightweight	Men	Muhammad Ashraf (PAK)	Sid Marsh (AUS)	Kurt Boese (CAN)
Welterweight	Men	Muhammad Bashir (PAK)	Philip Oberlander (CAN)	Len Allen (ENG)
Middleweight	Men	Muhammad Faiz (PAK)	Michael Benarik (AUS)	Fred Thomas (NZL)
Light Heavy weight	Men	Tony Buck (ENG)	Muhammad Saeed (PAK)	Jim Armstrong (AUS)
Heavyweight	Men	Muhammad Niaz (PAK)	Ray Mitchell (AUS)	Denis McNamara (ENG)

12

1966 British Empire and Commonwealth Games

The 1966 British Empire and Commonwealth Games were held in Kingston, Jamaica from 4 August to 13 August 1966. This was the first time that the Games had been held outside the so-called White Commonwealth countries. Kingston was elected host in Rome, Italy at the 1960 Summer Olympics. The vote was Kingston: 17, Edinburgh, Scotland: 12 and Salisbury, Rhodesia: 5.

Participants

Thirty four teams were represented at the 1966 British Empire and Commonwealth Games.

- Antigua
- Australia
- Bahamas
- Barbados
- Bermuda
- British Honduras
- Canada
- Ceylon

- England
- Fiji
- Ghana
- Gibraltar
- Guyana
- India
- Isle of Man
- Jamaica
- Jersey
- Kenya
- Malaysia
- Mauritius
- New Zealand
- Nigeria
- Northern Ireland
- Pakistan
- Papua & New Guinea
- Scotland
- Sierra Leone
- Singapore
- South Arabia
- St Vincent
- Tanzania
- Trinidad & Tobago
- Uganda
- Wales

Country-wise Medals

Rank	*Nation*	*Gold*	*Silver*	*Bronze*	*Total*
1	England	33	24	23	80
2	Australia	23	28	22	73
3	Wales	14	20	23	57
4	New Zealand	8	5	13	26
5	Ghana	5	2	2	9
6	Trinidad and Tobago	5	2	2	9
7	Pakistan	4	1	4	9
8	Kenya	4	1	3	8
9	India	3	4	3	10
10	Nigeria	3	4	3	10
11	Canada	3	2	2	7
12	Malaysia	2	2	1	5
13	Scotland	1	4	4	9
14	Northern Ireland	1	3	3	7
15	Isle of Man	1	0	0	1
16	Jamaica	0	4	8	12
17	Bermuda	0	1	0	1
18	Guyana	0	1	0	1
19	Uganda	0	1	0	1
20	Papua New Guinea	0	0	3	3
21	Barbados	0	0	1	1
	Total	110	110	120	340

Event-wise Medals

Athletics

Event		*Gold*		*Silver*		*Bronze*	
100 Yards	Women	Dianne Burge	10.6	Irene Piotrowski	10.8	Jill Hall	10.8
220 Yards	Women	Dianne Burge	23.73	Jenny Lamy	23.86	Irene Piotrowski	23.92

440 Yards	Women	Judy Pollock	53	Deirdre Watkinson	54.1	Una Morris	54.2
880 Yards	Women	Abby Hoffman	00:02:04	Judy Pollock	00:02:04	Anne Smith	00:02:05
80 Metres Hurdles	Women	Pam Kilborn	10.9	Carmen Smith	11	Jenny Wingerson	11
High Jump	Women	Michele Brown (Mason)	1.73	Dorothy Shirley	1.7	Robyn Woodhouse	1.7
Long Jump	Women	Mary Rand (Bignal)	6.36	Sheila Parkin	6.3	Violet Odogwu	6.15
Shot	Women	Val Young	16.5	Mary Peters	16.29	Nancy McCredie	15.34
Discus	Women	Val Young	49.78	Jean Roberts	49.2	Carol Martin	48.7
Javelin	Women	Margaret Parker	51.38	Anna Bocson (Pazera)	47.8	Jay Dahlgren	47.68
4 x 110 Yards Relay	Women	Australia	45.3	England	45.6	Jamaica	45.6
100 Yards	Men	Harry Jerome	9.41	Tom Robinson ()	9.44	Edwin Roberts	9.52
220 Yards	Men	Stanley Allotey	20.65	Edwin Roberts	20.93	David Njoke	20.95
440 Yards	Men	Wendell Mottley	45.08	Kent Bernard	46.06	Don Domansky	46.42
880 Yards	Men	Noel Clough	00:01:47	Wilson Kiprugut	00:01:47	George Kerr	00:01:47
1 Mile	Men	Kip Keino	00:03:55	Alan Simpson	00:03:57	Ian Studd	00:03:59
3 Miles	Men	Kip Keino	00:12:57	Ron Clarke	00:12:59	Allan Rushmer	00:13:09
6 Miles	Men	Naftali Temu	00:27:14	Ron Clarke	00:27:39	Jim Alder	00:28:15
Marathon	Men	Jim Alder	02:22:08	Bill Adcocks	02:22:13	Mike Ryan	02:27:59
3000 Metres Steeplechase	Men	Peter Welsh	00:08:29	Kerry O'Brien	00:08:33	Benjamin Kogo	00:08:33
120 Yards Hurdles	Men	David Hemery	14.1	Mike Parker	14.2	Ghulam Raziq	14.3
440 Yards Hurdles	Men	Ken Roche	50.95	Kingsley Agbabokha	51.46	Peter Warden	51.54
High Jump	Men	Lawrence Peckham	2.08	Samuel Igun	2.03	Anton Norris	2
Pole Vault	Men	Trevor Bickle	4.8	Mike Bull	4.72	Gerry Moro	4.65
Long Jump	Men	Lynn Davies	7.99	John Morbey	7.89	Wellesley Clayton	7.83
Triple Jump	Men	Samuel Igun	16.40w	George Ogan	16.08	Fred Alsop	15.96
Shot	Men	David Steen	18.79	Les Mills	18.37	George Puce	17.14
Discus	Men	Les Mills	56.18	George Puce	55.94	Robin Tait	55.02
Hammer	Men	Howard Payne	61.98	Praveen Kumar	60.12	Muhammad Iqbal	59.56
Javelin	Men	John FitzSimons	79.78	Nick Birks	76.16	Muhammad Nawaz	69.94

Decathlon	Men	Roy Williams	7270	Clive Longe	7123	Gerry Moro	6983
20 Miles Road Walk	Men	Ron Wallwork	02:44:43	Ray Middleton	02:45:19	Norman Read	02:46:29
4 x 110 Yards Relay	Men	Ghana	39.8	Jamaica	40	Australia	40
4 x 440 Yards Relay	Men	Trinidad and Tobago	00:03:03	Canada	00:03:05	England	00:03:07

Badminton

Event	*Gold*	*Silver*	*Bronze*
Men's Singles	Tan Aik Huang	Yew Cheng Hoe	Dinesk Khanna
Men's Doubles	Tan Aik Huang & Yew Cheng Hoe	Ng Boon Bee & Tan Yee Khan	David Horton & Roger Mills
Women's Singles	Angela Bairstow	Sharon Whittaker	Ursula Smith
Women's Doubles	Helen Horton & Ursula Smith	Angela Bairstow & Iris Rogers	Rosalind Singha Ang & Teoh Siew Yong
Mixed Doubles	Roger Mills & Angela Bairstow	Tony Jordan & Helen Horton	Robert McCoig & Muriel Ferguson

Boxing

Event		*Gold*	*Silver*	*Bronze*
Flyweight	Men	Sulley Shittu	Kenneth Campbell	Frank Scott John Rakowski
Bantamweight	Men	Edward Ndukwu	Darryl Norwood	Nderu Mwaura Brian Kendall
Featherweight	Men	Philip Waruinge	Pat Maguire	Amos Ajoo Harold West
Lightweight	Men	Anthony Andeh	Ron Thurston	Stephen Baraza Samuel Lockhart
Light Welter weight	Men	Jim McCourt	Aaron Popoola	Alex Odhiambo Ray Maguire
Welterweight	Men	Eddie Blay	Bobby Arthur	Nojim Maiyegun Andy Peace
Light Middleweight	Men	Mark Rowe	Tom Imrie	R. Okine Nojim Maiyegun
Middle-weight	Men	Joe Darkey	Arthur Trout	John Turpin Mathias Ouma
Light Heavy-weight	Men	Roger Tighe	Fatai Ayinla	Dennis Booth Sylvester Hines
Heavyweight	Men	Bill Kini	Adonis Ray	Danny McAlinden Benson Ocan

Diving

Event		*Gold*		*Silver*		*Bronze*	
3 Metres Spring board Diving	Men	Brian Phelps	154.55	Don Wagstaff	150.17	Chris Robb	136.52
10 Metres High board [Plat-form] Diving	Men	Brian Phelps	164.57	Don Wagstaff	148.44	Chris Robb	141.68
3 Metres Spring board Diving	Women	Kathy Rowlatt	147.1	Beverley Boys	134.92	Susan Knight	134.9
10 Metres High-board [Plat-form] Diving	Women	Joy Newman	98.87	Robyn Bradshaw	98.85	Beverley Boys	97.21

Cycling

Track

Event		*Gold*		*Silver*		*Bronze*	
Time Trial	Men	Roger Gibbon	00:01:10	Philip Bri-stow-Stagg	00:01:11	Richard Hine	00:01:11
Sprint	Men	Roger Gibbon		Jim Booker		Daryl Perkins	
Individual Pursuit	Men	Hugh Porter	00:04:57	John Bylsma	00:04:59	Richard Hine	00:05:04
10 Miles Scratch	Men	Ian Alsop	00:21:46	Hilton Clarke	00:21:46	Trevor Bull	00:21:47

Road

Event		*Gold*		*Silver*		*Bronze*	
Road Race	Men	Peter Buckley	05:07:52	Des Thomson	05:12:11	Laurie Byers	05:12:20

Fencing

Event		*Gold*	*Silver*	*Bronze*
Foil	Men	Allan Jay	Bill Hoskyns	Graham Paul
Foil - Team	Men	England	Australia	Scotland
Épée	Men	Bill Hoskyns	John Pelling	Robert Reynolds
Épée - Team	Men	England	Canada	Australia

Sabre	Men	Ralph Cooperman	Sandy Leckie	Gabor Arato
Sabre- Team	Men	England	Australia	Canada
Foil	Women	Janet Wardell-Yerburgh	Shirley Parker	Gaye McDermit
Foil - Team	Women	England	Australia	New Zealand

Shooting

Pistol

Event		Gold		Silver		Bronze	
Free Pistol	Men/Open	Charles Sexton	544	Jules Sobrian	538	Garfield McMahon	536
Centre-Fire Pistol	Men/Open	James Lee	576	Tony Clark	575	Julio Machado	571
Rapid-Fire Pistol	Men/Open	Tony Clark	585	Michael Papps	578	Jules Sobrian	572

Rifle

Event		Gold		Silver		Bronze	
Small Bore Rifle	Men/Open	Gilmour Boa	587	Brian Lacey	585	John Murphy	584
Full Bore Rifle	Men/Open	Lord John Swansea	394	Robert Stewart	381	Tom Sutherland	381

Swimming

Men's Events

Event	Gold		Silver		Bronze	
110 yd freestyle	Mike Wenden	54.0	Bobby McGregor	54.2	David Dickson	54.6
440 yd freestyle	Robert Windle	4:15.0	John Bennett	4:15.8	Ralph Hutton	4:16.1
1650 yd freestyle	Ron Jackson	17:25.9	Sandy Gilchrist	17:33.9	Ralph Hutton	17:38.9
110 yd backstroke	Peter Reynolds	1:02.4	Ralph Hutton	1:02.7	Neil Jackson	1:03.3
220 yd backstroke	Peter Reynolds	2:12.0	Ralph Hutton	2:13.5	Karl Byrom	2:18.8

110 yd breaststroke	Ian O'Brien	1:08.2	Tony Graham	1:12.9	Malcolm Tucker	1:13.9
220 yd breaststroke	Ian O'Brien	2:29.3	Tony Graham	2:36.9	Bill Mahony	2:38.9
110 yd butterfly	Ron Jacks	1:00.3	Graham Dunn	1:00.9	Keith Bewley	1:01.5
220 yd butterfly	David Gerrard	2:12.7	Brett Hill	2:12.8	Tom Arusoo	2:14.2
440 yd individual medley	Peter Reynolds	4:50.8	Ralph Hutton	4:51.8	Sandy Gilchrist	4:58.7
4×110 yd freestyle relay	Australia David Dickson John Ryan Michael Wenden Robert Windle	3:35.6	Canada J.A. Gilchrist Ralph Hutton Robert Kasting Ronald Jacks	3:42.3	England Anthony Jarvis John Martin-Dye Michael Turner Robert Lord	3:43.7
4×220 yd freestyle relay	Australia David Dickson Michael Wenden Peter Reynolds Robert Windle	7:59.5	Canada J.A. Gilchrist Ralph Hutton Robert Kasting Ronald Jacks	8:15.0	England Anthony Jarvis John Thurley Keith Bewley Michael Turner	8:24.0
4×110 yd medley relay	Canada J.A. Gilchrist Leonard Chase Ralph Hutton Ronald Jacks	4:10.5	England Keith Bewley Malcolm Tucker Michael Turner Neil Jackson	4:11.3	New Zealand David Gerrard Tony Graham Hilton Brown Paddy O'Carroll	4:17.5

Women's events

Event	*Gold*		*Silver*		*Bronze*	
110 yd freestyle	Marion Lay	01:02.3	Lynette Bell	01:03.2	Jan Murphy	01:03.4
440 yd freestyle	Kathy Wainwright	04:38.8	Jenny Thorn	04:44.5	Kim Herford	04:47.2
110 yd backstroke	Linda Ludgrove	01:09.2	Elaine Tanner	01:09.9	Janet Franklin	01:11.8
220 yd backstroke	Linda Ludgrove	02:28.5	Elaine Tanner	02:29.7	Margaret Macrae	02:34.7
110 yd breaststroke	Diana Harris	01:19.7	Jill Slattery	01:19.8	Heather Saville	01:21.6
220 yd breaststroke	Jill Slattery	02:50.3	Stella Mitchell	02:50.3	Vivien Haddon	02:53.9

110 yd butterfly	Elaine Tanner	01:06.8	Judy Gegan	01:09.3	Ann Barner	01:09.7
220 yd butterfly	Elaine Tanner	02:29.9	Marilyn Carson	02:34.8	Ann Barner	02:35.0
440 yd individual medley	Elaine Tanner	05:26.3	Jan Murphy	05:28.1	Jane Hughes	05:34.1
4×110 yd freestyle relay	Canada Elaine Tanner Jane Hughes Louise Kennedy Marion Lay	04:10.8	Australia Janet Steinbeck Janice Murphy Lynette Bell Marion Smith	04:11.1	England Diana Wilkinson Jeanette Cave Pauline Sillett Susan Cope	04:17.3
4×110 yd medley relay	England Diana Harris Judy Gegan Linda Ludgrove Pauline Sillett	04:40.6	Canada Donna Ross Elaine Tanner Louise Kennedy Marion Lay	04:44.5	Australia Allyson Mabb Heather Saville Jill Pauline Groeger Lynette Bell	04:45.7

Weightlifting

Event		Gold		Silver		Bronze	
Bantamweight-Overall	Men	Precious McKenzie	319.5	Martin Dias	307	Chun Hon Chan	304.5
Featherweight Overall	Men	Chung Kum Weng	337	Mahon Ghosh	334.5	Allen Salter	324.5
Lightweight Overall	Men	Hugo Gittens	367	George Newton	354.5	Ieuan Owen	349.5
Middleweight Overall	Men	Pierre St. Jean	404.5	Horace Johnson	382	Russell Perry	372
Light Heavy weight-Overall	Men	George Vakakis	419.5	Sylvanus Blackman	414.5	Mike Pearman	409.5
Middle Heavy weight - Overall	Men	Louis Martin	462	George Manners	429.5	Dudley Lawson	422
Heavyweight - Overall	Men	Don Oliver	497	Arthur Shannos	464.5	Brandon Bailey	462

Wrestling

Event		Gold	Silver	Bronze
Flyweight	Men	Muhammad Nazir	Shamrao Sable	Peter Michienzi
Bantam-weight	Men	Bishamber Singh	Kevin McGrath	Muhammad Saeed

Featherweight	Men	Muhammad Akhtar	Randhawa Singh	Albert Aspen
Lightweight	Men	Mukhtiar Singh	Ray Lougheed	Tony Greig
Welterweight	Men	Muhammad Bashir	Richard Bryant	Hukum Singh
Middleweight	Men	Muhammad Faiz	Sébastien Donison	Michael Benarik
Light Heavy-weight	Men	Robert Chamberot	Wallace Booth	Bishwanath Singh
Heavyweight	Men	Bhim Singh	Ikram Ilahi	Denis McNamara

13

1970 British Commonwealth Games

The 1970 British Commonwealth Games were held in Edinburgh, Scotland from 16 July to 25 July 1970. This was the first time the name British Commonwealth Games was adopted, the first time metric units rather than imperial units were used in events, and also the first time the games were held in Scotland. Also, these games saw the first unique Games trademark logo: an emblem showing the Games emblem intertwined with a St. Andrews Cross and a thistle. The bid election was held in Tokyo, Japan during the 1964 Summer Olympics. The vote result was Edinburgh: 18, Christchurch, New Zealand: 11.

Medals by Country

Rank	*Nation*	*Gold*	*Silver*	*Bronze*	*Total*
1	Australia	36	24	22	82
2	England	27	25	32	84
3	Canada	18	24	24	66
4	Scotland	6	8	11	25
5	Kenya	5	3	6	14
6	India	5	3	4	12
7	Pakistan	4	3	2	9
8	Jamaica	4	2	1	7
9	Uganda	3	3	1	7

10	Northern Ireland	3	1	5	9
11	New Zealand	2	6	6	14
12	Wales	2	6	4	12
13	Ghana	2	3	2	7
14	Nigeria	2	0	0	2
15	Malaysia	1	1	1	3
16	Hong Kong	1	0	0	1
17	Trinidad and Tobago	0	4	3	7
18	Zambia	0	2	2	4
19	Singapore	0	1	1	2
20	Barbados	0	1	0	1
	Tanzania	0	1	0	1*
22	Fiji	0	0	1	1
	Gambia	0	0	1	1*
	Guyana	0	0	1	1
	Isle of Man	0	0	1	1
	Malawi	0	0	1	1*
	Saint Vincent	0	0	1	1*
	Total	121	121	133	375

• * = First medal in the British Commonwealth Games.

Event-wise Medal

Athletics

Event		*Gold*		*Silver*		*Bronze*	
100 Metres	Women	Raelene Boyle (AUS)	11.26w	Alice Annum (GHA)	11.32w	Marion Hoffman (AUS)	11.36w
200 Metres	Women	Raelene Boyle (AUS)	22.75w	Alice Annum (GHA)	22.86w	Margaret Critchley (ENG)	23.16w
400 Metres	Women	Marilyn Neufville (JAM)	51.02	Sandra Brown (AUS)	53.66	Judith Ayaa (UGA)	53.77
800 Metres	Women	Rosemary Stirling (SCO)	00:02:06	Pat Lowe (ENG)	00:02:06	Cheryl Peasley (AUS)	00:02:06
1500 Metres	Women	Rita Ridley (ENG)	04:18:08	Joan Page (ENG)	04:19:00	Thelma Fynn (CAN)	04:19:01

Event		Gold		Silver		Bronze	
100 Metres Hurdles		Women Pam Kilborn (AUS)	13.27	Maureen Caird (AUS)	13.73	Christine Bell (ENG)	13.82
High Jump	Women	Debbie Brill (CAN)	1.78	Ann Wilson (ENG)	1.7	Moira Walls (SCO)	1.7
Long Jump	Women	Sheila Sherwood (Parkin) (ENG)	6.73	Ann Wilson (ENG)	6.5	Joan Hendry (CAN)	6.28
Shot	Women	Mary Peters (NIR)	15.93	Barbara Poulsen (NZL)	15.87	Jean Roberts (AUS)	15.32
Discus	Women	Rosemary Payne (SCO)	54.46	Jean Roberts (AUS)	51.02	Carol Martin (CAN)	48.42
Javelin	Women	Petra Rivers (AUS)	52	Anne Farquhar (ENG)	50.82	Jay Dahlgren (CAN)	49.54
Pentathlon	Women	Mary Peters (NIR)	5148	Ann Wilson (ENG)	5037	Jenny Wingerson (CAN)	4736
4 x 100 Metres Relay		Women Australia (AUS)	44.14	England (ENG)	44.28	Canada (CAN)	44.68
100 Metres	Men	Don Quarrie (JAM)	10.24w	Lennox Miller (JAM)	10.32w	Hasely Craw-ford (TRI)	10.33w
200 Metres	Men	Don Quarrie (JAM)	20.56	Edwin Roberts (TRI)	20.69	Charles Asati (KEN)	20.74
400 Metres	Men	Charles Asati (KEN)	45.01	Ross Wilson (AUS)	45.61	Saimoni Tamani (FIJ)	45.82
800 Metres	Men	Robert Ouko (KEN)	00:01:47	Benedict Cayenne (TRI)	00:01:47	William Smart (CAN)	00:01:47
1500 Metres	Men	Kip Keino (KEN)	00:03:37	Dick Quax (NZL)	00:03:38	Brendan Foster (ENG)	00:03:41
5000 Metres	Men	Ian Stewart (SCO)	00:13:23	Ian Mc-Cafferty (SCO)	00:13:23	Kip Keino (KEN)	13:27:06
10000 Metres	Men	Lachie Stewart (SCO)	00:28:12	Ron Clarke (AUS)	00:28:13	Dick Taylor (ENG)	00:28:15
Marathon	Men	Ron Hill (ENG)	02:09:28	Jim Alder (SCO)	02:12:04	Don Fair-cloth (ENG)	02:12:19
3000 Metres Steeplechase	Men	Tony Man-ning (AUS)	08:26:02	Ben Jipcho (KEN)	08:29:06	Amos Biwott (KEN)	08:30:08
110 Metres Hurdles	Men	David Hemery (ENG)	13.66w	Mal Baird (AUS)	13.86w	Godfrey Murray (JAM)	14.02w
400 Metres Hurdles	Men	John Sherwood (ENG)	50.03	William Koskei (KEN)	50 15	Charles Kipkwm-boi Yego (KEN)	50.19
High Jump	Men	Lawrence Peckham (AUS)	2.14	John Hawkins (CAN)	2.12	Sheikh Faye (GAM)	2.1
Pole Vault	Men	Mike Bull (NIR)	5.1	Alan Kane (CAN)	4.9	Robert Raftis (CAN)	4.9
Long Jump	Men	Lynn Davies (WAL)	8.06w	Phil May (AUS)	7.94w	Alan Lerwill (ENG)	7.94w
Triple Jump	Men	Phil May (AUS)	16.72	Mick McGrath (AUS)	16.41	Mohinder Singh Gill (IND)	15.9

Shot	Men	David Steen (CAN)	19.21	Jeff Teale (ENG)	18.43	Les Mills (NZL)	18.4
Discus	Men	George Puce (CAN)	59.02	Les Mills (NZL)	57.84	Bill Tancred (ENG)	56.68
Hammer	Men	Howard Payne (ENG)	67.8	Bruce Fraser (ENG)	62.9	Barry Williams (ENG)	61.58
Javelin	Men	Dave Travis (ENG)	79.5	John Mc-Sorley (ENG)	76.74	John Fitz-Simons (ENG)	73.2
Decathlon	Men	Geoff Smith (AUS)	7492	Peter Gabbett (ENG)	7469	Barry King (ENG)	7201
20 Miles Road Walk		Noel Free-man (AUS)	02:33:33	Bob Gard-iner (AUS)	02:35:55	Bill Suther-land (SCO)	02:37:24
4 x 100 Metres	Men	Jamaica (JAM)	39.46	Ghana (GHA)	39.82	England (ENG)	40.05
4 x 400 Metres Relay	Men	Kenya (KEN)	00:03:04	Trinidad & Tobago (TRI)	00:03:05	England (ENG)	00:03:06

Badminton

Event		*Gold*	*Silver*	*Bronze*
Men's Singles	Men	Jamie Paulson (CAN)	Paul Whetnall (ENG)	Ray Sharp (ENG)
Men's Doubles	Men	Ng Boon Bee & Punch Gunalan (MAS)	Ng Tat Wai & Tan Soon Hooi (MAS)	Yves Paré & Jamie Paulson (CAN)
Women's Singles	Women	Margaret Beck (ENG)	Gillian Perrin (ENG)	Margaret Boxall (ENG)
Women's Doubles	Women	Margaret Boxall & Sue Whetnall (ENG)	Gillian Perrin & Julie Rickard (ENG)	Rosalind Singha Ang & Teoh Siew Yong (MAS)
Mixed Doubles	Mixed	Derek Talbot & Margaret Boxall (ENG)	Roger Mills & Gillian Perrin (ENG)	David Eddy & Sue Whetnall (ENG)

Bowls

Event		*Gold*	*Silver*	*Bronze*
Singles	Men	David Bryant (ENG)	Neal Bryce (ZAM)	Roy Fulton (NIR)
Pairs	Men	Norman King & Peter Line (ENG)	Robert McDonald & Hugh Robson (NZL)	Jimmy Donnelly & Syd Thompson (NIR)
Fours	Men	Hong Kong (HKG)	Scotland (SCO)	Northern Ireland (NIR)

Boxing

Event		*Gold*	*Silver*	*Bronze*
Light Flyweight	Men	James Odwori (UGA)	Anthony Davies (WAL)	P.J. Butterfield (AUS) Michael Abrams (ENG)
Flyweight	Men	Dave Needham (ENG)	Leo Rwabwogo (UGA)	A. McHugh (SCO) Davy Larmour (NIR)
Bantam-weight	Men	Sulley Shittu (GHA)	Samuel Mbugua (KEN)	S. Ogilvie (SCO) Courtney Atherly (GUY)
Feather-weight	Men	Philip Waruinge (KEN)	Deogratias Musoke (UGA)	Mir Samar (PAK) Alan Richardson (ENG)
Light weight	Men	Abayomi Adeyemi (NGR)	John Gillan (SCO)	Tatu Ghionga (MAW) Moses Mbugua (KEN)
Light Wel-terweight	Men	Mohamed Muruli (UGA)	Dai Davies (WAL)	E.O. Lawson (GHA) Paul Kayula (ZAM)
Welter-weight	Men	Emma Ankudey (GHA)	John Olulu (KEN)	T. Joyce (SCO) Shivaji Bhonsle (IND)
Light Mid-dleweight	Men	Tom Imrie (SCO)	Julius Luipa (ZAM)	P.J. Doherty (NIR) David Attan (KEN)
Middle-weight	Men	John Conteh (ENG)	Titus Simba (TAN)	R. Murphy (AUS) Samuel Kasongo (ZAM)
Light Hea-vyweight	Men	Fatai Ayinla (NGR)	Oliver Wright (JAM)	Victor Attivor (GHA) John Rafferty (SCO)
Heavy-weight	Men	Benson Masanda (UGA)	John McKinty (NIR)	Jack Meda (CAN) Leslie Stevens (ENG)

Cycling

Track

Event		*Gold*		*Silver*		*Bronze*	
Time Trial	Men	Harry Kent (NZL)	00:01:09	Leslie King (TRI)	00:01:10	Jocelyn Lovell (CAN)	00:01:11
Sprint	Men	John Nicholson (AUS)		Gordon Johnson (AUS)		Leslie King (TRI)	
Individual Pursuit	Men	Ian Hallam (ENG)	00:05:01	Daniel Clark (AUS)	00:05:05	Blair Stockwell (NZL)	walk-over

10 Miles Scratch	Men	Jocelyn Lovell (CAN)	00:20:47	Brian Temple (SCO)	00:20:48	Vernon Stauble (TRI)	00:20:48
Tandem	Men	Gordon Johnson & Ron Jonker (AUS)	11.43	Jocelyn Lovell & Barry Harvey (CAN)		John Hatfield & John Beswick (WAL)	

Road

Event		*Gold*		*Silver*		*Bronze*	
Road Race	Men	Bruce Biddle (NZL)	04:38:06	Ray Bilney (AUS)	04:39:06	John Trevorrow (AUS)	04:40:03

Fencing

Event		*Gold*	*Silver*	*Bronze*
Foil	Men	Mike Breckin (ENG)	Barry Paul (ENG)	Graham Paul (ENG)
Foil – Team	Men	England (ENG)	Australia (AUS)	Canada (CAN)
Épée	Men	Bill Hoskyns (ENG)	Lester Wong (CAN)	Peter Jacobs (ENG)
Épée – Team	Men	England (ENG)	Scotland (SCO)	Canada (CAN)
Sabre	Men	Sandy Leckie (SCO)	Rodney Craig (ENG)	Richard Cohen (ENG)
Sabre- Team	Men	England (ENG)	Scotland (SCO)	Australia (AUS)
Foil	Women	Janet Wardell-Yerburgh (ENG)	Marion Exelby (AUS)	Susan Youngs (SCO)
Foil – Team	Women	England (ENG)	Scotland (SCO)	Canada (CAN)

Swimming

Men's events

Event	*Gold*		*Silver*		*Bronze*	
100 m freestyle	Mike Wenden (AUS)	53.06	Greg Rogers (AUS)	54.26	William Devenish (AUS)	54.28
200 m freestyle	Mike Wenden (AUS)	1:56.69	Ralph Hutton (CAN)	1:58.45	Rogers Greg (AUS)	1:58.63
400 m freestyle	Graham White (AUS)	4:08.48	Ralph Hutton (CAN)	4:08.77	Greg Brough (AUS)	4:12.16
1500 m freestyle	Graham Windeatt (AUS)	16:23.82	Max Travasci (AUS)	16:34.46	Mark Treffers (NZL)	16:44.69
100 m	Bill Kennedy	1:01.65	Mike Richards	1:01.69	Erik Fish	1:02.02

backstroke	(CAN)		(WAL)		(CAN)	
200 m backstroke	Mike Richards (WAL)	00:02:15	Ray Terrell (ENG)	00:02:15	Neil Rogers (AUS)	00:02:16
100 m breaststroke	Bill Mahony (CAN)	1:09.0	Peter Cross (CAN)	1:09.4	Paul Jarvie (AUS)	1:10.0
200 m breaststroke	Bill Mahony (CAN)	2:30.29	Paul Jarvie (AUS)	2:30.70	David Wilkie (SCO)	2:32.87
100 m butterfly	Byron MacDonald (CAN)	58.44	Tom Arusoo (CAN)	58.98	Ron Jacks (CAN)	59.01
200 m butterfly	Tom Arusoo (CAN)	2:08.97	Martyn Wood- (WAL) roffe	2:09.14	James Findlay (AUS)	2:09.4
200 m individual medley	George Smith (CAN)	2:13.72	Ken Campbell (CAN)	2:16.57	Martyn Woodroffe (WAL)	2:16.64
400 m indivi dual medley	George Smith (CAN)	4:48.87	Ray Terrell (ENG)	4:49.85	James Findlay (AUS)	4:51.92
4×100 m freestyle relay	Australia (AUS) Graham White Gregory Rogers Michael Wenden William Devenish	3:36.02	Canada (CAN) George Smith Ralph Hutton Robert Kasting Ronald Jacks	3:37.65	England (ENG) Anthony Jarvis Ivan Myall Malcolm B. Windeatt Raymond Terrell	3:41.24
4×200 m freestyle relay	Australia (AUS) Graham White Gregory Rogers Michael Wenden William Devenish	7:50.77	Canada (CAN) George Smith Ralph Hutton Robert Kasting Ronald Jacks	8:00.69	England (ENG) Anthony Jarvis Ivan Myall John Mills Raymond Terrell	8:10.60
4×100 m medley relay	Canada (CAN) Byron MacDonald Robert Kasting William Mahony Bill Kennedy	4:01.10	Australia (AUS) James Findlay Michael Wenden Neil Rogers Paul Jarvie	4:04.55	Wales (WAL) Kevin Moran Martin Richards Martyn Woodroffe Nigel Johnson	4:08.05

Women's events

Event	*Gold*		*Silver*		*Bronze*	
100 m freestyle	Angela Coughlan (CAN)	1:01.22	Lynne Watson (AUS)	1:01.45	Jenny Watts (AUS)	1:01.80
200 m freestyle	Karen Moras (AUS)	2:09.78	Angela Coughlan (CAN)	2:10.83	Alex Jackson (IOM)	2:13.52
400 m freestyle	Karen Moras (AUS)	4:27.38	Denise Langford (AUS)	4:31.42	Robyn Risson (AUS)	4:39.75
800 m freestyle	Karen Moras (AUS)	9:02.45	Helen Gray (AUS)	9:27.48	Robyn Risson (AUS)	9:37.89
100 m backstroke	Lynne Watson (AUS)	1:07.10	Debra Cain (AUS)	1:07.73	Donna Gurr (CAN)	1:08.87

200 m backstroke	Lynne Watson (AUS)	2:22.86	Donna Gurr (CAN)	2:24.33	Debra Cain (AUS)	2:26.02
100 m breaststroke	Beverley Whitfield (AUS)	1:17.40	Dorothy Harrison (ENG)	1:17.60	Chris Jarvis (ENG)	1:19.83
200 m breaststroke	Beverley Whitfield (AUS)	2:44.12	Dorothy Harrison (ENG)	2:46.18	Amanda Radnage (ENG)	2:50.11
100 m butterfly	Diane Lansley (ENG)	1:07.90	Susan Smith (CAN)	1:08.18	Allyson Mabb (AUS)	1:08.67
200 m butterfly	Maree Robinson (AUS)	2:24.67	Jane Comerford (AUS)	2:24.95	Allyson Mabb (AUS)	2:31.09
200 m individual medley	Denise Langford (AUS)	2:28.89	Shelagh Ratcliffe (ENG)	2:29.65	Diana Rickard (AUS)	2:30.80
400 m individual medley	Denise Langford (AUS)	5:10.74	Gail Neall (AUS)	5:15.82	Shelagh Ratcliffe (ENG)	5:17.89
4×100 m freestyle relay	Australia (AUS) Debra Cain Denise Langford Jennifer Watts Lynette Watson	4:06.41	Canada (CAN) Angela Coughlan Karen James Linda Hall Susan Smith	4:12.16	England (ENG) Diane Sutherland Kathryn Smith Lesley Allardice Sally Pickering	4:14.90
4×100 m medley relay	Australia (AUS) Allyson Mabb Beverley Whitfield Denise Langford Lynette Watson	4:30.66	England (ENG) Diane Lansley Dorothy Harrison Kathryn Smith Sylvia Platt	4:38.94	Canada (CAN) Angela Coughlan Donna-Marie Gurr Susan Smith Sylvia Dockerhill	4:39.65

Diving

Event		*Gold*		*Silver*		*Bronze*	
3 Metres Springboard Diving	**Men**	Don Wagstaff (AUS)	557.73	Ken Sully (CAN)	497.37	Ronald Friesen (CAN)	495.9
10 Metres Highboard [Platform] Diving	**Men**	Don Wagstaff (AUS)	485.73	Philip Drew (ENG)	429.24	Andy Gill (ENG)	421.47
3 Metres Springboard Diving	**Women**	Beverley Boys (CAN)	432.87	Elizabeth Carruthers (CAN)	391.2	Gaye Morley (AUS)	389.04
10 Metres Highboard [Platform] Diving	**Women**	Beverley Boys (CAN)	352.95	Nancy Robertson (CAN)	350.49	Shelagh Burrow (ENG)	330.63

Weightlifting

Event		*Gold*		*Silver*		*Bronze*	
Flyweight - Overall	**Men**	George Vasiliades (AUS)	290	Abdul Ghafoor (PAK)	287.5	John McNiven (SCO)	265

Bantamweight Overall	Men	Precious Mc-Kenzie (ENG)	335	Tony Phillips (BAR)	317.5	Tung Chye Hong (SIN)	302.5
Featherweight Overall	Men	George Perrin (ENG)	342.5	Chua Phung Kim (SIN)	340	Alexander Navis (IND)	335
Lightweight Overall	Men	George New-ton (ENG)	372.5	Ieuan Owen (WAL)	355	Bruce Came-ron (NZL)	335
Middleweight ron (NZL) Overall	Men	Russell Perry (AUS)	412.5	Tony Ebert (NZL)	402.5	Pierre St. Jean (CAN)	400
Light Heavy-weight - Overall	Men	Nicolo Ciancio (AUS)	447.5	John Bolton (NZL)	445	Peter Arthur (WAL)	427.5
Middle Heavy-weight Overall	Men	Louis Martin (ENG)	457.5	Robert San-tavy (CAN)	425	George Man-ners SVG (VIN)	410
Heavy - Overall weight	Men	Russ Prior (CAN)	490	Dave Hancock (ENG)	470	Price Morris (CAN)	470
Super Heavy-weight - Overall	Men	Ray Rigby (AUS)	500	Terry Perdue (WAL)	500	Grant Ander-son (SCO)	432.5

Wrestling

Event		*Gold*	*Silver*	*Bronze*
Light Flyweight Overall	**Men**	**Ved Prakash (IND)**	**Ken Shand (CAN)**	**Masih Sadiq (PAK)** **Don Urquhart (SCO)**
Flyweight	**Men**	**Sudesh Kumar (IND)**	**Muhammad Nazir (PAK)**	**David Stitt (CAN)**
Bantamweight	**Men**	**Muhammad Sardar (PAK)**	**Herbert Singerman (CAN)**	**Terence Robinson (ENG)**
Featherweight	**Men**	**Muhammad Saeed (PAK)**	**Patrick Bolger (CAN)**	**Randhawa Singh (IND)**
Lightweight	**Men**	**Udey Chand (IND)**	**Muhammad Yaqub (PAK)**	**Ole Sorensen (CAN)**
Welterweight	**Men**	**Mukhtiar Singh (IND)**	**Alfred Wurr (CAN)**	**Gordon Mackay (NZL)**
Middleweight	**Men**	**Harish Rajindra (IND)**	**Nick Schori (CAN)**	**David Aspin (NZL)** **Ron Grinstead (ENG)**
Light Heavy-weight	**Men**	**Muhammad Faiz (PAK)**	**Sajjan Singh (IND)**	**Claude Pilon (CAN)**
Heavyweight	**Men**	**Edward Millard (CAN)**	**Bishwanath Singh (IND)**	**Muhammad Riaz (PAK)**
Super Heavy-weight	**Men**	**Ikram Ilahi (PAK)**	**Maruti Mane (IND)**	**Denis McNamara (ENG)**

14

1978 Commonwealth Games

The 1978 Commonwealth Games were held in Edmonton, in the province of Alberta in Canada, from 3 to 12 August 1978, two years after the 1976 Summer Olympics were held in Montreal, Quebec. They were boycotted by Nigeria, in protest at New Zealand's sporting contacts with apartheid-era South Africa. The Bid Election was held at the 1972 Munich Summer Olympics.

Medals (Country-wise)

Rank	*Nation*	*Gold*	*Silver*	*Bronze*	*Total*
1	Canada	45	31	33	109
2	England	27	27	33	87
3	Australia	24	33	27	84
4	Kenya	7	6	5	18
5	New Zealand	5	6	9	20
6	India	5	5	5	15
7	Scotland	3	6	5	14
8	Jamaica	2	2	3	7
9	Wales	2	1	5	8
10	Northern Ireland	2	1	2	5

11	Hong Kong	2	0	0	2
12	Malaysia	1	2	1	4
13	Ghana	1	1	1	3
14	Guyana	1	1	1	3
15	Tanzania	1	1	0	2
16	Trinidad and Tobago	0	2	2	4
17	Zambia	0	2	2	4
18	Bahamas	0	1	0	1
19	Papua New Guinea	0	1	0	1
20	Western Samoa	0	0	3	3
21	Isle of Man	0	0	1	1
	Total	128	129	138	395

Medals by Event

Athletics

Men's Events

Event	*Gold*		*Silver*		*Bronze*	
100 Metres	Don Quarrie (JAM)	10.03w	Allan Wells (SCO)	10.07w	Hasely Crawford (TRI)	10.09w
200 Metres	Allan Wells (SCO)	20.12w	James Gilkes (GUY)	20.18w	Colin Bradford (JAM)	20.43w
400 Metres	Rick Mitchell (AUS)	46.34	Joseph Coombs (TRI)	46.54	Glenn Bogue (CAN)	46.63
800 Metres	Mike Boit (KEN)	00:01:46	Seymour Newman (JAM)	00:01:47	Lemashon Peter (KEN)	00:01:48
1500 Metres	David Moorcroft (ENG)	00:03:35	Filbert Bayi (TAN)	00:03:36	John Robson (SCO)	00:03:36
5000 Metres	Henry Rono (KEN)	00:13:23	Mike Musyoki (KEN)	00:13:30	Brendan Foster (ENG)	00:13:31
10000 Metres	Brendan Foster (ENG)	00:28:14	Mike Musyoki (KEN)	00:28:19	Mike McLeod (ENG)	00:28:34
Marathon	Gidamis Shahanga (TAN)	02:15:40	Jerome (CAN)	02:16:14	Paul Bannon Drayton (CAN)	02:16:52

3000 Metres Steeplechase	Henry Rono (KEN)	00:08:27	James Munyala (KEN)	00:08:32	Kip Rono (KEN)	00:08:34
110 Metres Hurdles	Berwyn Price (WAL)	13.70w	Max Binnington (AUS)	13.73w	Warren Parr (AUS)	13.73w
400 Metres Hurdles	Daniel Kimaiyo (KEN)	49.48	Garry Brown (AUS)	50.04	Alan Pascoe (ENG)	50.09
High Jump	Claude Ferragne (CAN)	2.2	Greg Joy (CAN)	2.18	Dean Bauck (CAN)	2.15
					Brian Burgess (SCO)	
Pole Vault	Bruce Simpson (CAN)	5.1	Don Baird (AUS)	5.1	Brian Hooper (ENG)	5
Long Jump	Roy Mitchell (ENG)	8.06w	Chris Commons (AUS)	8.04w	Suresh Babu (IND)	7.94w
Triple Jump	Keith Connor (ENG)	17.21w	Ian Campbell (AUS)	16.93w	Aston Moore (ENG)	16.69
Shot	Geoff Capes (ENG)	19.77	Bruno Pauletto (CAN)	19.33	Bishop Dolegiewicz (CAN)	18.45
Discus	Borys Chambul (CAN)	59.7	Brad Cooper (BAH)	57.3	Rob Gray (CAN)	55.48
Hammer	Peter Farmer (AUS)	71.1	Scott Neilson (CAN)	69.92	Chris Black (SCO)	68.14
Javelin	Phil Olsen (CAN)	84	Michael O'Rourke (NZL)	83.18	Peter Yates (ENG)	78.58
Decathlon	Daley Thompson (ENG)	8467	Peter Hadfield (AUS)	7623	Alan Drayton (ENG)	7484
30 km Road Walk	Olly Flynn (ENG)	02:22:04	Willi Sawall (AUS)	02:22:59	Tim Erickson (AUS)	02:26:34
4 x 100 M. Relay	Scotland (SCO)	39.24	Trinidad & Tobago (TRI)	39.29	Jamaica (JAM)	39.33
4 x 400 M. Relay	Kenya (KEN)	00:03:04	Jamaica (JAM)	00:03:04	Australia (AUS)	00:03:04

Women's Events

Event	*Gold*		*Silver*		*Bronze*	
100 Metres	Sonia Lannaman (ENG)	11.27w	Raelene Boyle (AUS)	11.35w	Denise Boyd (AUS)	11.37w
200 Metres	Denise Boyd (AUS)	22.82w	Sonia Lannaman (ENG)	22.89w	Colleen Beazley (AUS)	22.93w
400 Metres	Donna Hartley (ENG)	51.69	Verona Elder (ENG)	52.94	Bethanie Nail (AUS)	53.06

800 Metres	Judy Peckham (AUS)	00:02:03	Tekla Chemabwai (KEN)	00:02:03	Jane Colebrook (ENG)	00:02:03
1500 Metres	Mary Stewart (ENG)	00:04:06	Chris Benning (ENG)	00:04:08	Penny Werthner (CAN)	00:04:08
3000 Metres	Paula Fudge (ENG)	00:09:13	Heather Thomson (NZL)	00:09:21	Ann Ford (ENG)	00:09:24
100 Metres Hurdles	Lorna Boothe (ENG)	12.98w	Shirley Strong (ENG)	13.08w	Sharon Colyear (ENG)	13.17w
High Jump	Katrina Gibbs (AUS)	1.93	Debbie Brill (CAN)	1.9	Julie White (CAN)	1.83
Long Jump	Sue Reeve (ENG)	6.59	Erica Hooker (AUS)	6.58	June Griffith (GUY)	6.52
Shot	Gael Mulhall (AUS)	17.31	Carmen Ionescu (CAN)	16.45	Judy Oakes (ENG)	16.14
Discus	Carmen Ionescu (CAN)	62.16	Gael Mulhall (AUS)	57.6	Lucette Moreau (CAN)	56.64
Javelin	Tessa Sanderson (ENG)	61.34	Alison Hayward (CAN)	54.52	Laurie Kern (CAN)	53.6
Pentathlon	Diane Konihowski (CAN)	4768	Sue Mapstone (ENG)	4222	Yvette Wray (ENG)	4211
4 x 100 M. Relay	England (ENG)	43.7	Canada (CAN)	44.26	Australia (AUS)	44.78
4 x 400 M. Relay	England (ENG)	00:03:27	Australia (AUS)	00:03:29	Canada (CAN)	00:03:36

Badminton

Event	*Gold*	*Silver*	*Bronze*
Mixed Team	England (ENG)	Canada (CAN)	Malaysia (MAS)
Men's Singles	Prakash Padukone (IND)	Derek Talbot (ENG)	Ray Stevens (ENG)
Men's Doubles	Ray Stevens Mike Tredgett (ENG)	Moo Foot Lian Ong Beng Teong (MAS)	Bryan Purser Richard Purser (NZL)
Women's Singles	Sylvia Meow Eng Ng (MAS)	Katherine Swee Phek Teh (MAS)	Wendy Clarkson (CAN)
Women's Doubles	Nora Perry Anne Statt (ENG)	Claire Backhouse Jane Youngberg (CAN)	Ami Ghia Kanwal Singh (IND)
Mixed Doubles	Mike Tredgett Nora Perry (Gardner) (ENG)	Billy Gilliland Joanna Flockhart (SCO)	Derek Talbot Barbara Sutton (ENG)

Bowls

Event	*Gold*	*Silver*	*Bronze*
Men's Singles	David Bryant (ENG)	John Snell (AUS)	John Russell Evans (WAL)
Men's Pairs	Clementi Delgado Eric Liddell (HKG)	Alex McIntosh Willie Wood (SCO)	James Morgan Ray Williams (WAL)
Men's Fours	Hong Kong (HKG)	New Zealand (NZL)	Wales (WAL)

Boxing

Event	*Gold*	*Silver*	*Bronze*
Light Flyweight	Stephen Muchoki (KEN)	Francis Kabala (ZAM)	Birender Thapa (IND) Kid Jumalia (GHA)
Flyweight	Michael Irungu (KEN)	Ian Clyde (CAN)	Peter Wighton (AUS) Hugh Russell (NIR)
Bantamweight	Barry McGuigan (NIR)	Tumat Sugolik (PNG)	Douglas Maina (KEN) William Rannelli (CAN)
Featherweight	Azumah Nelson (GHA)	John Sichula (ZAM)	Guy Boutin (CAN) Maurice O'Brien (ENG)
Lightweight	Gerry Hamill (NIR)	Patrick Waweru (KEN)	Teddy Makofi (ZAM) John McAllister (SCO)
Light Welter-weight	Winfield Braithwaite (GUY)	James Douglas (SCO)	John Raftery (CAN) Michael Mawangi (KEN)
Welterweight	Mike McCallum (JAM)	Ken Beattie (NIR)	Derrick Hoyt (CAN) Anthony Freal (WAL)
Light Middle-weight	Kelly Perlette (CAN)	Abdurahman Athuman (KEN)	Ropati Vipo Samu (SAM) Enock Chama (ZAM)
Middleweight	Philip McElwaine (AUS)	Delroy Parkes (ENG)	Roddy MacDonald (CAN) Richard Betham (SAM)
Light Heavy weight	Roger Fortin (CAN)	Ron Smith (ENG)	Fautala Su'a (SAM) Edward Thande (KEN)
Heavy-weight	Julius Awome (ENG)	Adamah Mensah (GHA)	George Stankovich (NZL)

Cycling

Track

Event	*Gold*		*Silver*		*Bronze*	
Men's Time Trial	Jocelyn Lovell (CAN)	00:01:06	Kenrick Tucker (AUS)	00:01:07	Gordon Singleton (CAN)	00:01:08
Men's Sprint	Kenrick Tucker (AUS)		Trevor Gadd (ENG)		David Weller (JAM)	
Men's Individual Pursuit	Michael Richards (NZL)	00:04:50	Gary Campbell (AUS)	00:04:56	Tony Doyle (ENG)	00:04:56
Men's Team Pursuit	Australia Colin Fitzgerald Kevin Nichols Gary Sutton Shane Sutton	00:04:29	New Zealand Kevin Blackwell Anthony Cuff Neil Lyster Jack Swart	00:04:38	England Tony Doyle Paul Fennell Tony James Glen Mitchell	00:04:51
Men's 10 Miles Scratch	Jocelyn Lovell (CAN)	00:20:06	Shane Sutton (AUS)	00:20:06	Gary Sutton (AUS)	00:20:06
Men's Tandem	Jocelyn Lovell Gordon Singleton (CAN)	15.52	Trevor Gadd David Le Grys (ENG)		Ron Boyle Stephen Goodall (AUS)	

Road

Event	*Gold*		*Silver*		*Bronze*	
Men's Road Race	Phil Anderson (AUS)	04:22:34	Pierre Harvey (CAN)	04:22:35	Garry Bell (NZL)	04:22:35

Diving

Event	*Gold*		*Silver*		*Bronze*	
Men's 3 Metres Springboard	Chris Snode (ENG)	643.83	Scott Cranham (CAN)	595.53	Don Wagstaff (AUS)	572.16
10 Metres Highboard [Platform]	Chris Snode (ENG)	538.98	Ken Armstrong (CAN)	534.99	Scott Cranham (CAN)	512.37
Women's 3 Metres Springboard	Janet Nutter (CAN)	477.33	Beverley Boys (CAN)	469.95	Eniko Kiefer (CAN)	447.42
Women's 10 Metres Highboard [Platform]	Linda Cuthbert (CAN)	397.44	Valerie McFarlane (AUS)	383.4	Janet Nutter (CAN)	374.67

Gymnastics

Event	*Gold*		*Silver*		*Bronze*	
Men's All-Around	Philip Delesalle (CAN)	56.4	Lindsay Nylund (AUS)	54.95	Jean Choquette (CAN)	54.25
Men's Team	Canada (CAN)	165.55	England (ENG)	161.95	Australia (AUS)	158.5
Women's All-Around	Elfi Schlegel (CAN)	38.25	Monica Goermann (CAN) Sherry Hawco (CAN)	37.25		
Women's Team	Canada (CAN)	113.25	England (ENG)	107.4	New Zealand (NZL)	106.35

Shooting

Pistol

Event	*Gold*		*Silver*		*Bronze*	
Men's/Open Free Pistol	Yvon Trempe (CAN)	543	Edward Jans (CAN)	540	Bertram Manhin (TRI)	536
Men's/Open Rapid-Fire Pistol	Jules Sobrian (CAN)	587	John Cooke (ENG)	581	Jeff Farrell (AUS)	581

Rifle

Event	*Gold*		*Silver*		*Bronze*	
Men's/Open Small Bore Rifle	Alister Allan (SCO)	1194	Bill Watkins (WAL)	1191	Stewart Watterson (IOM)	1187
Men's/Open Full Bore Rifle	Desmond Vamplew (CAN)	391	James Spaight (ENG)	388	Patrick Vamplew (CAN)	387

Shotgun

Event	*Gold*		*Silver*		*Bronze*	
Men's/Open Trap	John Primrose (CAN)	186	George Leary (CAN)	185	Terry Rumbel (AUS)	183
Men's/Open Skeet	John Woolley (NZL)	193	Paul Bentley (ENG)	191	Joe Neville (ENG)	190

Swimming

Men's events

Event	Gold		Silver		Bronze	
100 m freestyle	Mark Morgan *Australia (AUS)*	52.70	Bill Sawchuk *Canada (CAN)*	52.81	Gary MacDonald *Canada (CAN)*	52.9
200 m freestyle	Ron McKeon *Australia (AUS)*	1:52.06	Graeme Brewer *Australia (AUS)*	1:52.86	Mark Morgan *Australia (AUS)*	1:53.16
400 m freestyle	Ron McKeon *Australia (AUS)*	3:54.43	Simon Gray *England (ENG)*	3:56.87	Max Metzker *Australia (AUS)*	3:58.83
1500 m freestyle	Max Metzker *Australia (AUS)*	15:31.92	Simon Gray *England (ENG)*	15:39.39	Andrew Astbury *England (ENG)*	15:42.89
100 m backstroke	Glenn Patching *Australia (AUS)*	57.90	Gary Abraham *England (ENG)*	58.48	Jay Tapp *Canada (CAN)*	59.05
200 m backstroke	Gary Hurring *New Zealand (NZL)*	2:04.37	Glenn Patching *Australia (AUS)*	2:05.76	Paul Moorfoot *Australia (AUS)*	2:05.99
100 m breaststroke	Graham Smith *Canada (CAN)*	1:03.81	Duncan Goodhew *England (ENG)*	1:04.24	Paul Naisby *England (ENG)*	1:06.36
200 m breaststroke	Graham Smith *Canada (CAN)*	2:20.86	Duncan Goodhew *England (ENG)*	2:21.92	Lindsay Spencer *Australia (AUS)*	2:22.49
100 m butterfly	Dan Thompson *Canada (CAN)*	55.04	John Mills *England (ENG)*	56.22	Bill Sawchuk *Canada (CAN)*	56.37
200 m butterfly	George Nagy *Canada (CAN)*	2:01.99	Claus Bredschneider *Canada (CAN)*	2:02.49	Phil Hubble *England (ENG)*	2:02.53
200 m individual medley	Graham Smith *Canada (CAN)*	2:05.25	Bill Sawchuk *Canada (CAN)*	2:05.61	Peter Dawson *Australia (AUS)*	2:09.05
400 m individual medley	Graham Smith *Canada (CAN)*	4:27.34	Simon Gray *England (ENG)*	4:27.70	Bill Sawchuk *Canada (CAN)*	4:27.99
4×100 m freestyle relay	Canada Bill Sawchuk Gary MacDonald Graham Smith Peter Szmidt	3:27.94	Australia Glenn Patching Graeme Brewer Mark Morgan Ronald McKeon	3:28.62	England David Dunne Kevin Burns Martin Smith Richard Burrell	3:30.10
4×200 m freestyle relay	Australia Graeme Brewer Mark Morgan Maxwell Metzker Ronald McKeon	7:34.83	Canada Bill Sawchuk Dennis Corcoran Peter Szmidt Robert Baylis	7:36.58	England David Dunne Martin Smith Philip Hubble Simon Gray	7:42.02

4×100 m medley relay	Canada Bill Sawchuk Dan Thompson Graham Smith Jay Tapp 3:49.76	England Duncan Goodhew Gary Abraham John Mills Martin Smith 3:50.22	Australia Glenn Patching Graeme Brewer Lindsay Spencer Mark Morgan 3:53.16

Women's Events

Event	*Gold*	*Silver*	*Bronze*
Cana			
100 m freestyle	Carol Klimpel *Canada (CAN)* 57.78	Rosemary Brown *Australia (AUS)* 58.30	Wendy Quirk *Canada (CAN)* 58.41
200 m freestyle	Rebecca Perrott *New Zealand (NZL)* 2:00.63	Tracey Wickham *Australia (AUS)* 2:01.50	Michelle Ford *Australia (AUS)* 2:01.64
400 m freestyle	Tracey Wickham *Australia (AUS)* 4:08.45	Michelle Ford *Australia (AUS)* 4:10.25	Rebecca Perrott *New - Zealand (NZL)* 4:16.70
800 m freestyle	Tracey Wickham *Australia (AUS)* 8:24.62	Michelle Ford *Australia (AUS)* 8:25.78	Rebecca Perrott *New - Zealand (NZL)* 8:44.87
100 m backstroke	Debra Forster *Australia (AUS)* 1:03.97	Hélène Boivin *Canada (CAN)* 1:04.54	Cheryl Gibson *Canada (CAN)* 1:04.68
200 m backstroke	Cheryl Gibson *Canada (CAN)* 2:16.57	Lisa Forrest *Australia (AUS)* 2:17.66	Glenda Robertson *Australia (AUS)* 2:18.32
100 m breaststroke	Robin Corsiglia *Canada (CAN)* 1:13.56	Maggie Kelly *England (ENG)* 1:13.69	Marion Stuart *Canada (CAN)* 1:13.72
200 m breaststroke	Lisa Borsholt *Canada (CAN)* 2:37.70	Debbie Rudd *England (ENG)* 2:38.07	Maggie Kelly *England (ENG)* 2:38.63
100 m butterfly	Wendy Quirk *Canada (CAN)* 1:01.92	Penny McCarthy *New - Zealand (NZL)* 1:02.27	Linda Hanel *Australia (AUS)* 1:02.69
200 m butterfly	Michelle Ford *Australia (AUS)* 2:11.29	Wendy Quirk *Canada (CAN)* 2:13.65	Linda Hanel *Australia (AUS)* 2:14.52
200 m individual medley	Sharron Davies *England (ENG)* 2:18.37	Rebecca Perrott *New Zealand (NZL)* 2:18.70	Becky Smith *Canada (CAN)* 2:18.95
400 m indivi dual medley	Sharron Davies *England (ENG)* 4:52.44	Becky Smith *Canada (CAN)* 4:57.83	Cheryl Gibson *Canada (CAN)* 4:59.39
4×100 m freestyle relay	Canada Carol Klimpel Gail Amundrud Sue 3:50.28	England Cheryl Brazendale Heidi Turk 3:53.27	Australia Lisa Burnes Michelle Ford 3:54.11

	Sloan Wendy Quirk		Kaye Lovatt Sharron Davies		Rosemary Brown Tracey Wickham	
4×100 m	Canada Carol Klimpel Helene Boivin Marian Stuart Wendy Quirk	4:15.26	Australia Debra Forster Lisa Curry-Kenny Rosemary Brown Tracey Wickham	4:16.75	England Helen Gilyard Margaret Kelly Sharron Davies Sue Jenner	4:19.87

Weightlifting

Event	*Gold*		*Silver*		*Bronze*	
Flyweight Overall	Ekambaram Karunakaran (IND)	205	Charlie Revolta (SCO)	197.5	Roger Crabtree (AUS)	190
Bantamweight Overall	Precious McKenzie (NZL)	220	Tamil Selvin (IND)	220	Jeffrey Brice (WAL)	215
Featherweight Overall	Michael Mercier (CAN)	237.5	Ivan Katz (AUS)	235	Darrell Schultz (CAN)	230
Lightweight Overall	Bill Stellios (AUS)	272.5	Adrian Kebbe (AUS)	267.5	Philip Sue (NZL)	262.5
Middleweight - Overall	Sam Castiglione (AUS)	300	Newton Burrowes (ENG)	290	Steve Pinsent (ENG)	290
Light Heavyweight - Overall	Robert Kabbas (AUS)	322.5	Charles Quagliata (AUS)	287.5	Gary Shadbolt (ENG)	277.5
Middle Heavyweight - Overall	Gary Langford (ENG)	335	Terry Hadlow (CAN)	330	Brian Marsden (NZL)	312.5
Sub Heavy weight - Overall	John Burns (WAL)	340	Steve Wyatt (AUS)	325	Robert Santavy (CAN)	315
Heavyweight - Overall	Russ Prior (CAN)	347.5	Wayne Smith (CAN)	337.5	Andy Drzewiecki (ENG)	335
Super Heavyweight - Overall	Jean-Marc Cardinal (CAN)	365	Bob Edmond (AUS)	322.5	John Hynd (SCO)	305

Wrestling

Event	*Gold*	*Silver*	*Bronze*
Light Flyweight	Ashok Kumar (IND)	George Gunouski (CAN)	Mark Dunbar (ENG)
Flyweight	Ray Takahashi (CAN)	Sudesh Kumar (IND)	Ken Hoyt (AUS)
Bantamweight	Satbir Singh (IND)	Michael Barry (CAN)	Amrik Singh (ENG)
Featherweight	Egon Beiler (CAN)	Jagminder Singh (IND)	Brian Aspen (ENG)
Lightweight	Zsigmund Kelevitz (AUS)	Joe Gilligan (ENG)	Jagdish Kumar (IND)
Welterweight	Rajinder Singh (IND)	Victor Zilberman (CAN)	Keith Howard (ENG)

Middleweight	Richard Deschatelets (CAN)	Wally Koenig (AUS)	Ivan Weir (NIR)
Light Heavy weight	Stephen Danier (CAN)	Mick Pikos (AUS)	Kartar Singh (IND)
Heavyweight	Wyatt Wishart (CAN)	Satpal Singh (IND)	Murray Avery (NZL)
Super Heavy-weight	Robert Gibbons (CAN)	Albert Patrick (SCO)	Ishwar Singh (IND)

15

Commonwealth Games 1982

Edition XII, the 1982 Commonwealth Games were held in Brisbane, Queensland, Australia from 30 September—9 October 1982. The Opening Ceremony was held at the QEII Stadium (named for Queen Elizabeth II), in the Brisbane suburb of Nathan. The QEII Stadium was also the venue which was used for the athletics and archery competitions during the Games. Other events were held at the purpose-built Sleeman Sports Complex in Chandler.

The Chairman of the 1982 Commonwealth Games was Sir Edward Williams KCMG, KBE. Sir Edward later became the Commissioner General of Expo '88. He was also the Chairman of the Queensland Turf Club in the 80's until the early 90's.

12th Commonwealth Games

Logo

The 1982 Commonwealth Games Logo was designed by Hugh Edwards, who was the winner of a nation-wide competition held in 1978. The symbol is derived from the form of a bounding kangaroo. The three bands, forming stylized A's (for Australia), are in colours which are common to flags of many Commonwealth countries.

Matilda the kangaroo mascot for the 1982 Commonwealth Games was represented by a cartoon kangaroo, and a gigantic 13-metre (42 feet 8 inches) high mechanical "winking" kangaroo, who travelled around the stadium and winked at the crowd. The games were officially opened by the Duke of Edinburgh.

Bidding for the XII Commonwealth Games was held in Montreal at the 1976 Summer Olympics: Lagos (Nigeria), Brisbane (Australia), Kuala Lumpur (Malaysia) and Birmingham (England).

Brisbane won the rights to stage the Games after the other candidate cities withdrew bids early in 1976. The Montreal Summer Olympics were plagued with cost overruns and bidding on a sports festival anywhere in the world was not good politically.

Brisbane was awarded by default of being the only Candidate City left at the bid election. Nigeria's boycott of the Montreal Summer Olympics made Lagos' bid lobbying impractical.

Participating Nations

45 Commonwealth nations and territories took part at the 1982 Commonwealth Games.

Sports

Sports contested during the 1982 Commonwealth Games included the following:

Athletics | Archery | Badminton | Bowls | Boxing | Cycling
Shooting | Swimming | Diving | Weightlifting | Wrestling

Highlights

Opening Ceremony (30 September)

The ceremony at the QEII Stadium was held on a fine but extremely windy day.

Day 1 (1 October)

The first event of the Games was 100 km Road Trial in cycling. England won the Gold Medal in the event, and Australia won the Silver Medal — coming second to England by only six seconds.

Other sports which were contested on the first day of competition included swimming and diving, weightlifting, shooting and bowls.

Day 2 (2 October)

Sports contested included swimming, diving, weightlifting, shooting, cycling, bowls and archery.

The day was marred by both Australia and Canada being disqualified in the 4 x 100 metres relay in swimming (both problems occurring during change-overs. The medals awarded for this race went to England, Scotland and New Zealand.

Day 4 (4 October)

Sports contested included swimming, diving, àcycling, athletics, archery, hammer throwing and shooting.

The day was marred when Canada was again disqualified, this time in the 4 x 200 metres freestyle relay. Canada protested against the winners, Australia, as well as against their own disqualification.

Queen Elizabeth closed the Games during a colourful ceremony, which included parachute jumpers (who had originally been also intended as part of the Opening Ceremony display) jumping and landing in a special target area within the stadium and red, white and blue balloons. Matilda the Kangaroo also winked at the Queen. Following the closing of the Games, the Queen and Duke left the stand to be driven from the stadium. However, nobody wanted the Games to end and the Australian team formed a 'guard of honour' and ran beside and behind the car in which Queen Elizabeth and Prince Philip were travelling, as it circled the stadium several times before finally leaving. Team members from other countries also joined in running after the royal car.

Medals Table

This is the full table of the medal count of the 1982 Commonwealth Games. These rankings sort by the number of gold medals earned by a country. The number of silvers is taken into consideration next and then the number of bronze. If, after the above, countries are still tied, equal ranking is given and they are listed alphabetically. This follows the system used by the IOC, IAAF and BBC.

Rank	*Nation*	*Gold*	*Silver*	*Bronze*	*Total*
1	Australia	39	39	29	107
2	England	38	38	32	108
3	Canada	26	23	33	82
4	Scotland	8	6	12	26
5	New Zealand	5	8	13	26
6	India	5	8	3	16
7	Nigeria	5	0	8	13
8	Wales	4	4	1	9

9	Kenya	4	2	4	10
10	Bahamas	2	2	2	6
11	Jamaica	2	1	1	4
12	Tanzania	1	2	2	5
13	Malaysia	1	0	1	2
14	Fiji	1	0	0	1
15	Hong Kong	1	0	0	1
16	Zimbabwe	1	0	0	1
17	Northern Ireland	0	3	3	6
18	Uganda	0	3	0	3
19	Zambia	0	1	5	6
20	Guernsey	0	1	1	2
21	Bermuda	0	0	1	1
	Singapore	0	0	1	1
	Swaziland	0	0	1	1
	Total	143	141	153	437

Aboriginal Movement Protests

The Brisbane Commonwealth Games were also noted by large-scale protests by the Aboriginal rights movement in Australia, which brought to the centre of international media attention the lack of land rights, poor living condition and suppression of personal and political rights in Queensland in particular, and in Australia as a whole. The protests, which were followed by large-scale arrests, are a significant event in the history of the Australian Aboriginal movement.

16

1986 Commonwealth Games

Edition XIII, the 1986 Commonwealth Games were held in Edinburgh, Scotland for the second time. The Games were held from 24 July-2 August 1986.

Despite the popular success of the previous 1970 British Commonwealth Games in Edinburgh, the 1986 Games are remembered with considerable notoriety due to a large political boycott and financial mismanagement. The games were boycotted by a large number of African, Asian and Caribbean countries, reducing them almost to a whites-only affair. In all 32 of the 59 Commonwealth nations due to take part boycotted the Games. The boycott was over the Thatcher Government's attitude towards British sporting links with apartheid-era South Africa. Further controversy came about when it was revealed that due to the lack of participation and associated decline in anticipated broadcasting and sponsorship revenues, the Organising Committee was facing a serious financial black hole, and the boycott ended any prospect of securing emergency government assistance. Businessman Robert Maxwell stepped in to offer funding, taking over as chairman, but despite promising to invest £2m, Maxwell's contribution was just £250,000. On a budget of £14m, the Games opened with a deficit of £3m, which grew to £4.3m. Instead of putting enough money into the event to save it, the new chairman of the Games asked creditors to forego half the payment due to them to keep the event out of liquidation. The debt was finally paid off in 1989, with the city of Edinburgh losing approximately £500,000.

Several participants were excluded because they breached the amateurism rules; lawn bowlers Phil Skoglund from New Zealand and Willie Wood from Scotland, both of whom have competed in subsequent games.

Participants

Because of the boycott only 28 countries took part in the games with the Maldives and Norfolk Island making their first appearance in the games.

- Cayman Islands
- Cook Islands
- Samoa
- Norfolk Island
- Fiji
- Gibraltar
- Lesotho
- Malta
- Swaziland
- Falkland Islands
- Vanuatu
- Maldives
- Singapore
- England

- Canada
- Australia
- New Zealand
- Wales
- Scotland
- Northern Ireland
- Isle of Man
- Guernsey
- Swaziland
- Hong Kong
- Malawi
- Botswana
- Jersey

It is pertinent to note that Bermuda (Took part in opening ceremony but boycotted rest of the games)

Opening Ceremony

The theme of the opening ceremony celebrated the "Spirit of Youth", and included 6500 Scottish schoolchildren taking part in a series of large Mass Games-style Gymnastics routines. The theme song "Spirit of Youth" was written by Gerard Kenny. The ceremony began on the esplanade of Edinburgh Castle with hundreds of schoolchildren running from there down the Royal Mile, through Holyrood Park to Meadowbank Stadium. The Bermudan team took part in the opening ceremony, before being ordered to boycott the games and leave.

Venues

- Meadowbank Stadium
- Royal Commonwealth Pool
- Strathclyde Park
- Barry Buddon
- Balgreen, Bowls

Sponsors

- Allied Lyons - Bell's, Gordon's, Harp Lager, Johnnie Walker Red Label, Kailber, White Horse (whisky), Wimpy
- Bhs
- British Caledonian
- British Gas
- British Telecom
- Coca-Cola
- De La Rue
- Dewar's
- Elf Aquitaine UK
- Europcar
- Ford
- McEwan's
- Mirror Group - Daily Mirror, Daily Record (Scotland), Sunday Mail, Daily Mirror, The People, The Sporting Life
- Nissan
- Omega SA (Timing)
- Rank Xerox

- Rover Group
- Royal Dutch Shell
- Royal Mail
- Safeway (UK)
- WANG Computers

Country-wise Medals

Rank	*Nation*	*Gold*	*Silver*	*Bronze*	*Total*
1	England	52	43	49	144
2	Canada	51	34	31	116
3	Australia	40	46	35	121
4	New Zealand	8	16	14	38
5	Wales	6	5	12	23
6	Scotland	3	12	18	33
7	Northern Ireland	2	4	9	15
8	Isle of Man	1	0	0	1
9	Guernsey	0	2	0	2
10	Swaziland	0	1	0	1
11	Hong Kong	0	0	3	3
12	Malawi	0	0	2	2
13	Botswana	0	0	1	1
14	Jersey	0	0	1	1
15	Singapore	0	0	1	1
	Total	163	163	176	502

17

1990 Commonwealth Games

Edition XIV, the 1990 Commonwealth Games were held in Auckland, New Zealand from 24 January-3 February 1990. It was the 14th Commonwealth Games, and part of New Zealand's 1990 sesquicentennial celebrations. Participants competed in ten sports: athletics, aquatics, badminton, boxing, cycling, gymnastics, judo, lawn bowls, shooting and weightlifting. The Triathlon was a demonstration event.

Remarkably the main venue was the Mt Smart Stadium, see New Zealand at the 1990 Commonwealth Games. The Games were awarded to Auckland July 27. 1984 at the Los Angeles Summer Olympics. Perth, Australia had withdrawn from the bid contest leaving New Delhi, India as the sole opponent to Auckland 1990.

The Opening Ceremony consisted many events including the arrival of The Queen's Representative Prince Edward, arrival of the Queen's Baton and many Mâori ceremonial stories.

The Opening Ceremony started off with the Auckland Commonwealth Games Choir singing the *Song of Welcome* before the Queen's Representative, Prince Edward arrived to the stadium. When Prince Edward came, the Mâori in attendance, gave Prince Edward a *Challenge of a welcome*.

This is conducted by a Mâori placing a wooden batton on the ground. To see if the visitor comes in peace or not, the visitor must pick it up.

The New Zealand National Anthem God Defend New Zealand was sung during a ceremonial fourteen gun salute from nearby One Tree Hill. This was followed by the New Zealand Army Guard Commander allowing Prince Edward to inspect the Guard of honour. After which was the introduction of the participating countries of the Commonwealth. During the introduction of the countries, the choir at attendance would display the flag of the announced country with boards.

When all the athletes finally sat down, the main Mâori ceremonies began. First of the Mâori ceremonies was all the Mâori women performing a "Song of Welcome" for the athletes in a spectacular fashion with the use of Poi. The Mâori women then gave some of the athletes a Hongi.

Next was the Mâori story of how New Zealand was formed, performed by many New Zealanders and organised by Logan Breha. It involved a narration of how the Polynesians found their way to what was to become New Zealand. In the middle of the performance, a re-enactment was performed of how New Zealand was formed between Rangi and Papa (the sky father and earth mother). The story then moved on to the coming of religion and European migration. This was demonstrated with a formation of the Union Jack, to show the colonisation by the British. Dame Whina Cooper then made a speech about the Treaty of Waitangi signed in 1840 that brought about peace and stability of modern New Zealand.

Introduction of the European communities was next with music and native European dancing from Scotland,

Ireland, Austria, Wales and England. From here, many of the neighbouring Pacific Islanders made their entrance with the rhythmic tempo of the Pacific Island drum beat. This was to show the then complete migration of people to New Zealand.

New Zealand performer Sir Howard Morrison then lead New Zealand in singing the folk song Tukua-a-hau. After Howard Morrison, the Queen's Baton arrived at the stadium where Prince Edward announced the opening of the games which was followed by the *Athletes Pledge*.

Fireworks followed and was capped off with a night time flyover by nine A-4 Skyhawk jets of the Royal New Zealand Air Force. The Opening Ceremony was concluded by the singing of the game's motto "This is the moment" as performers and athletes exited the stadium.

Closing Ceremony

A more relaxed affair was held for the 14th Commonwealth Games closing ceremony, reflecting that of Christchurch in 1974. Attended by Her Majesty Queen Elizabeth II, formality and respect played their due part in the beginning with formal salute and the acceptance of the Commonwealth Games flag to the next host city, Victoria, Canada. This was followed by a Native American and modern Canadian dancing display.

Then the fun began with thousands of children entering the stadium with a mass jumprope demonstration, followed by the Athletes themselves. The Queen then made the traditional closing speech and called for all the Commonwealth's athletes to assemble in four years time in Victoria BC in 1994. As the evening wore on, opera singer Dame Kiri Te Kanawa sang "Now is the Hour" a favorite New Zealand hymn as the Royal New Zealand

Airforce's A4 Skyhawks made one final swooping flyover of Mt Smart Stadium followed by fireworks. It was then Her Majesty, Prince Phillip, and the popular Prince Edward exited the stadium standing in open top vehicles.

Medals

This is the full table of the medal count of the 1990 Commonwealth Games. These rankings sort by the number of gold medals earned by a country. The number of silvers is taken into consideration next and then the number of bronze. If, after the above, countries are still tied, equal ranking is given and they are listed alphabetically. This follows the system used by the IOC, IAAF and BBC.

Rank	*Nation*	*Gold*	*Silver*	*Bronze*	*Total*
1	Australia	52	54	58	164
2	England	47	40	43	130
3	Canada	35	43	38	116
4	New Zealand	17	14	27	58
5	India	13	8	11	32
6	Wales	10	3	12	25
7	Kenya	6	9	3	18
8	Nigeria	5	13	7	25
9	Scotland	5	7	10	22
10	Malaysia	2	2	0	4
11	Jamaica	2	0	2	4
12	Uganda	2	0	2	4
13	Northern Ireland	1	3	5	9
14	Nauru	1	2	0	3
15	Hong Kong	1	1	3	5
16	Cyprus	1	1	0	2

17	Bangladesh	1	0	1	2
18	Jersey	1	0	1	2
19	Bermuda	1	0	0	1
20	Guernsey	1	0	0	1
21	Papua New Guinea	1	0	0	1
22	Zimbabwe	0	2	1	3
23	Ghana	0	2	0	2
24	Tanzania	0	1	2	3
25	Zambia	0	0	3	3
26	Bahamas	0	0	2	2
27	Western Samoa	0	0	2	2
28	Guyana	0	0	1	1
29	Isle of Man	0	0	1	1
30	Malta	0	0	1	1
	Total	205	205	236	646

REFERENCES

1. Medals by country from: Commonwealth Games Other Information From: The Bateman New Zealand Encyclopedia

18

1994 Commonwealth Games

Edition XV, the 1994 Commonwealth Games were held in Victoria, in the province of British Columbia in Canada, from 18 August to 28 August 1994.

The XV Commonwealth Games marked South Africa's return to the Commonwealth Games following the apartheid era, and over 30 years (1958) since the country last competed in the Games. It was also Hong Kong's last appearance at the games before reverting to Chinese rule.

The official mascot of the Games was an anthropomorphic killer whale named "Klee Wyck". "Klee Wyck" - "the laughing one" - was a nickname given to Canadian painter and sculptor Emily Carr by the Ucluelet First Nation.

Ten types of sports were featured at the Victoria Games: athletics (track and field), aquatics, badminton, boxing, cycling, gymnastics, lawn bowling, shooting, weightlifting, and wrestling.

The "Lightweight Games"

Victoria 1994 was considered by many in the Commonwealth movement to be a version of a minimalistic games. Some considered them a mild letdown from the high memories of Auckland's games four years previously. Facilities were temporary and none more so than the large scaffolding built Stands that totally transformed the University of Victoria's Centennial Stadium. Still the games were successful and proved to many that smaller cities could manage hosting a large event as a Commonwealth Games.

The Last "Original Games"

1994 was also the last time Team Sports were excluded, The Commonwealth Games Federation deemed the current set up of ten sports as obsolete and from 1998 allowed team sports such as Sevens, Basketball, and Hockey to be added. This was to encourage revenue streams from television by making the games more attractive to TV networks.

Opening Ceremony

A simple friendly atmosphere was the theme to the Opening Ceremonies. In the presence of HRH Prince Edward, the Athletes had a long march past to their seated area (an idea created four years previously but not emulated since). Welcome speeches and flag raisings were followed by a precision horse riding display by the Royal Canadian Mounted Police. A wonderful visual and theatrical display by the Four Nations Tribes culminated in a massive Thunderbird symbol covering the entire inner field. This was followed by a spectacular flypast by the "Snowbirds" Canadian Forces aerobatic display team.

Commonwealth Games Associations

- Antigua and Barbuda
- Australia
- Bahamas

- Bangladesh
- Barbados
- Belize
- Bermuda
- Botswana
- British Virgin Islands
- Brunei
- Canada
- Cayman Islands
- Cook Islands
- Cyprus
- Dominica
- England
- Falkland Islands
- Gambia
- Ghana
- Gibraltar
- Grenada
- Guernsey
- Guyana
- Hong Kong
- India
- Isle of Man
- Jamaica
- Jersey
- Kenya

- Lesotho
- Malaui
- Malaysia
- Maldives
- Malta
- Mauritius
- Montserrat
- Namibia
- Nauru
- New Zealand
- Nigeria
- Norfolk Island
- Northern Ireland
- Pakistan
- Papua New Guinea
- Saint Kitts and Nevis
- Saint Lucia
- Saint Vincent and the Grenadines
- Scotland
- Seychelles
- Sierra Leone
- Singapore
- Solomon Islands
- South Africa
- Sri Lanka
- Swaziland

- Tanzania
- Tonga
- Trinidad and Tobago
- Uganda
- Vanuatu
- Wales
- Western Samoa
- Zambia
- Zimbabwe

19

1998 Commonwealth Games

Edition XVI, the 1998 XVI Commonwealth Games were held in Kuala Lumpur, Malaysia from 11 September to 21 September 1998 making it the first Asian country to act as host and the last Commonwealth Games for the 20th century. A record 70 nations (34 of which collected medals) supplied 3638 athletes.

The 16th Games was declared open by His Majesty the King of Malaysia, Yang di-Pertuan Agong Tuanku Jaafar ibni Almarhum Tuanku Abdul Rahman on 11 September. The main focus for the games and the venue for the opening and closing ceremonies was the newly built National Stadium Bukit Jalil, a 100,000 spectator capacity stadium.

The logo for these games was inspired by the national flower of Malaysia, the Hibiscus, and was the first time that the colour yellow was introduced in the logo. (All previous logos had been red, white and blue to reflect the colours of the British Union Flag). The official mascot for the games was Wira (Malay for "warrior" or "hero") the orang utan.

The host nation was thrilled at achieving its best ever haul of ten gold medals. The 16th Commonwealth Games' host newly introduced team sports of cricket, field hockey, netball and Rugby Sevens.

These joined athletics (track and field), badminton, boxing, cycling, gymnastics, lawn bowls, shooting, squash, swimming, ten-pin bowling and weightlifting to make a total of 15 different categories of events.

In front of 20,000 fans at the Petaling Jaya Stadium, Rugby Sevens in particularly were an enormous success with New Zealand collecting its 100th Commonwealth Games medal with a 21-12 win over the plucky Fiji, (the reigning world champions). Man of the match was the giant Jonah Lomu who had worked tirelessly during the 10-minutes each way final.

Led by veteran star David Campese, Australia took the bronze beating Samoa 33-12.

In the squash event many had anticipated a close match between Michelle Martin and Sarah Fitz-Gerald who had both comfortably won their respective semi finals. Sarah had won the previous two years world open and Michelle the three prior to that and so it was with some surprise too many that Michelle took the gold in three straight sets 9-0, 9-6, 9-5. Sarah did avenge this defeat in the final of the world championship later that year, in what many people regard as the greatest women's final ever, coming back from 8-2 down in the fifth to retain her title.

Michelle also teamed up with Craig Rowland to take the commonwealth mixed doubles gold.

Erika-Leigh Stirton took five of the six available golds in the rhythmic gymnastics only being beaten into second place in the team event in the hosts took gold.

September 21 saw Her Majesty Queen Elizabeth II, Head of the Commonwealth and Patron of the Commonwealth Games Federation declare the ceremony closed on a night that saw both international star Céline Dion and Rod Stewart entertain the crowd.

The nation that won the most medals during the 1998 Commonwealth Games was Australia. England and Canada came second and third respectively, while Malaysia came in fourth place.

Main Venues

National Sports Complex, Bukit Jalil

- National Stadium, Bukit Jalil — Opening/Closing Ceremony, Athletics
- Putra Stadium, (Indoor) Bukit Jalil — Gymnastics
- National Aquatic Centre—Swimming
- National Hockey Stadium — Hockey
- National Squash Centre—Squash

Bukit Kiara Sports Complex

- Juara Stadium — Netball
- National Lawn Bowls Centre — Lawn Bowls

Other Venues

- Cheras Veledrome, Kuala Lumpur — Track cycling
- Kuala Lumpur Badminton Stadium — Badminton
- Mines Convention Centre — Weightlifting
- Shah Alam — Cycling road racing
- Melawati Stadium, Shah Alam — Boxing
- Pyramid Bowl, Sunway Pyramid, Subang Jaya — Tenpin bowling
- Petaling Jaya Stadium, Petaling Jaya — Rugby
- Langkawi International Shooting Range (Lisram) — Shooting

Corporate Sponsors

- Telekom Malaysia
- Bank Bumiputra
- Malaysia Airlines
- Siemens
- Proton
- Maybank
- Panasonic
- Toyota
- Pepsi
- Nestle's Milo
- Pro-Sport
- MasterCard
- Percetakan Nasional Malaysia Berhad (PNMB) (National Printing Malaysia Berhad)
- Astro
- Spritzer

Medal Table

Rank	*Nation*	*Gold*	*Silver*	*Bronze*	*Total*
1	Australia	82	61	57	200
2	England	36	49	53	138
3	Canada	30	31	40	101
4	Malaysia	10	14	12	36
5	South Africa	9	11	14	34
6	New Zealand	8	6	20	34
7	India	7	10	8	25

8	Kenya	7	5	4	16
9	Jamaica	4	2	0	6
10	Wales	3	4	8	15
11	Scotland	3	2	7	12
12	Nauru	3	0	0	3
13	Northern Ireland	2	1	1	4
14	Zimbabwe	2	0	3	5
15	Ghana	1	1	3	5
16	Mauritius	1	1	2	4
17	Cyprus	1	1	1	3
18	Tanzania	1	1	1	3
19	Trinidad and Tobago	1	1	1	3
20	Bahamas	1	1	0	2
21	Mozambique	1	1	0	2
22	Barbados	1	0	2	3
23	Lesotho	1	0	0	1
24	Cameroon	0	3	3	6
25	Namibia	0	2	1	3
26	Seychelles	0	2	0	2
27	Sri Lanka	0	1	1	2
28	Bermuda	0	1	0	1
29	Fiji	0	1	0	1
30	Isle of Man	0	1	0	1
31	Pakistan	0	1	0	1
32	Papua New Guinea	0	0	1	1
33	Uganda	0	0	1	1
34	Zambia	0	0	1	1
	Total	215	215	245	675

20

2002 Commonwealth Games

Edition XIII, the 2002 Commonwealth Games were held in Manchester, England from 25 July to 4 August 2002. The XVII Commonwealth Games was the largest multi-sport event ever to be held in England, eclipsing London's 1948 Summer Olympics in numbers of teams and athletes participating.

After the 1996 Manchester bombing, the Games formed the catalyst for the widespread regeneration and heavy development of Manchester, and bolstered its reputation as a European and Global City internationally. Rapid economic development and continued urban regeneration of the now thriving city continued after the Games and has helped cement its place as one of the main cities in the United Kingdom.

Events were held across Greater Manchester. The opening and closing ceremonies, the athletic and the rugby sevens events were held at the City of Manchester Stadium, which was purpose built for the Games. Unusually for a large multi-sport event – the second largest competition by number of countries and athletes participating – the shooting events were held in the National Shooting Centre in Bisley, Surrey, some 200 miles (322 km) from the main focus of the Games in Manchester. Seventy-two nations competed in 14 individual sports and 3 team sports events.

There were the maximum of 17 sports included in the schedule for the 2002 Commonwealth Games.

Further information: 2002 Commonwealth Games results

Sport	*Venue*	*Number of medal events*
Aquatics	Manchester Aquatics Centre	50
Athletics	City of Manchester Stadium	46
Badminton	Bolton Arena	05
Boxing	Wythenshawe Forum, MEN Arena	12
Cycling	Manchester Velodrome (track events), Rivington (mountain biking)	17
Gymnastics	G-MEX Centre	15
Hockey	Belle Vue Complex	02
Judo	G-MEX Centre	14
Lawn bowls	Heaton Park	06
Netball	MEN Arena	01
Rugby Sevens	City of Manchester Stadium	01
Shooting	Bisley Shooting Centre	40
Squash	National Squash Centre	05
Table tennis	Table Tennis Centre, Sportcity	08
Triathlon	Salford Quays	02
Weightlifting	Manchester International Conference Centre	46
Wrestling	G-MEX Centre	07

After experimenting with it on a smaller scale at the 1994 Commonwealth Games and dropping it at the 1998 Games, disabled competitions were held in swimming, athletics, bowls, table tennis and weightlifting (powerlifting). The medals were added to the final tally for each nation.

Participating Teams

There were 72 participating countries, territories, and Commonwealth regions at the 2002 Commonwealth Games. In alphabetical order, these included:

- Anguilla
- Antigua and Barbuda
- Australia
- Bahamas
- Bangladesh
- Barbados
- Belize
- Bermuda
- Botswana
- British Virgin Islands
- Brunei
- Cameroon
- Canada
- Cayman Islands
- Cook Islands
- Cyprus
- Dominica
- England
- Falkland Islands
- Fiji

- Gambia
- Ghana
- Gibraltar
- Grenada
- Guernsey
- Guyana
- India
- Isle of Man
- Jamaica
- Jersey
- Kenya
- Kiribati
- Lesotho
- Malawi
- Malaysia
- Maldives
- Malta
- Mauritius
- Montserrat
- Mozambique
- Namibia
- Nauru
- New Zealand
- Nigeria
- Niue
- Norfolk Island

- Northern Ireland
- Pakistan
- Papua New Guinea
- Saint Helena
- Saint Kitts and Nevis
- Saint Lucia
- Saint Vincent and the Grenadines
- Samoa
- Scotland
- Seychelles
- Sierra Leone
- Singapore
- Solomon Islands
- South Africa
- Sri Lanka
- Swaziland
- Tanzania
- Tonga
- Trinidad and Tobago
- Turks and Caicos Islands
- Tuvalu
- Uganda
- Vanuatu
- Wales
- Zambia
- Zimbabwe

Queen's Jubilee Baton Relay

The 2002 Queen's Jubilee Baton Relay, the continuation of a tradition that started with the 1958 Games, consisted of the relay of an electronic baton, containing a personal message from Queen Elizabeth II across 23 Commonwealth nations. The relay culminated in the arrival of the baton at the City of Manchester Stadium, opening the Games. The speech was then removed electronically from the baton, and read by Her Majesty to open the Games.

The 2002 Baton itself was designed by a company called IDEO, and was constructed of machined aluminium with the handle plated for conductivity. It weighed 1.69 kg, reached over 710 mm, and was 42.5 mm to 85 mm in diameter. The Queen's message itself was held in an aluminium capsule inserted into the top of the Baton. On either side of the Baton were two sterling silver coins; designed by Mappin and Webb, which celebrated the City of Manchester as host of the XVII Commonwealth Games.

In fact, the Baton was also equipped with sensors that detected and monitored the Runner's pulse rate. This information was then conveyed to a series of light-emitting diodes (LEDs), via a light behaviour module. The lens then transformed the LEDs into a shaft of bright blue pulsating light which synchronised with each new Runner. The hearts of the Runner and the Baton then beat as one until it was passed on, symbolising the journey of humanity and the essence of life. The Queen's Jubilee Baton Relay passed through over 500 cities, towns and villages across the UK and the Baton was carried by 5,000 individuals, with each Runner carrying the Baton up to 500 yards, however on Saturday 15 June, the baton was snatched from a runners hand in the town of Connah's Quay, Deeside.

The UK Baton Runners were made up of people from all walks of life including athletes, celebrities and local heroes from all over the country. Around 2500 Jubilee Runners were nominated by the community to carry the Baton, because they made a special contribution to their community or achieved a personal goal against the odds.

The judging of the Jubilee Runners was conducted by a panel of judges under the supervision of The Duke of Edinburgh's Award in January 2002. The relay was sponsored by Cadbury Schweppes, a major UK confectionery and soft drinks manufacturer.

The Opening Ceremony was produced by Jack Morton Worldwide. David Zolkwer was the Project & Artistic Director, Julie Brooks was Executive Producer.

Five-time Olympic champion Sir Steve Redgrave got the two-and-a-quarter-hour opening ceremony underway by banging a huge drum, which initiated a huge co-ordinated dance and fireworks act.

The champion rower was joined on the stage by sporting stars including yachtswoman Ellen MacArthur, heptathlete Denise Lewis, long-distance runner Moses Kiptanui, swimmer Susie O'Neill and sprinter Donovan Bailey.

The Grenadier Guards shared the arena with pop band S Club and Salford-born opera singer Russell Watson sang the Games' theme, "Faith of the Heart", while the arrival of Her Majesty the Queen was greeted with a flypast by the Red Arrows.

England football captain David Beckham helped chaperone Queen's Baton final runner Kirsty Howard, assisting the terminally ill six-year-old to hand the baton to the Queen. A 4,000-strong cast took part in the £12m spectacular, which in theme and tone consisted of a mix of "pomp and pop", combining the ceremonial aspects of the Games with a party-style atmosphere, based on Manchester's reputation as the party city of "Madchester". The ceremony was voiced by broadcaster Anthony Davis.

The traditional athletes' parade was led by previous hosts Malaysia, and England brought up the rear before the Queen as the Head of the Commonwealth, declared the Games open:

> "All of us participating in this ceremony tonight, whether athletes or spectators, or those watching on television around the world, can share in the ideals of this unique association of nations."
>
> "We can all draw inspiration from what the Commonwealth stands for, our diversity as a source of strength, our tradition of tolerance...our focus on young people, for they are our future."

Venues

The Games' main venue was the City of Manchester Stadium, which hosted all athletics events, the rugby sevens and the opening and closing ceremonies. The stadium was a downscaled version of that proposed during Manchester's bid for the 2000 Summer Olympics. Construction started in January 2000, and was completed shortly before the Games. The cost was approximately £110 million, £77 million of which was provided by Sport England, with the remainder funded by Manchester City Council. For the Commonwealth Games the stadium featured a single lower tier running around three sides of the athletics track, and second tiers to the two sides, with an open-air temporary stand at one end, giving an overall capacity of 38,000. The stadium formed the centrepiece of an area known as

Sportcity. Other venues in Sportcity include the Manchester Velodrome, which hosted cycling, and the £3.5m National Squash Centre, which was built specifically for the Games.

Swimming and diving events took place at Manchester Aquatics Centre, another purpose-built venue, and the only one in the United Kingdom with two 50m pools.

The shooting events were held at the National Shooting Centre, Bisley (located in Surrey). The NSC saw major redevelopment of all its ranges in order to host the fullbore rifle, smallbore rifle, pistol and clay target events.

New Records or Other Notable Events

- Australian, Ian Thorpe set a world record in the 400 metre freestyle swimming.
- English Zoe Baker set a world record in the 50 metre breaststroke.
- English track athlete Paula Radcliffe won her first major gold medal in the 5,000 metres, to record a time of 14:31.42, over 20 seconds ahead of silver medallist Edith Masai of Kenya and 1 minute 21 seconds faster than the inaugural running of the event four years earlier.
- In the final of the 100 m for men (athletics), the two English favourites (Dwain Chambers & Mark Lewis-Francis) both pulled up with injuries. The race was won by Kim Collins of Saint Kitts and Nevis, winning the country's first Commonwealth title.
- Simon Whitfield of Canada, the 2000 and 2008 Olympic champion, won gold in the triathlon.
- On the last day of track competition, England won

gold in both the men's 4x100 and 4x400 relays by tiny margins, recording the same time (38.62) as the Jamaican quartet in sprint relay and holding off a fast finishing Welsh team by 1/100th of a second in the longer race, with a winning time of 3:00.40.

- The women's 4x400 relay was won by Australia after the favoured Jamaican team dropped the baton.
- In winning the triple jump England's Jonathan Edwards simultaneously held the World, Olympic, European and Commonwealth championships and the World record. He would lose the European title a week later in Munich.
- Another world record was set in the 4000 metre team pursuit at the track cycling by the Australian team. Scot Chris Hoy took the individual time trial and 19-year old Nicole Cooke of Wales won the women's cycling road race.
- South African swimmer Natalie du Toit created history. As well as winning her events in the newly-included disabled swimming event, the 18-year-old, missing the lower section of her left leg, made the final of the 800 metre able-bodied freestyle event in one of a small number of disabled sporting events integrated into the games.
- In gymnastics England's Beth Tweddle and Kanukai Jackson took gold in the asymmetric bars and all around events respectively. Herodotos Giorgallas also won the first gymnastics gold ever for Cyprus when tying with Scotland's Steve Frew.

Medal Table by Country

Rank	*Nation*	*Gold*	*Silver*	*Bronze*	*Tota*
1	Australia	82	62	63	207
2	England	54	52	60	166
3	Canada	31	41	46	118
4	India	30	22	17	69
5	New Zealand	11	13	21	45
6	South Africa	9	20	17	46
7	Cameroon	9	1	2	12
8	Malaysia	7	9	18	34
9	Wales	6	13	12	31
10	Scotland	6	8	16	30
11	Nigeria	5	3	11	19
12	Kenya	4	8	4	16
13	Jamaica	4	6	7	17
14	Singapore	4	2	7	13
15	Bahamas	4	0	4	8
16	Nauru	2	5	8	15
17	Northern Ireland	2	2	1	5
18	Cyprus	2	1	1	4
19	Pakistan	1	3	4	8
20	Fiji	1	1	1	3
	Zambia	1	1	1	3
22	Zimbabwe	1	1	0	2
23	Namibia	1	0	4	5
24	Tanzania	1	0	1	2
25	Bangladesh	1	0	0	1
	Guyana	1	0	0	1

	Mozambique	1	0	0	1
	Saint Kitts and Nevis	1	0	0	1
29	Botswana	0	2	1	3
30	Uganda	0	2	0	2
31	Samoa	0	1	2	3
32	Trinidad and Tobago	0	1	0	1
33	Barbados	0	0	1	1
	Cayman Islands	0	0	1	1
	Ghana	0	0	1	1
	Lesotho	0	0	1	1
	Malta	0	0	1	1
	Mauritius	0	0	1	1
	Saint Lucia	0	0	1	1
	Total	282	280	336	898

Cultureshock and Festival Live

Cultureshock was the Commonwealth Games Cultural Programme which ran alongside the Games themselves. The events ranged from images of the athlete as hero in sculpture and photography (Go! Freeze, which ran at Turton Tower in Bolton) to a Zulu performance at The Lowry. There was an exhibition at the Whitworth Art Gallery called Tales of Power: West African Textiles, and a performance of the film Monsoon Wedding at Clwyd Theatr Cymru. The geographical range was from Cheshire in the south to Blackburn and Cumbria in the north, and included that year the various Melas that take place around the region. Cultureshock also ensured that a wide range of cultural events and acts reached the "man on the street", with the city centre of Manchester filled with bands, performers, and artists of various forms entertaining the thousands of visitors to the Games. It also coincided with the BBC's 2002 Festival Live series of open air concerts and celebrations around the country, held to celebrate the Queen's Golden Jubilee.

The Closing Ceremony was produced by Jack Morton Worldwide. David Zolkwer was the Project & Creative Director, Julie Brooks was the Executive Producer and Nigel Jameson was Artistic Director.

Highlights of Closing Ceremony

- Children covering themselves with red, blue and white paint to portray a giant British flag before unveiling a giant portrait of the Queen as a Golden Jubilee gift.
- The athletes bringing their national flags into the stadium
- South African swimmer Natalie du Toit being honoured as the outstanding athlete of the Games.
- The symbolic handover of the Commonwealth Games Ceremonial Flag to Melbourne, host city for the 2006 Games.
- A spectacular presentation with over 1,700 lanterns, which ended with the message 'Seek Peace' lit up in vast letters on the floor of the arena.
- Coronation Street stars Steve Arnold and Tracy Shaw (who played characters Ashley and Maxine Peacock) arriving in one of 40 Morris Minors which became the centre of a song-and-dance showpiece.
- Hip-hop DJ Grandmaster Flash encouraging the massed ranks to "make some noise" as athletes and volunteers poured into the arena to music from the likes of Will Young, Dave Stewart, Heather Small, Jimmy Cliff and Toploader.
- Australian singer Vanessa Amorosi sang her signature tune, *Shine* and a song about the city of Melbourne, "I'll always be a Melbourne girl" just as it began to pour with rain.

The Queen ended 11 days of competition at a rain-drenched closing ceremony in the City of Manchester Stadium. She declared the Games closed in front of a 38,000 sell-out crowd gathered in the stadium.

She also called on the athletes to assemble again in four years in Melbourne and to continue displaying the "friendship" they had shown in Manchester. The ceremony, attended by Prime Minister Tony Blair and several other dignitaries, took place in pouring rain and like the opening ceremony, mixed "pomp with pop". Australian Ian Thorpe, the star of the Games with his six swimming golds, carried his national flag into the arena, along with athletes from each of the other competing countries. Around 40,000 balloons were released into the rainy Manchester sky as the ceremony concluded with a spectacular fireworks display.

In terms of infrastructure, the Games were the catalyst for the widespread redevelopment of the east of the city, an area which had remained derelict since the departure of heavy industry some decades before. To many these Commonwealth Games are the benchmark for the new era in CWG hosting and for cities wishing to bid for them.

A new commercial centre for East Manchester, known as SportCity, was created based on the stadium. Legacy sporting facilities include the Northern Regional Tennis Centre, the National Squash Centre, the City of Manchester Stadium for football, the Manchester Velodrome and facilities for athletics, as well as shops, supermarkets and new housing. Legacy facilities for aquatics, the Manchester Aquatics Centre, and comprehensive upgrades of Belle Vue and Moss Side leisure centres serve their local communities.

Olympic president Jacques Rogge said the Games had

gone a long way to restoring Britain's credibility in terms of hosting big sporting events. It has since been said that the success of the games was a major factor in reassuring the UK's sporting authorities and the government that the country could successfully stage major successful international sporting events and that, without them, London's successful bid for the 2012 Summer Olympics would not have come about.

Public houses and restaurants in Manchester reported a threefold increase in takings during the Games, and local tourism board Marketing Manchester estimate some 300,000 more visitors will come to the city each year as a result of its increased profile. It is estimated that by 2008 £600m has been invested in the region as a result of the Games and that about 20,000 jobs had been created.

REFERENCES

"England's Northwest set to reap rewards of 2012" (http). *Liverpool is European capital of culture*. North west Development Agency. 2006-01-13.

James, Gary (2006). *Manchester City - The Complete Record*. Derby: Breedon.

"London 2012- what's in it for us?" (http). *Inside Out North West*. BBC. 2008-02-04.

"Manchester games hailed a success" (http). *Commonwealth Games 2002*. BBC Sport. 2002-08-03.

"Rogge rules out joint Olympic bid" (http). *Commonwealth Games 2002*. BBC Sport. 2002-08-03.

21

2006 Commonwealth Games

Edition XVIII, the 2006 Commonwealth Games were held in Melbourne, Victoria, Australia between 15 March and 26 March 2006. It was the largest sporting event to be staged in Melbourne, eclipsing the 1956 Summer Olympics in terms of the number of teams competing, athletes competing, and events being held.

The site for the opening and closing ceremonies was the Melbourne Cricket Ground which was also used during Melbourne's 1956 Olympic Games. The mascot for the games was Karak, a Red-tailed Black Cockatoo (a threatened species).

Early concerns arose about the large cost of staging the Games, with projected costs likely to be over 1 billion Australian dollars and a high likelihood the Victorian taxpayer would have to cover the expense. The cost was described in some local media as excessive. National Party leader Peter Ryan said that the Labor government should win "gold (medal) for burning money" However, not all of this money was wasted. Prior to the Games, accountants at KPMG were estimating that the gross income generated by this event could be as high as 1.5 billion dollars.

Melbourne's premier sporting ground, the Melbourne

Cricket Ground (MCG), was redeveloped in preparation for the Games. An athlete's village in the inner suburb of Parkville housed approximately 7,000 athletes and support staff during the Games, and has been transformed into commercial housing with a distinctly eco-friendly image. The creation of this village attracted controversy, with critics claiming it was created by alienating public parkland, while proponents maintained that it represented the renewal of an otherwise derelict inner-city area

The change from Daylight Saving Time to Standard Time in Australian states that follow it was delayed from 26 March to 2 April for 2006 to avoid affecting the games. In addition, state and private schools amended their usual term times so as to allow the first term holidays to coincide with the Games.

Melbourne's public transport system - train, tram and bus - ran to altered timetables with some amended or substituted services for the duration of the Games. For the most part, timetabled services were unchanged but suffered due to higher loads.

For the first time ever, the Melbourne 2006 Commonwealth Games appointed a Goodwill Partner, Plan International Australia.

Venues

The following venues were used at the 2006 Commonwealth Games. The sport(s) which were played at that venue is listed after it.

Melbourne Venues

- Docklands Precinct: Walks
- Melbourne Cricket Ground: Opening and Closing Ceremonies, and Athletics

- Melbourne Convention and Exhibition Centre: Badminton, Boxing and Weightlifting
- Melbourne Gun Club: Clay Target Shooting
- Melbourne International Shooting Club: Small Bore and Pistol Shooting
- Melbourne Sports and Aquatic Centre: Aquatics, Squash and Table tennis
- Multi Purpose Venue (Melbourne Park): Basketball Finals, Track Cycling and Netball Finals
- Rod Laver Arena (Melbourne Park): Gymnastics
- Royal Botanic Gardens Circuit: Cycling Road Race events
- State Lawn Bowls Centre: Lawn Bowls
- State Netball and Hockey Centre: Netball preliminaries and Hockey
- St Kilda Foreshore and Beach Road: Triathlon and Cycling Time Trial
- Telstra Dome: Rugby 7s

Regional and Suburban Venues

Ballarat

Ballarat Minerdome: Basketball with Tim O'Shea

Bendigo

Bendigo Stadium: Basketball

Wellsford Rifle Range: Full Bore Shooting

Geelong

Geelong Arena: Basketball

Lysterfield Park

State Mountain Bike Course: Mountain Bike Cycling

Traralgon

Traralgon Sports Stadium: Basketball

Broadcasting

1. The host broadcaster was Trans World International, while the domestic rights-holding broadcaster was the Nine Network in Australia. They showed rolling coverage, except for a break for the evening news and overnight.
2. In Australia Fox Sports broadcast the Games on eight dedicated digital Pay-TV channels. These were available on the Foxtel, Austar and Optus Vision networks.
3. The BBC covered the Commonwealth Games in the UK on BBC One and BBC Two. BBCi included a choice of two extra video streams on Freeview and four streams on Digital Satellite and Cable. Users with Broadband in the UK could also view all 5 video streams on bbc.co.uk, and the BBC Sport website.
4. CBC, CBC Newsworld, and CBC Country Canada aired a daily one-hour highlights show of the Commonwealth Games in Canada. Compared to past games, the CBC's coverage was minimally staffed, with commentary from other broadcasting partners. At first, they did not even consider bidding for the broadcasting rights due to scheduling conflicts with events Canadians are more interested in, such as the Tim Hortons Brier, World Figure Skating Championships, and the 2006 Winter Paralympics *(which itself had been reduced to five-to-ten minute daily coverage)*. None of Canada's metropolitan

newspapers sent any journalists to report on the Games, instead relying on news agencies

5. TVNZ covered the games for the residents of New Zealand
6. In Malaysia, TV1 broadcast live coverage of the Games for three hours starting at 10 a.m. Malaysian time and for two hours starting at 3 p.m., with highlights at 12:30 a.m.. Astro also included 3 dedicated channels to broadcast the Games live & delayed broadcast 24 hours to it Sports package subscribers.
7. Singapore's MediaCorp TV had supposedly not broadcast the games due to the high cost of telecast rights, satellite charges and the lack of sponsors. However, on 17 March, the MediaCorp found other sponsors which is the Ministry of Community Development, Youth and Sports and the Singapore Sports Council. Broadcast started from 18 March till the end of the games.
8. In the United States, selected coverage was carried by Fox College Sports
9. Altogether an estimated 4 billion viewers watched the 2006 Commonwealth Games worldwide.

Games

Opening Ceremony

Both the Melbourne Cricket Ground and the Yarra River were centrepieces for the ceremony, which included many fireworks, and other spectacle. The Games were opened by Queen Elizabeth II, in her capacity as Head of the Commonwealth. The Queen is also Head of State of a number of Commonwealth countries, including Australia.

Sports

The 2006 Commonwealth Games included 16 sports, with 12 individual sports and 4 team sports. In total there are 247 events at the Games.

- Aquatics
  - Diving
  - Swimming
  - Synchronized swimming
- Athletics
- Badminton
- Basketball
- Boxing
- Cycling
  - Road
  - Track
  - Mountain biking
- Gymnastics
  - Artistic gymnastics
  - Rhythmic gymnastics
- Hockey
- Lawn bowls
- Netball
- Rugby sevens
- Shooting
- Squash
- Table tennis
- Triathlon

- Weightlifting
- The athletics, swimming, table tennis and weightlifting sports included fully integrated events for elite athletes with a disability (EAD). These events were included in the official medal tally.

Closing Ceremony

Both the Melbourne Cricket Ground and the Yarra River were again centrepieces for the ceremony. Samresh Jung of India was given the David Dixon Award at the closing ceremony. He was the "Best Athlete of the 18th Commonwealth Games". The games were closed by HRH Prince Edward.

Medal Table

Rank	Nation	Gold	Silver	Bronze	Total
1	Australia	84	69	68	221
2	England	36	40	34	110
3	Canada	26	29	31	86
4	India	22	17	11	50
5	South Africa	12	13	13	38
6	Scotland	11	7	11	29
7	Jamaica	10	4	8	22
8	Malaysia	7	12	10	29
9	New Zealand	6	12	13	31
10	Kenya	6	5	7	18

Participation

There were 71 countries, territories and bodies competing at the 2006 Commonwealth Games. The only difference between the 2006 games and the 2002 games was the absence of Zimbabwe, which withdrew from the Commonwealth of Nations.

- Anguilla
- Antigua and Barbuda
- Australia
- Bahamas
- Bangladesh
- Barbados
- Belize
- Bermuda
- Botswana
- British Virgin Islands
- Brunei Darussalam
- Cameroon
- Canada
- Cayman Islands
- Cook Islands
- Cyprus
- Dominica
- England
- Falkland Islands
- Fiji
- The Gambia
- Ghana
- Gibraltar
- Grenada
- Guernsey
- Guyana

- India
- Isle of Man
- Jamaica
- Jersey
- Kenya
- Kiribati
- Lesotho
- Malawi
- Malaysia
- Maldives
- Malta
- Mauritius
- Montserrat
- Mozambique
- Namibia
- Nauru
- New Zealand
- Nigeria
- Niue
- Norfolk Island
- Northern Ireland
- Pakistan
- Papua New Guinea
- Saint Helena
- Saint Kitts and Nevis
- Saint Lucia

- Saint Vincent and the Grenadines
- Samoa
- Scotland
- Seychelles
- Sierra Leone
- Singapore
- Solomon Islands
- South Africa
- Sri Lanka
- Swaziland
- Tanzania
- Tonga
- Trinidad and Tobago
- Turks and Caicos
- Tuvalu
- Uganda
- Vanuatu
- Wales
- Zambia

Trivia

On 20 March 2006 it was reported that two athletes had gone missing from the Commonwealth Games village: Tanzanian boxer Omari Idd Kimweri and Bangladeshi runner Mohammad Tawhidul Islam.

On 22 March 2006 it was reported that seven athletes from Sierra Leone (three women and four men) had also disappeared. A further seven Sierra Leonean athletes also went missing during the course of the Games, bringing the total runaway count to fourteen (two thirds of the team). Victoria Police believed that they had fled to Sydney where the Sierra Leonean community is much larger than Melbourne's.

Two hours before the Closing Ceremony on 26 March, officials from the Cameroon team reported to police that nine of their members had also vanished.

These incidents were not without precedent: 27 athletes similarly disappeared from the 2002 Commonwealth Games in Manchester, England (21 from Sierra Leone, 5 from Bangladesh and one from Pakistan), and over 80 athletes and officials overstayed their visas after the 2000 Summer Olympics in Sydney.

On request of Sierra Leone officials, the Commonwealth Games Federation cancelled those athletes' Games accreditation, allowing the Australian Department of Immigration and Multicultural Affairs (DIMA) to cancel their visas at midnight on 27 March, and begin investigating their disappearance.

At 7.20am on that day, New South Wales Police located six of the Sierra Leonean athletes in a house at Freshwater near Manly Beach in Sydney. All six indicated they wished to seek political asylum in Australia, and were granted bridging visas by DIMA while their refugee applications were arranged. The athletes claimed to have been subjected to violence and torture in their home country; seventeen-year-old Isha Conteh stated she could be forced into female genital cutting if she returned. On Tuesday 28 March, six further Sierra Leoneans turned themselves in to immigration authorities in Sydney and were also granted bridging visas.

Two of the missing Cameroon athletes were later found in Perth, Western Australia.

REFERENCES

"Athletes 'go missing from Games'". *BBC News Online*. 23 March 2006.

"Nine athletes vanish from Commonwealth Games". *Reuters*. 22 March 2006.

"Visas for second group of athletes". *The Age*. 28 March 2006.

Whinnett, Ellen (22 March 2006). "Mystery of missing athletes". *Herald Sun*.

Bibliography

Bath, Richard (ed.) *The Complete Book of Rugby* (Seven Oaks Ltd, 1997.

Bawlf, R. Samuel (2003). *The Secret Voyage of Sir Francis Drake: 1577–1580*. Walker & Company.

Cooper, Glynis (2005). *Salford: An Illustrated History*. The Breedon Books Publishing Company.

Cubby, Ben (2009-09-23). "Global warning: Sydney dust storm just the beginning". *Brisbane Times* (Brisbane).

Dale, William (July 1982). "Is the Commonwealth an International Organisation?". *International and Comparative Law Quarterly* 31 (3): 451–73.

Daniel Sankey and Tony Moore (19 July 2007). "Coldest day on record for Brisbane". The Brisbane Times.

Davies, John (1994). *A History of Wales*. London: Penguin. pp. 17 18.

Fact Files: London "Government Offices for the English Regions". Office for National Statistics.

Francis, Daniel (2004). *L.D.:Mayor Louis Taylor and the Rise of Vancouver*. Vancouver: Arsenal Pulp Press.

Frangopulo, Nicholas (1977). *Tradition in Action. The historical evolution of the Greater Manchester County*. Wakefield: EP Publishing.

Fraser, W. Hamish (2004). "Second City of The Empire: 1830s to 1914".

Fremantle, John (1928). *Diary & Letters of Admiral Sir C. H. Fremantle, G.C.B. Relating the Founding of the*

Colony of Western Australia 1829. London: Hazell, Watson & Viey.

Growth of the Commonwealth Games. Commonwealth Games Federation.

Gwynne, Michael (1985). *Ballroom Sequence Dancing* (2nd ed.). Hightstown: Princeton Book Company. p. 202.

Hardy, Clive (2005). "The blitz". *Manchester at War* (2nd ed.). Altrincham: First Edition Limited. pp. 75–99.

High Achievers. Australian Commonwealth Games Association.

Hull, Raymond; Soules, Christine; Soules, Gordon (1974). *Vancouver's Past*. Seattle: University of Washington Press.

Hutton, T. (2008). *The New Economy of the Inner City*. London & New York: Routledge.

Hylton, Stuart (2003). *A History of Manchester*. Phillimore & Co.

James, Gary (2006). *Manchester City - The Complete Record*. Derby: Breedon.

Jenkins, H Geraint (1997). *The Welsh Language before the Industrial Revolution*. Cardiff.

Jones, Bill; Kavanagh, Dennis; Moran, Michael; Norton, Philip (2007). *Politics UK*. Pearson Education. p. 868.

Jones, J.R. *Encyclopedia of Rugby Union Football* (Robert Hale, London, 1976.

Kidd, Alan (2006). *Manchester: A History*. Lancaster: Carnegie Publishing.

Kimberly, W. B. (1897). *History of West Australia*. Melbourne: F. W. Niven & Co.

Kottek, M.; J. Grieser, C. Beck, B. Rudolf, and F. Rubel (2006). "World Map of the Köppen-Geiger climate classification updated". *Meteorol. Z.* 15: 259–263.

Leach (2005a) is a heavily annotated chronology of cricket 1300-1730 and the source for numerous entries here.

Lee, Brian (1999-04-15). *Butetown and Cardiff Docks*. The History Press.

Letter XII from "A tour thro' the whole island of Great Britain" by Daniel Defoe.

Lewis, Miles (1995). 2nd. ed. *Melbourne: the city's history and development*. Melbourne: City of Melbourne. p. 25.

Linacre, Edward; Geerts, Bart (1997). *Climates and Weather Explained*. London: Routledge. p. 379.

Lynch, Michael (2001). *The Oxford Companion to Scottish History*. Oxford: Oxford University Press.

Major, Richard Henry (1859). "Early Voyages to Terra Australis, now called Australia". *Project Gutenberg of Australia*.

Manley, John (1994). "Canadian Communists, Revolutionary Unionism, and the 'Third Period': The Workers' Unity League," (PDF). *Journal of the Canadian*

Massie, Allan *A Portrait of Scottish Rugby* (Polygon, Edinburgh;.

Matthews, J.S. "Skit" (1936). *Early Vancouver*. City of Vancouver.

McCandless, R. C. (1974). "Vancouver's 'Red Menace' of 1935: The Waterfront Situation". *BC Studies* (22): 68.

Mckinley, James C., Jr (1999-03-26). "Baseball; Clash of Cultures, Pride and Passion". *The New York Times*.

Mills, A.D. (2003). *A Dictionary of British Place-Names*. Oxford: Oxford University Press.

Morton, James (1973). *In the Sea of Sterile Mountains: The Chinese in British Columbia*. Vancouver: J.J. Douglas.

Newcomb,John. A source of Victoria's power, 18 March 2001 (pdf 140K). geog.Uvic.ca

Parkinson-Bailey, John J (2000). *Manchester: an Architectural History*. Manchester: Manchester University Press.

Patai, Raphael; Jennifer Patai (1989). *The Myth of the Jewish Race*. Wayne State University Press. p. 43.

Peter Dunn (27 August 2005). "The Battle Of Brisbane — 26 & 27 November 1942".

Rees, William (1969). *Cardiff: A History of the City*. The Corporation of the City of Cardiff. p. 1.

Regent Theatre [1930-1976] (from the Canterbury Film Society website).

Richards, Huw (2007). *A Game for Hooligans: The History of Rugby Union*. Edinburgh: Mainstream Publishing.

Sevens World Series Media Guide" (PDF). International Rugby Board.

Speake, Jennifer, ed (2003). *The Oxford Dictionary of Proverbs* (4th ed.). Oxford University Press.

Staples, John (5 September 2002). "Secret plot to strip Glasgow of influence". The Scotsman. Archived from the original on 19 January 2005.

Statham-Drew, Pamela (1990). *The Origin of Australia's Capital Cities*. Cambridge University Press. pp. 257.

Steve Baily, *A Noble Ally and Olympic Disciple: The Reverend Robert S. de Courcy Laffan, Coubertin's 'man' in England* (PDF).

Whinnett, Ellen (22 March 2006). "Mystery of missing athletes". *Herald Sun*

Index